Texas Rangers

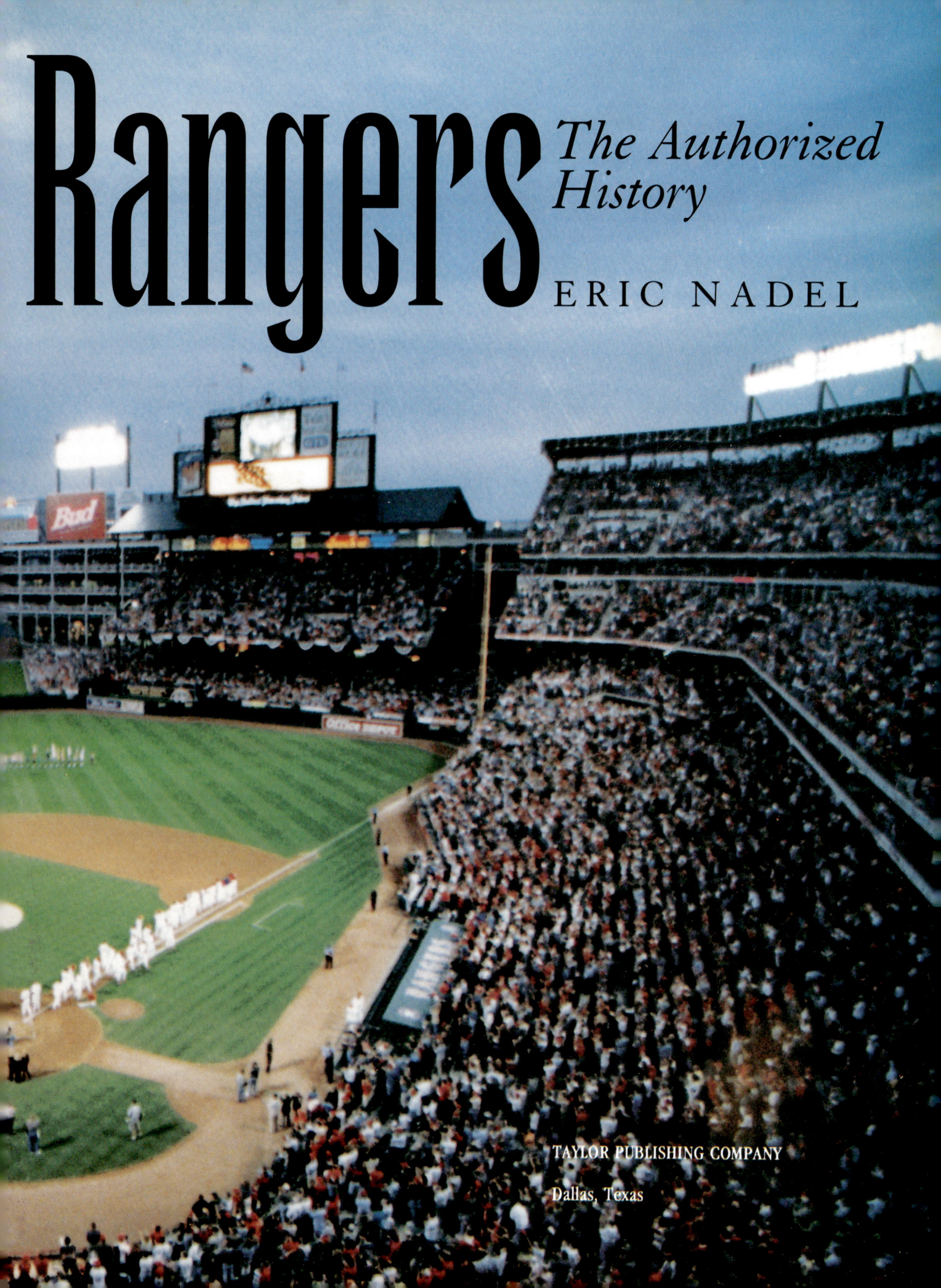

Rangers
The Authorized History

ERIC NADEL

TAYLOR PUBLISHING COMPANY

Dallas, Texas

Photo Acknowledgments

To gather more than 300 photographs for this volume took a great deal of labor and effort on the part of many people and institutions. Particularly, I want to mention the splendid cooperation from the *Fort Worth Star-Telegram*; Special Collections, The University of Texas at Arlington; and the Texas/Dallas History Division, Dallas Public Library. For everyone's help, I am grateful and appreciative. Also, I want to recognize the photographers who, over the twenty-five years of the team's history, have captured the Texas Rangers Baseball Club on film and helped to preserve the story of this wonderful game. I hope I have not overlooked anyone:

Public Relations, Texas Rangers: John Blake; Texas/Dallas History and Archives Division, Dallas Public Library: Jimm Foster, Carol Roark; Special Collections, The University of Texas at Arlington: Jerry Stafford; *Fort Worth Star-Telegram*: Max Faulkner, Tonya Harris, Cathy Belcher, Teddy Sparman, and Katherine Brush; *The Dallas Morning News*: Dave Smith; Legend of the Game Baseball Museum and Learning Center: Peggy Riddle, Wende Eudy, Margaret Bales, Cynthia Firestone; Photographers for the Texas Rangers Baseball Club: Linda Kaye, Brad Newton.

Photographers (in alphabetical order) for the *Fort Worth Star-Telegram, The Dallas Times-Herald,* and *The Dallas Morning News*: Milton Adams, Brian Anderson, Charles Baker, Doug Campbell, James Crittenden, Louis DeLuca, Kevin Fujii, Skeeter Hagler, Ron Heflin, Phil Huber, Paul Iverson, Bob Jackson, Ron Jenkins, Dan Levine, John Mazziotta, Rick Moon, Paul Moseley, Layne Murdock, Ed Panzera, Mark Pearlstein, Tom Pennington, Kurt Wallace, Jeffery Washington, Michael S. Wirtz.

Other photographers: Barry Chin, *The Boston Globe;* Dick Darcy, *The Washington Post;* Glenn Patterson, Sky Cam; Ron Kuntz, Reuters News Service; James F. Mahoney, *The Boston Herald*; Paul Tepley Photography, Inc.; Corky Trewin; The White House Photo Office; The National Baseball Hall of Fame and Museum; The Washington D.C. Public Library; *St. Paul Pioneer Press; The Sporting News; Sports Illustrated*; Public Relations, Kansas City Royals; Public Relations, Detroit Tigers; Yomiuri Shimbun, Tokyo, Japan.

Thomas H. Smith
Photo Editor

Copyright © 1997 by Eric Nadel

All rights reserved.

No part of this book may be reproduced in any form or by any means without written permission from the publisher.

Published by Taylor Publishing Company
1550 West Mockingbird Lane
Dallas, Texas 75235

Designed by David Timmons

Pages ii–iii: First playoff game at The Ballpark in Arlington, October 4, 1996. (*Fort Worth Star-Telegram*)

Library of Congress Cataloging-in-Publication Data
Nadel, Eric.
    Texas rangers : the authorized history by Eric Nadel.
        p.   cm.
    ISBN 0-878330139-5 (cloth)
    1. Texas Rangers (Baseball team)—History. I. Title.
GV875.T4N33 1997
796.357'64'09764531—dc21   97-9629
                                                  CIP

Printed in the United States of America

10 9 8 7 6 5 4 3 2 1

Baseball's all-time strikeout king, Nolan Ryan, is carried off the field after pitching his seventh career no-hitter, May 1, 1991. (*Fort Worth Star-Telegram*)

Contents

	Introduction	*1*
1.	*Prelude to a Championship*	*5*
2.	*Exorcising the Demons*	*13*
3.	*Red October*	*37*
4.	*Good-bye, Washington*	*51*
5.	*Hello, Texas*	*61*
6.	*Whitey, We Hardly Knew You*	*73*
7.	*Billy the Kid*	*85*
8.	*The Strangest Year of All*	*101*
9.	*Wheeling and Dealing with Brad*	*113*
10.	*Mad Eddie*	*125*
11.	*The Rooster*	*139*
12.	*Bobby V.*	*151*
13.	*A New Combination*	*165*
14.	*The End of an Era*	*185*
15.	*Changing Philosophy*	*207*
	Records and Statistics	*212*

Six-time Gold Glove winner Buddy Bell. (Texas Rangers Archives)

Rusty Greer and teammates celebrate the Rangers' greatest comeback win ever, June 8, 1995, won by Greer on a 10th-inning home run. (*Fort Worth Star-Telegram*)

Knuckleballer Charlie Hough, the Rangers' career leader in wins, innings and strikeouts, was 139–123 in 11 seasons with the club. (Texas Rangers Archives)

Jeff Russell, the Rangers' all-time leader in saves and games pitched. (Texas Rangers Archives)

Five-time Gold Glove winner Pudge Rodriguez, the only Ranger to appear in five All-Star Games. (Texas Rangers Archives)

Six-time Gold Glove winner Jim Sundberg. (Linda Kaye)

Hall-of-Famers Gaylord Perry (left photo) in 1977 and Fergie Jenkins (right photo) in 1978—both reached milestones while pitching for the Rangers. Check the scoreboard clock for an uncanny coincidence. (Courtesy *Fort Worth Star-Telegram*, Special Collections Division, University of Texas at Arlington Libraries.)

Creatively killing a spring training rain delay in 1990. From right: Brad Arnsberg, Jeff Russell, Dean Palmer, Geno Petralli, Mike Stanley, Chad Kreuter, Juan Gonzalez. (Texas Rangers Archives)

Introduction

There were twenty-four years of futility...of unfulfilled hopes...of second-half collapses...of front-office instability.

That is the undeniable history that the 1996 Texas Rangers finally overcame.

But there's another way to view the first quarter-century of Ranger baseball—as an era of colorful, unforgettable characters. As a series of talented individuals who never quite meshed into a winning combination, but who provided Ranger fans with a long list of unforgettable memories and plenty of laughs.

This book chronicles Ranger history from both points of view. As one who has been privileged to cover the team for eighteen years, I assure you that the pleasant memories far outnumber the painful ones.

Of course, I have been lucky enough to team with several outstanding broadcast partners, ever since a brave man named Roy Parks decided in 1978 to allow a young hockey announcer to broadcast Ranger games. To Roy and all my partners, I am eternally grateful.

I am thankful as well to the Rangers' eight managers, five general managers, and hundreds of players and employees with whom I have worked. And to three different Ranger ownership groups and two radio stations, all of whom allowed me to be frank and honest in describing happenings that frequently were not pretty.

I work in constant admiration of the dedicated baseball writers who have covered this team and were responsible for eliciting the many memorable quotes appearing in this book.

My thanks to the Rangers' outstanding media relations staffs, past and present, under current Vice President John Blake and under his predecessor, Burt Hawkins, who remains an inspiration to all of us in the baseball community.

And for their countless hours of effort in helping to produce this book, I owe a debt of gratitude to my photo editor, Tom Smith, and his staff at the Legends of the Game Baseball Museum and Learning Center and to John Ralph of the National Baseball Hall of Fame.

> THIS SUMMER, I WAS NEVER LOOKING OVER MY SHOULDER AT ANOTHER TEAM. THE THING I KEPT SEEING OVER MY SHOULDER WAS TEXAS RANGERS HISTORY. THAT WAS MUCH TOUGHER TO DEAL WITH, IN MY MIND, THAN ANY TEAM CHASING US."
>
> *Manager Johnny Oates, after clinching the A.L. West championship, September 28, 1996*

And finally, to the thousands of Ranger fans whose lives were profoundly affected when the magic moment arrived last September, I say, "Thanks for waiting…and as always, thanks for listening."

ERIC NADEL
DECEMBER 1996

Manager Bobby Valentine drags Oddibe McDowell out of the dugout for a reluctant curtain call after McDowell homered to become the only Ranger ever to hit for the cycle, July 23, 1985. (Linda Kaye)

1

Prelude to a Championship

In many ways, the Texas Rangers' 1996 spring training was not unlike the twenty-four that had preceded it.

Manager Johnny Oates and his staff were working long days at the complex in Port Charlotte, Florida, hoping to decide on a fifth starting pitcher and the final member of their bullpen. The Rangers' starting line-up was set, with competition centered around the need for a utility infielder or two. Oates's primary hope was to avoid the sort of major injury that had spoiled the club's '95 pennant hopes.

This spring training, however, had a different feel to it. Having finished just $4\frac{1}{2}$ games out in '95, their most successful season ever, this group of Rangers brought more than the usual spring hopes and dreams to Port Charlotte. Heartily endorsing the team concept that General Manager Doug Melvin had emphasized in his player acquisitions, every one of the Ranger players reported early for spring training.

Among those early reportees was left fielder Juan Gonzalez, the two-time American League home run champion who missed 54 games in '95 because of a back problem. At the urging of team doctors, Gonzalez had worked hard all winter to lose twenty pounds of upper-body mass to lessen the load on his back. The man called "Igor" appeared physically and mentally ready for the challenge of returning to the ranks of baseball's power elite.

Adding to the depth of Gonzalez's task was a new defensive assignment. Oates had decided that due to the unusual dimensions of The Ballpark in Arlington, Gonzalez would be better off playing right field, with Rusty Greer shifting to more spacious territory in left. The manner in which Gonzalez accepted the move would go a long way toward determining the Rangers' fortunes.

By his uncustomary early arrival and frequent extra work with outfield coach Ed Napoleon, Gonzalez demon-

A healthy Dean Palmer, who played only 36 games in '95, would be critical to the club's offensive production. (Texas Rangers Archives)

"THIS YEAR I'M COMING IN EARLY TO WORK HARD AND PREPARE MY MIND AND BODY FOR A LONG SEASON.... I FEEL LIGHT AND STRONG AND LOOSE."

Juan Gonzalez, February 21, 1996

A streamlined Juan Gonzalez was among the early arrivals in Port Charlotte, ready for a huge year. (*Fort Worth Star-Telegram*)

strated that his commitment to an improved Ranger defense was as strong as anyone's. The Rangers had vaulted from last in the league in team fielding in '94 to fourth in '95 as Oates and Melvin made defense a major priority. And the shift of Greer and Gonzalez could help turn more hits into outs.

Offensively, a healthy Gonzalez and Dean Palmer (whose '95 season had ended in June with a freak biceps injury) were counted on to return the Rangers to offensive prominence. As Oates was fond of saying, "We traded for two big hitters this winter and didn't have to give up anyone. Their names are Juan Gonzalez and Dean Palmer."

The only other addition to the Ranger lineup would be Darryl Hamilton, signed as a free agent to replace Otis Nixon as center fielder and leadoff hitter. Batting behind him in the No. 2 slot, if Oates's experiment succeeded, would be All-Star catcher Ivan Rodriguez. A free swinger with power, Pudge was hardly the classic No. 2 hitter. Oates, however, felt that Rodriguez would hit well in that spot and would thrive with the additional at-bats.

First baseman Will Clark, in his third year with the club after leaving the Giants as a free agent, would bat third, followed by Gonzalez and designated hitter Mickey Tettleton. Having signed a one-year contract with the Rangers in '95, the thirty-five-year-old switch-hitter had spurned a larger offer from the Yankees to re-sign with the Rangers for '96.

Palmer would play third base and bat sixth, Greer seventh, and Mark McLemore eighth. The versatile McLemore, one of the first free agents signed by Melvin in December 1994, would hopefully play every day at second base, after spending much of '95 in the outfield as a result of Gonzalez's injury.

The Rangers were expecting a big year out of their No. 9 hitter, shortstop Benji Gil, who was coming off a promising rookie year and a strong season in the Mexican Winter League.

General Manager Doug Melvin was active in the free agent market, looking to bridge the gap between the Rangers and the Mariners. (Texas Rangers Archives)

Oates would have two new outfielders to utilize off the bench. Veteran Warren Newson had been signed as a free agent. And young defensive whiz Damon Buford came over in a trade with the Mets.

There would be a new man fronting the pitching staff. Thirty-year-old right-hander Ken Hill had been signed in the off-season to replace Kenny Rogers as the No. 1 starter after Rogers failed to accept the club's multiyear offer. During a breakfast meeting with Oates while visiting Texas in December, Hill had decided he wanted to be a Ranger, and the manager became certain that Hill was the man he wanted at the front of his rotation.

Following Hill would be returnees Roger Pavlik, Kevin Gross, and Bobby Witt, with the hope that lefty Darren Oliver would be sufficiently recovered from shoulder surgery to man the fifth spot. Former Tiger Mike Henneman had been signed as the bullpen closer, and Gil Heredia had been added to work in long and middle relief. Returning from '95 were relievers Dennis Cook, Ed Vosberg, Matt Whiteside, and Mark Brandenburg.

Things were rolling along smoothly in mid-March. The outfield switch was working out well, Rodriguez loved batting second, and Oliver was way ahead of schedule. The bullpen became stronger when the club's all-time save leader, Jeff Russell, agreed to a contract allowing him to rejoin the team in May. But one lingering problem was becoming serious.

Manager Johnny Oates and his coaching staff returned for their second year in Texas. From left, top row: Third base coach Jerry Narron, bullpen coach Larry Hardy, Oates, pitching coach Dick Bosman. Bottom row: Dugout and infield coach Bucky Dent, hitting coach Rudy Jaramillo, first base and outfield coach Ed Napoleon. (Texas Rangers Archives)

Former Brewer Darryl Hamilton was signed as a free agent, hoping to leave his injury problems behind him. (Texas Rangers Archives)

Shortstop Gil had injured his back during the winter, was not responding to treatment, and was unable to play. Veteran Kevin Elster, who was given a Ranger tryout only after his brother/agent Patrick persuaded Melvin to issue a nonroster invitation, was now getting most of the playing time at shortstop.

Having come to camp competing for a utility job, the usually sure-handed Elster committed two errors in the exhibition opener. But he also had three hits in that game and went on to demonstrate more offensive power than he had shown in his years with the Mets.

After his shaky first game in the field, Elster caught everything hit his way the rest of the spring. Despite having played only 49 big league games since '92 due to shoulder injuries, Elster was Oates's choice to start at shortstop after Gil underwent disk surgery on March 26.

And so it happened that a major spring injury, the kind that had helped ruin numerous Ranger seasons, helped ensure that this year would be different from all the others.

Elster would go on to be the Rangers Player of the Month in April, set a major league record for RBI by a No. 9 hitter, and win *The Sporting News'* Comeback Player of the Year Award.

The Rangers went 19–11 in spring training, equaling their most spring wins ever. And the winning did not stop until October. Yes, this would be the special season that Ranger fans had been waiting for.

Mickey Tettleton re-signed with the Rangers, providing power, versatility, and the ability to produce despite a variety of injuries. (Texas Rangers Archives)

Mike Henneman, a resident of Colleyville, Texas, came to the Rangers with 160 career saves. (Texas Rangers Archives)

Darren Oliver's return from shoulder surgery ended speculation regarding the fifth spot in the starting rotation. (Texas Rangers Archives)

An injury to Benji Gil left the Rangers' shortstop job up for grabs in spring training. (Texas Rangers Archives)

Kevin Elster beat out Kurt Stillwell and Rene Gonzales to become the starting shortstop and had a storybook season, while Stillwell and Gonzales contributed in utility roles. (Linda Kaye)

2

Exorcising the Demons

Actually, there was a multitude of reasons that explained the absence of a division title in the Rangers' first twenty-four years. Longtime observers cited bad trades, bad drafts, bad health, bad luck, even bad weather (too much heat). But the most frequent culprit was bad pitching.

On Opening Day at The Ballpark, on Monday, April 1, new staff ace Ken Hill showed a crowd of 40,484 fans that he would help put an end to their years of frustration. The right-hander outpitched Boston star Roger Clemens on the way to a 5–3 victory.

In the first inning, Rodriguez began what would be a brilliant year in the No. 2 spot by walking on a 3–2 pitch and scoring on Clark's double to right-center. Then in the second, backup third baseman Craig Worthington led off with a home run. Worthington, playing because of a minor hamstring injury to Palmer, added another RBI later in the game and turned in a dazzling defensive play.

Worthington's Opening Day heroics provided the first of many major contributions by the Rangers' bench players. But the home run was the only one of the season for the veteran third baseman, who ended the season playing in Japan.

With two outs in the ninth, Vosberg relieved Hill and recorded the save—the first of five for the lefty in the Rangers' first 15 wins—as Oates skillfully maneuvered Vosberg and Henneman in save situations.

Two blowout wins over Boston and a 4–2 victory over New York left the Rangers undefeated going into a Sunday doubleheader against the Yankees. Hill was matched up in the first game against former National League Cy Young Award winner Dwight Gooden. Batting

Ivan Rodriguez scored all the way from first on Gonzalez' single to give the Rangers a 2–1 lead on the night they clinched the title. Pudge led the team in runs (116), hit .300 for the second straight year, won his fifth consecutive Gold Glove, and became the first Ranger to play in five All-Star Games. (Fort Worth Star-Telegram)

"THERE'S ONLY ONE WAY OF STOPPING THE QUESTION. WIN. UNTIL WE DO IT, THAT QUESTION WILL BE THERE EVERY YEAR."

Johnny Oates, March 30, 1996, responding to the frequently asked question, "Why have the Rangers never won?"

Opening Day starter Ken Hill tied for the team lead with 16 victories, tied for the major league lead with three shutouts, and ranked in the top six in the league in ERA, innings and complete games. (Texas Rangers Archives)

for the first time ever against his former Mets teammate, Elster homered on the first pitch he saw in the second inning. Tettleton's three-run blast to the upper porch in the fifth broke the game open as Texas rolled to a 7–2 win.

The nightcap was the season's first cliffhanger, a pitchers' duel between Pavlik and another former Cy Young Award winner, David Cone. Newson, starting for the first time, tied the game, 1–1, with a home run in the bottom of the second. Pavlik and Cone proceeded to hang zeros on the scoreboard until the bottom of the eighth, when former Ranger Steve Howe came out of the Yankee bullpen.

With two men on and two outs, Oates allowed the left-handed-hitting Newson to face the southpaw Howe. Newson responded with a line-drive single to left, putting the Rangers on top, 2–1. Palmer and Greer followed with RBI singles, and Vosberg pitched a scoreless ninth for his second save.

The Rangers' 6–0 home stand equaled their best start ever and gave them a two-game lead in the West. They outscored two 1995 playoff teams by a margin of 40–12 and trailed in only one half-inning. Naturally, the club was brimming with confidence as it headed to Chicago for the White Sox' home opener at Comiskey Park.

On a forty-two-degree Tuesday afternoon, Elster's run-scoring double snapped a 2–2 tie in the seventh. Texas held on to the 3–2 lead with clutch relief work by Heredia and Henneman, a brilliant play by Elster, and a bit of luck. A Frank Thomas smash that would have driven in the tying run in the seventh caromed off an umpire and stayed in the infield.

For the first time ever, the Rangers had started a season with seven straight wins. And the formula for their success had become clear—scoring early to ease the pressure on the starters, strong starting pitching (starters picked up the victories in all seven games), and a tight defense that committed just two errors during the streak and frequently turned hits into outs. The bullpen pitched effectively in every game, saving four of them.

The seven-game winning streak, the club's longest since 1992, marked only the sixteenth time in major league history that a team had started a season 7–0. But the Rangers' bid for win No. 8 fell short the next day when the White Sox rallied to win against Henneman after Clark's homer had put Texas in front in the top of the 10th.

THE BIGGEST INNING

The Rangers concluded their first road trip by losing two out of three in New York, then made club history upon returning to Arlington on April 19. Leading the Orioles, 10–7, after 7½ innings, Texas sent 19 batters to the plate in a 16-run, fifty-six-minute eighth inning.

Exorcising the Demons

The Rangers' biggest inning ever was capped by an Elster grand slam, which was surrendered by Baltimore's reserve infielder Manny Alexander. Gonzalez, who had crushed a three-run homer in the first inning, also drove in three runs in the record frame with a two-run double and a bases-loaded walk.

The 26–7 final score represented the most runs ever scored by a Rangers team and moved the Rangers back into a first-place tie with the Mariners, who had briefly taken over the top spot. Two more wins over the Orioles extended the winning streak to five games. But a four-game losing streak followed, a skid that included an 11–9 disaster at Fenway Park in which the Rangers blew a seven-run lead for the first time ever.

The team's resiliency—the invaluable trait that would ultimately save the season—was then displayed for the first time. The Rangers rebounded to win three straight in Baltimore while compiling a club-record, nine-game errorless string. They lost the series finale in Baltimore and came home with a one-game lead to face second-place Seattle, the defending West Division champs.

Craig Worthington starred on Opening Day with a home run and a diving play at third base. (Texas Rangers Archives)

After arriving home from Baltimore in the wee hours of the morning on April 30, the Rangers were wiped out, 8–0, by a well-rested Seattle club that improved its record to 16–10—the best start in team history and good enough for a first-place tie. But that would be the last time the Mariners would taste the division lead.

The Rangers moved back into the top spot the following night with a 5–4 win that foretold volumes of what was to come for both teams. Seattle's Cy Young Award winner, Randy Johnson, pitching despite a stiff lower back, allowed four runs and left after two innings. Shortly thereafter, Johnson went on the disabled list, where he remained for the majority of the season.

While the Mariners were losing their most important pitcher, the Rangers were regaining one of theirs. The team's all-time leader in saves and games pitched, Jeff Russell, returned to the club, hurled three shutout innings, and picked up the win when Clark homered in the seventh to snap a 4–4 deadlock. Without Johnson, the Mariners' staff was never the same. And with Russell, the Rangers added an important arm to their bullpen.

After losing in Detroit to open a road trip, the Rangers started another

TEXAS RANGERS

five-game winning streak, with Hill and Pavlik turning in remarkable back-to-back one-hitters at Tiger Stadium. But as the Rangers were defeating the Blue Jays in Toronto on May 7, Gonzalez suffered a torn left quadriceps muscle and was lost to the club for 21 games.

WINNING WITHOUT JUAN AND RUSTY

Despite playing without Gonzalez and Greer, who missed nine games after separating his shoulder on a wall-crashing catch, the Rangers surged to a 5½-game lead at the end of May. But there were some anxious moments along the way.

On May 24, the club was slumping and had lost six of eight when Oates called his first team meeting of the season. After an 8–0 whitewash by Mark Gubicza in Kansas City, the skipper angrily questioned his team's intensity in a rare tirade that helped reverse the slide.

Equally helpful was a superb performance by right-hander Rick Helling the next night. Called up from Oklahoma City to start in place of the ailing Gross, the former No. 1 draft choice shut down the Royals for eight innings in a tense 2–1 win. Helling's only win of the season triggered a six-game winning streak for the club, which closed out the month of May with a 34–19 record.

A three-game home sweep of defending A.L. champion Cleveland began with a dramatic 3–2 win in which Palmer homered in the eighth to tie the game, 2–2. Then, with two outs in the ninth, Hamilton doubled into the right-field corner to score Elster from first with the winning run. Pavlik went the distance to run his record to 7–1.

The Rangers had gone 18–9 in May, paced by Hamilton's .352 batting average. But primarily, it was outstanding pitching that allowed the Rangers to go 13–8 without Gonzalez. In June and July, the Rangers would scuffle to play .500 ball. But the return of Igor on June 1 prevented a more serious tumble.

Ed Vosberg saved five games in April and finished with a total of eight, the most by a Ranger lefty since 1990. (Texas Rangers Archives)

Left fielder Rusty Greer led the team in batting (.332), finishing fifth in the A.L. batting race, and played brilliantly in left field. (Fort Worth Star-Telegram)

JUAN CARRIES THE LOAD

The month of June began with two demoralizing ninth-inning losses to the Twins in Arlington. But the club bounced back with four straight victories to open a gap of 6½ games on June 10—the largest lead in club history.

Seattle reduced the lead to five games by winning two of three from the Rangers at the Kingdome on the last three days of June. The Rangers went 14–13 in the month, paced by McLemore hitting .472—a club record for any month—and 11 homers and 27 RBI from Gonzalez.

The Mariners came to The Ballpark for the last four games before the All-Star break, trailing by six games. Three consecutive sellout crowds endured Seattle victories as the lead shrank to three games before the final game of the series.

With the Mariners threatening to sweep, Hill, who had suffered through a miserable June, permitted just one unearned run in 7⅓ innings. Newson and Gonzalez connected off Seattle's top winner, Bob Wells, early in the game, and the Rangers won, 8–3, to lead by four games at the break.

Rodriguez and Pavlik represented the club at the All-Star Game in Philadelphia. But it was Gonzalez who delivered at a superhuman pace after the break. Dividing his time between right field and designated hitter to allow his quadriceps to heal completely, Juan tied a major league record with 15 home runs in July. He set a club record with 38 RBI in the 27 games and batted .407 to capture the American League Player of the Month Award.

Between June 25 and July 19, Gonzalez hit safely in 21 consecutive

Warren Newson came off the bench to hit 10 home runs, filling in admirably while Gonzalez and Greer were injured. Here he bowls over Mike Matheny to score against the Brewers. (*Fort Worth Star-Telegram*)

Rick Helling's only win of the season, May 25 in Kansas City, ignited a six-game winning streak. (Texas Rangers Archives)

Kevin Elster dives past Sandy Alomar to score on Darryl Hamilton's ninth-inning double which beat the Indians on May 27. Rich Garcia makes the call at the plate. (Linda Kaye)

games. Almost incredibly, he matched that streak with another 21-gamer in August.

The Rangers' mediocre July (13–14), which left them just 2½ games in front, was attributable in part to injuries to Clark, Tettleton, Gross, and Henneman. But in yet another Cinderella story, first baseman Lee Stevens was called up to replace Clark on July 20. Returning to the big leagues for the first time since 1992, the former Angel banged out three hits in each of his first two games and also tripled home the winning run in a 10-inning win at Chicago.

On July 31, Melvin traded rookie reliever Mark Brandenburg and minor leaguer Kerry Lacy to Boston for left-handed reliever Mike Stanton. The acquisition of Stanton, a veteran of several pennant races, was a key factor in a strong finish by the Texas bullpen.

THE MEETING

Leading by just one game on August 6, the Rangers opened a road trip with a 4–2 win in Detroit but stranded 12 runners the next night in a 4–2 loss. The final day of that series, August 8, would prove to be one of the season's most noteworthy, begin-

Roger Pavlik got off to a 12–2 start, pitched two innings in the All-Star Game, and finished with a 15–8 record. (Texas Rangers Archives)

Exorcising the Demons

First baseman Lee Stevens tied a club record with two triples in his first game after being called up on July 20 to replace the injured Clark. (Texas Rangers Archives)

ning with the announcement that Melvin had acquired right-handed starter John Burkett from the Florida Marlins for minor league pitching prospect Ryan Dempster and a player to be selected later, who turned out to be Helling.

A few hours later, Gross, who would soon be moved to the bullpen to make room for Burkett in the rotation, went to the mound and pitched his best game of the year, taking a 2–1 lead to the eighth inning. But the bullpen could not hold the lead, and the Tigers won in the ninth, 3–2. The Rangers offense had gone dead, managing just one hit in the last five innings.

After the game, Oates exploded, closing the clubhouse for several minutes as he lambasted the club. The Rangers' lead was down to two games, and when the players showed up at Toronto's Skydome the next day, backup catcher David Valle had a few things on his mind.

Valle called a players-only meeting in which he addressed every player individually, asking each man if he would make a commitment to the team's winning, surrendering individual goals in the process. Valle made each player respond, "Yes, I will," before going on to the next locker.

How effective was Valle's meeting? Dennis Cook recalled, "I was so pumped up I wanted to wear my uniform home to bed."

Later, on the Skydome turf, the Rangers responded with a 5–4 win behind Witt. Gonzalez's 100th RBI, a line-drive single in the seventh, snapped a 4–4 tie, and Russell, Vosberg, and Henneman combined to hold the lead. The Rangers blew out the Blue Jays the next day, 12–1, as Oliver collected his 10th win. Then on Sunday afternoon Burkett debuted with a masterful six-hit shutout to win, 6–0. Five days later the former Giants 20-game winner followed up his shutout by beating the Royals to complete another Ranger winning streak of seven games.

On August 19, the Rangers opened a seven-game lead by winning in Cleveland, 10–3. While doing so, Texas set an A.L. record by playing its 15th consecutive errorless game. An Elster miscue ended the errorless streak the next night in a 10–4 loss. But in the series finale, the Rangers pulled off one of their most satisfying wins of the season.

Mike Stanton posted a 3.22 ERA in 22 games after coming over from the Red Sox on July 31. (Texas Rangers Archives)

TEXAS RANGERS

Storming back from a 6–1 deficit, the Rangers knocked out Charles Nagy with a seven-run sixth inning, only to blow an 8–6 lead when the Tribe scored two in the bottom of the ninth. Vosberg then escaped a bases-loaded jam to send the game to the 10th inning, in which Greer hit a mammoth two-run homer to win the game. At the end of that four-hour marathon, the Rangers flew to Minnesota with an eight-game lead, their largest yet.

SURGING TO A NINE-GAME LEAD

Despite losing seven of their next eleven, the Rangers led by a healthy six games on September 6 when they began a six-game trip to Milwaukee and Toronto. Outstanding outings by Burkett, Hill, and Witt keyed a three-game sweep of the Brewers.

The second win was made possible by several huge defensive plays, including one on an eighth-inning squeeze bunt toward first. With David Hulse racing for the plate with the tying run, Valle blocked the plate long enough to catch the throw from Clark and tag out the diving Hulse. Then McLemore closed out the 2–1 win with a brilliant stab to rob Turner Ward of a hit. The Rangers swept the series, although Greer, who had become their No. 3 hitter, was on the bench with a fractured rib suffered when he was hit by a pitch.

The clutch performances kept on coming in Toronto. In the first game, Tettleton's RBI double in the sixth broke a 3–3 tie, and

Backup catcher David Valle, being restrained here by third base coach Jerry Narron, hit .302 and inspired the club in an August team meeting. (Texas Rangers Archives)

American League Most Valuable Player Juan Gonzalez belted 47 HRs and drove in 144 runs, both club records, despite missing 28 games due to injuries. (Fort Worth Star-Telegram)

Damon Buford hit .283 and played errorless ball in 80 games in the outfield. (Texas Rangers Archives)

Gross, Stanton, and Henneman protected the lead the rest of the way. The next night, Oliver battled control trouble early but survived to win, 11–8, aided by a big three-run homer off the bat of Clark. Again, a combination of relievers shut the door in the late innings, with Henneman finishing up to post his 30th save.

The Mariners lost that night for the third time in four games, swelling the Rangers' lead to an unprecedented nine games on September 11. Texas' five-game winning streak ended at Toronto the next night, but the Mariners lost again to the Royals.

The Rangers' magic number, which had been printed on the front page of the Metroplex newspapers when it was still above 30, was now down to 10. The Rangers' first division title appeared to be in sight with only 17 games remaining. Unfortunately, however, that is when the Rangers stopped hitting—and winning.

IT AIN'T OVER 'TIL IT'S OVER

An average of forty-three thousand fans a night on Nolan Ryan Appreciation Weekend watched in dismay as the Brewers won the first three games of a four-game series at The Ballpark on September 9–12. The Rangers appeared sloppy in the field and over-anxious at the plate, failing to hit with men on base at a most inopportune time. The Mariners had turned things around that same weekend, winning three straight to cut the lead back to six games.

On the last day of the Brewers series, following pregame ceremonies to retire Ryan's uniform No. 34, the Rangers rallied from a 2–1 deficit to win on sixth-inning homers by McLemore and Tettleton, as Oliver went seven strong innings in a 6–2 victory. That ended the four-game losing streak and finally reduced the magic number to nine. The Mariners won their fourth in a row and were six games behind as the Rangers flew to Seattle for a four-game series.

Seattle's 1995 West Division title was miraculously won after the M's overcame a 13-game California lead in the last two months. Envisioning a repeat performance, Seattle fans packed the Kingdome for Game 1 of the series on Monday, September 16. Needing a sweep to reduce the Rangers' margin to two games, the Mariners got off to a good start with two runs in the first off Burkett. That would be all that former Ranger Jamie Moyer needed. The Mariners breezed to a 6–0 win.

Kevin Gross won nine games as a starter then moved to the bullpen in August and did a great job in long relief. (Texas Rangers Archives)

Third baseman Dean Palmer (left) established career highs in HRs (38), RBI (107), and batting average (.280). Designated hitter Mickey Tettleton contributed 24 HRs, 83 RBI, and filled in at first base. (Texas Rangers Archives)

The next two nights would be no better for Texas fans as the Rangers came unraveled at key moments in a pair of 5–2 defeats. Before the series finale, Oates held a brief pregame meeting, after which the Rangers played much better but still lost, 7–6. The Mariners had done the unthinkable, sweeping the four-game set to reduce the Rangers' lead to two games. As the Rangers boarded their buses for the trip to the airport, they were taunted mercilessly by Seattle fans.

Somehow, through it all, Oates remained calm, positive, and upbeat, reiterating often that no matter what happened in Seattle, the Rangers would leave town in first place. Oates's approach may have kept his team from panicking and was instrumental in the rally that would soon begin. But no soothing words from the manager could prepare the Rangers for what would befall them in Anaheim the next night.

Seemingly uplifted by escaping the house of horrors that the Kingdome had become, the Rangers jumped to an immediate lead when Hamilton homered to lead off the game. A two-run homer by Palmer in the third made it 3–0, but the Angels rallied, and the game went into extra innings tied, 4–4. McLemore appeared to win it for Texas with an RBI single in the 10th. But with two outs and no one on base in the bottom of the 10th, the Angels came back to win against Stanton on two singles and a heartbreaking two-run double by Garret Anderson.

Bobby Witt tied for the club lead with 16 wins, eight of them coming after a Rangers' loss. (Texas Rangers Archives)

Despite three stints on the disabled list, Will Clark hit .284 and set a club record for fewest errors (4) in a season by a first baseman. (Texas Rangers Archives)

DOWN BUT NOT OUT

The Rangers' spirits had never been lower. The Mariners demolished the Athletics, 12–2, for their ninth straight win, and the once-large Texas lead was down to a single game. The Rangers had eight games to play, while Seattle still had 10 games left on their schedule.

All the arithmetic that the newspapers had shown just ten days earlier, establishing the near impossibility of a Seattle comeback, had been rendered insignificant. The Rangers were fighting for their lives and were desperate for a victory. The club had lost nine out of 10, scoring only 37 runs in the 10 games. Never had the Rangers needed a well-pitched game as badly as they did that Saturday, September 21 in California.

Years from now, those telling the tale of the Rangers' first championship will recall that it was Burkett who halted the notorious slide and got the Rangers back on track. Oates placed Valle behind the plate, as he had done in Burkett's brilliant A.L. debut, and the bat-

THE RANGERS WON IN '96 BECAUSE ...

- **They led the majors in fielding,** committing only 87 errors—the fewest in club history and only three more than the major league record.
- **Texas starting pitchers led the majors in wins (75)** as the club ranked sixth in the A.L. in ERA.
- **They set club records in almost every offensive category,** including home runs, with 221, matching the seventh-highest total in major league history. The Rangers finished fourth in the league in homers and runs scored, averaging 5.7 runs per game and outscoring their opponents by a total of 129 runs.

THE RANGERS WON IN '96 DESPITE ...

- Not winning a single game in which they trailed after 8 innings.
- Losing twelve times when leading after 8 innings or later.
- Winning only 3 of 13 games against second-place Seattle.

Native Texan Dennis Cook led the club in appearances (60) and relief wins (5). (Texas Rangers Archives)

tery teamed perfectly. Moving the ball expertly on and off the corners, the wily veteran blanked the Angels for seven innings. Meanwhile, the Rangers offense came alive when Greer returned to the lineup after a 15-game absence.

Despite still suffering from the rib injury, Rusty homered in his second at-bat to make the score 2–0 in the third. Gonzalez went deep on the very next pitch, Valle did the same in the seventh, and Burkett did the rest. The 7–1 win reduced the magic number to eight, and kept the Rangers a game in front of the Mariners, who won their 10th in a row.

Ranger fans wondering if the Mariners would ever lose again were frequently reminded that Seattle's final eight games would be played on the road. The Mariners had just one more home game the next day, which they proceeded to lose to the A's, 13–11, to end their winning streak.

Texas took advantage of the rare Seattle loss with another well-pitched win over the Angels, a complete-game 4–1 victory by Hill. Another Gonzalez homer opened the scoring, giving Juan a career-high and club-record 47. Palmer blasted his 37th and started another rally with an eighth-inning single. Rodriguez provided defensive heroics, nailing a would-be base stealer when the game was scoreless, then pouncing on a seventh-inning bunt to start an amazing 2-6-4 double play. Of all the sensational plays turned in by the Gold Glove catcher, the double play may have been the very best.

With their magic number at six, the Rangers lost the opener of a two-game set in Oakland, 5–3, but the Mariners began their season-ending road trip with a 4–3 loss to the Angels. The magic number was down to five, but the Ranger offense was still sputtering.

Fortunately, the Texas bullpen came up big on Tuesday afternoon in the last game of the trip. Pavlik was pulled in the fifth inning with a 6–1 lead, but Cook, Russell, and Henneman did not allow a baserunner after the fifth. The Rangers won, 7–3, helped by four Oakland errors. But the go-ahead runs were earned the old-fashioned way—Tettleton smashing a two-run homer.

The Rangers were met by a large contingent of fans and media upon their arrival at DFW Airport that evening. By the time they reached their homes, most had learned that the Mariners were losing again in Anaheim, eventually falling by the score of 11–6. The magic number was then three, and the Rangers could take matters into their own hands and clinch the title by winning three of the last four from the Angels.

SCOREBOARD WATCHING AS NEVER BEFORE

The Rangers enjoyed a day off while the Mariners won at California, then opened the final home stand with a 2½-game lead, still needing three wins or Mariner losses to clinch the crown. As the Rangers and then the Angels took batting practice on that unusually cool and gray late afternoon, everyone in The Ballpark kept an eye on the out-of-town score-

Above: Nolan Ryan addresses the crowd on September 15, the day the Rangers retired his No. 34. Seated behind Ryan are club president Tom Schieffer (far left) and play-by-play announcer Mark Holtz. (Texas Rangers Archives)

Left: Ryan's number now adorns the home run porch in right field. (Texas Rangers Archives)

John Burkett went 5–2 after being acquired from Florida on August 8, and posted the critical victory September 26 in Anaheim which stopped the Rangers' five-game losing streak. (Texas Rangers Archives)

board in left field. The Mariners were playing in Oakland, and the scoreboard was being updated with each development.

The long-honored baseball tradition of scoreboard watching was raised to new heights as the Mariners fell behind, rallied to take the lead, then gave up four runs in the bottom of the eighth to lose, 7–5. An hour before they took the field, the Rangers knew that their magic number had been sliced to two.

The Rangers then fell behind the Angels, 3–0, but scored four times in the third to take the lead. The tying run scored on a Gonzalez smash through the legs of third baseman Randy Velarde, after which Clark put the Rangers in front to stay with a sacrifice fly. At just about the same time that the huge moon above The Ballpark was totally obscured in a rare lunar eclipse, a sixth-inning triple by Elster padded the lead to 6–3.

With Burkett on the mound, things seemed under control until the Angels scored single runs in the seventh and eighth to narrow the gap to 6–5. Vosberg retired the last batter in the eighth with the tying run on, and Stanton recorded the first two outs of the ninth before Henneman was summoned with the tying run at second. After walking pinch-hitter Jack Howell, Henneman got Gary Disarcina to loft a soft pop fly to left.

As Greer settled under that fly ball and the magic number dropped to one, even the most cynical among us could no longer deny the inevitable. Greer made the catch, and the Rangers had clinched at least a tie for first place.

THE FAT LADY SINGS...IN OAKLAND

A sellout crowd of 46,764 crammed The Ballpark on Friday, September 27, hoping to witness a division-clinching win. This they did not see. They did, however, experience the unforgettable moment when the Rangers became division champions for the first time.

With Hill on the mound

Kevin Elster won the A.L. Comeback Player of the Year Award, achieving career highs in home runs (24) and RBI (99), and providing a reliable glove at shortstop. (Texas Rangers Archives)

1996 AWARD WINNERS

Juan Gonzalez—American League Most Valuable Player
Johnny Oates—*The Sporting News* American League Manager of the Year, Baseball Writers Association of America American League Co-Manager of the Year
Doug Melvin—*The Sporting News* Major League Executive of the Year
Kevin Elster—*The Sporting News* American League Comeback Player of the Year
Ivan Rodriguez—Rawlings Gold Glove Winner

against California rookie Jason Dickson, the Rangers broke a 1–1 tie in the fifth. Rodriguez was at first with two outs when Gonzalez smoked a single that caromed off the glove of left fielder Garret Anderson. Third-base coach Jerry Narron kept waving his right arm until Rodriguez slid in at the plate with the go-ahead run, having scored all the way from first on a single.

That was Gonzalez's 144th and last RBI of the season, and it would have been fitting for it to have stood up as the division clincher. Nothing, however, had ever gone exactly as planned for the Rangers, and that tradition lived on as Anderson singled in the seventh to tie the game, 2–2.

Johnny Oates, who held the club together through a difficult September, shared A.L. Manager of the Year honors with New York's Joe Torre. (Texas Rangers Archives)

TEXAS RANGERS

A rare lunar eclipse on September 26 gave a special glow to the Rangers' last victory before clinching the title. (*Fort Worth Star-Telegram*)

The out-of-town scoreboard, meanwhile, showed Oakland with an early 2–0 lead over Seattle. A Ranger win would render that game meaningless, and the Rangers battled all night trying make it so. But as the Texas and California bullpens took over in the eighth, the scoring at The Ballpark came to a halt. Both teams had chances, but neither could push across a run before the next major development in Oakland—a six-run seventh inning for the A's that sent The Ballpark crowd into a frenzy.

The Rangers and Angels were now in extra innings, but the out-of-town scoreboard was offering more immediate signs of satisfaction. In Oakland, the Mariners went quickly in the eighth and ninth, and while the Angels were batting at The Ballpark in the top of the 13th with a runner at second and nobody out, the letter "F" was posted on the out-of-town scoreboard next to the 8–1 score of the Oakland-Seattle game. At 11:53 P.M., the Mariners' score was a final.

The Rangers were West Division champions! The crowd rejoiced, and the electronic message board flashed the news. But what were the Ranger players to do? There was a game going on, and they were trying to get out of a 13th-inning jam. Finally, Stanton got them out of the inning, and the players allowed themselves some mild celebrating in the dugout.

The Angels finally won, 4–3, in the 15th inning of a game that took over five hours to play. When the final out was made at 12:45 A.M., the Rangers massed in front of their dugout, with many players waving and tossing souvenirs to the remaining fans. The real party occurred in the clubhouse, starting moments later and extending long into the morning.

The Rangers had been in first since May 1 and held the top spot for all but four days of the season. Certainly, it was a source of frustration to players and fans alike that the final act of clinching took place not in Arlington but rather in Oakland. The slightly bizarre ending is yet another unique moment in

Mike Henneman celebrates the final out which reduced the Rangers' magic number to one. Henneman tied for fifth in the A.L. in saves with 31, the third most in team history. (Linda Kaye)

At 11:53 p.m., the out-of-town scoreboard relayed the news that Seattle had lost and the Rangers were West Division champions. (Linda Kaye)

the history of a franchise that has been anything but conventional.

The fact is that the Rangers had bounced back from a near-fatal skid by winning four out of five games until the title was clinched. The ability to keep its composure and win those four games demonstrated the remarkable character for which this team will be remembered.

"My confidence didn't waver at all," said Oates, referring to the way his team bounced back after the nightmarish loss in Anaheim. "We've lost a number of very tough games this season, but we always came back the next day and played well.

"We had a unique kind of pressure this year. Since the All-Star break, we've heard a lot about how the Rangers always collapse. I have all the respect in the world for the Mariners, A's, and Angels, but the biggest obstacle we've had to overcome was our history."

Club President Tom Schieffer viewed the division title as the start of a new chapter in team history. "This team has carried an extra burden of twenty-five years of not winning," he said. "But by winning, we put all that behind us. This is confirmation that things have changed, that we're not a sad-sack franchise anymore."

The Rangers' first postseason was about to begin.

At 12:45 A.M., after their 15-inning loss to the Angels, the Rangers and their fans celebrated their first division title. (*Fort Worth Star-Telegram*)

(Fort Worth Star-Telegram)

FRIDAY NIGHT FOOTBALL

Full report, Section D	Sam Houston 16 Azle 0	Southwest Christian 27 Oakridge 13	Cleburne 24 Alvarado 7	Eastern Hills 48 Mineral Wells 0	Killeen Ellison 24 Lamar 21
Wyatt 27 Southwest 0	Everman 21 Midlothian 7	Grapevine 28 Dallas Kimball 24	Granbury 13 Ennis 7	Springtown 21 Northwest 14	Weatherford 17 Denton 12

IN BUSINESS

It's official. Full-size pickups will be built at the Arlington GM plant starting in June, company officials announced yesterday at the State Fair.
Page 11B

CITY FINAL

Fort Worth Star-Telegram

SATURDAY, SEPTEMBER 28, 1996 — Tarrant County, Texas ★ "Where The West Begins" — 50 CENTS

RANGERS CLINCH!

Despite marathon loss, team captures first AL West title

Rangers centerfielder Darryl Hamilton, right, hugs a teammate after Texas clinched the American League West title.
Star-Telegram/Rick Moon

By MEDE NIX
Star-Telegram Staff Writer

ARLINGTON — A quarter-century of baseball futility ended late last night for the Rangers, not with a victory but because of a loss by the Seattle Mariners that came as the Rangers played in the 13th inning of a marathon battle with the California Angels.

The Rangers, who lost to California, 4-3, when the 15-inning game ended at 12:45 this morning, clinched the American League West division title in unlikely fashion, as a sellout crowd of 46,764 fans at The Ballpark in Arlington started watching the left-field scoreboard along with the game.

Because the Rangers' magic number was one, a Seattle loss or a Texas victory clinched the team's first division title. The Mariners lost, 8-1, to the A's in Oakland.

Seattle's loss brought cheers from the boisterous fans, most of whom remained in the stands until California went ahead of the Rangers, 4-2, in the top of the 15th. But after the cheers for the Seattle loss, the crowd lost much of its momentum. About half had left by the time fireworks celebrating the title were set off after the Rangers' longest game of the year and the Rangers players came out to wave to the crowd.

The Rangers open a best-of-five playoff series against the New York Yankees or Chicago
(More on RANGERS on Page 2)

Jim Reeves
SPORTS

We'll never be quite the same again

ARLINGTON — It had to be this way, of course. They had to bleed us dry one more time, push us to the limits of emotional endurance and then beyond, squeeze out one last drop of sweat, one final gasp of anguish, one ultimate, unendurable moment of agony.

Make that five hours worth of unendurable moments.

So there we were again, snagged and flopping on the hook of a sordid history that simply refused to let go.

We should have known. This has not come easy all season, not even in a quarter of a century. Why would it now?

And then, in a heartbeat, the Texas Rangers were champions. *Champions!*

At 11:51 p.m., in a moment of anticlimax that found the Rangers still on the field in the 13th inning, trying to find a way to beat the California Angels, the Oakland Athletics put the Seattle Mariners — and I suppose the Rangers, too — out of their misery.

In that incredible moment, all the heartache, all the tears, all the accumu-
(More on REEVES on Page 2)

IN SPORTS: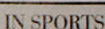

- Rangers fans gathered early and hung on every pitch .... Page 2D
- Championship helps team put ghosts of past behind it .... Page 3D
- Rangers roots run deep in rocky rebirth of the Washington Senators .... Page 6D
- Game-by-game in 1996 .... Page 7D

Clinton comes to town with victory in mind

President Clinton waves a hat given to him in Sundance Square by *Star-Telegram* President and Publisher Richard L. Connor.
Star-Telegram/Harry W. Hoover

President says he can top GOP in state

By MAX B. BAKER
Star-Telegram Staff Writer

FORT WORTH — Using a rejuvenated downtown Fort Worth as his backdrop, President Clinton campaigned for re-election in Sundance Square yesterday, promising new opportunities and a common vision that will take America into the 21st century.

"I want us to go into the next century with the American dream of opportunity alive for every single person who's willing to work for it — without regard to their race, their gender and what they start out with in life," Clinton said during the noontime rally in Fort Worth.

"If you are willing to work hard, you ought to have a chance," he said.

INSIDE:
A photographic presentation of the warm reception for President Clinton .... Page 8A
Bud Kennedy: Bill the Thrill had fans at high pitch of excitement ... Page 10A
Many saw this as a once-in-a-lifetime chance to see president. ... Page 10A
Clinton's rating as president climbs to 47 percent in Texas .... Page 11A

An estimated 20,000 people waited in line for hours under chilly gray skies, then squeezed onto two blocks to catch a glimpse of the first sitting president to stump for votes on Main Street in nearly three decades.

Ironically, it was a president who until recently had been given little
(More on VISIT on Page 11)

Visit brings back Texas memories

By RON HUTCHESON
Star-Telegram Washington Bureau

FORT WORTH — After spotting a former prom date and eight old high school buddies in Sundance Square yesterday, President Clinton was ready to reminisce when he eased into his limousine and propped a black Justin boot on the seat across from him.

But the small talk on the ride out of town ended when Clinton was asked why conservative Texans should choose him over Republican Bob Dole on Nov. 5.

"I'll bet you," he said, "if you took a survey of the people in Texas and got away from the labels, more of them would agree
(More on CLINTON on Page 9)

INSIDE

CLASSIFIED	.... G
COMICS	.... 4-5F
CROSSWORDS	...10E, 2G
EDITORIALS	.... 6B
ENCORE	.... 4A
HOROSCOPE	.... 2E
MOVIES	.... 8-9E
NEWS FEATURES	...17-38A
OBITUARIES	.... 2-3B
TELEVISION	.... 12E

Today: Mostly clear and warmer. High in the middle 70s, low in the middle 50s.
Full report on Page 22B

91st year, No. 158, 142 pages
Copyright © Fort Worth Star-Telegram 1996
To subscribe, dial DEL-IVER

Second baseman Mark McLemore, who hit .290 and led the club with 26 stolen bases, celebrates the division championship. Rookie reliever Danny Patterson is grinning behind McLemore. (*Fort Worth Star-Telegram*)

Jeff Russell, the Rangers' all-time leader in saves (134) and appearances (445), spent ten seasons with the Rangers before finally getting to celebrate a championship. Russell, who appeared in 55 games in '96, the most by a Ranger right-hander, lights Darryl Hamilton's victory cigar. (Linda Kaye)

Center fielder Darryl Hamilton, who set an A.L. record for most chances by an outfielder (389) without an error, salutes the crowd after the final regular season game. (*Fort Worth Star-Telegram*)

3

Red October

The first two playoff games in Ranger history would be played at Yankee Stadium, home of the East Division champion Yankees, twenty-two world championship flags, and the most abusive fans in baseball.

The Ranger rotation for the best-of-five Division Series had actually been determined way back on August 26, when Oates and pitching coach Dick Bosman set up their pitching plans for the month of September. Burkett would pitch before Hill, and Oliver would get extra rest between starts, a strategy that had worked brilliantly in the season's final month.

Burkett and Hill had pitched in three of the team's crucial last four victories before clinching the division title, and Oliver was 3–0 in the month. Declaring Burkett and Hill to be "Co-no. 1 Starters," Oates would send Burkett to the mound for Game 1 of the playoffs, followed by Hill and Oliver. For a possible Game 4, Oates selected Witt, with Pavlik moving to the bullpen.

Yankee manager Joe Torre countered in the first game with playoff-tested David Cone, the ace right-hander whose late-season comeback from an aneurism in his right shoulder had sparked the Yankees in September.

> "It won't be any tougher than playing in Seattle."
>
> *Johnny Oates, on having to open the playoffs at Yankee Stadium, September 29, 1996*

BURKETT WINS GAME 1

Despite the fact that the Rangers had won the season series from the Yankees, 7–5, most media observers rated the Yankees as heavy favorites, based on their playoff experience and the league's best bullpen. Plus, the Yankee Stadium crowd could quickly intimidate the Rangers.

"Señor Octubre," Gonzalez, homers for the fourth straight game to give the Rangers a 3–0 lead in Game Four. (*Fort Worth Star-Telegram*)

Gonzalez high-fives hitting coach Rudy Jaramillo as he returns to the dugout. (*Fort Worth Star-Telegram*)

John Burkett was masterful in Game One at Yankee Stadium, going all the way to win, 6–2. (©1996 Rich Pilling/MLB Photos)

Dean Palmer watches the flight of his fourth inning homer in Game One, which gave the Rangers a 5–1 lead. (*Fort Worth Star-Telegram*)

That forecast could not possibly have been more off target in Game 1. With 57,205 fans roaring on Tuesday, October 1, the Yankees put runners on second and third with nobody out in the first inning. Paul O'Neill then rifled a one-hop shot toward third that Palmer speared while diving toward the line. Bouncing to his feet and holding the runner at third, the Ranger third baseman gunned a throw across the diamond to nail O'Neill at first.

Thanks to Palmer's defensive gem, the Yankees were held to just one run on what otherwise might have been a big inning. Palmer's play may very well have kept the Rangers in the game.

Still trailing, 1–0, the Rangers unloaded on Cone in the fourth. Rodriguez led off with a single, and Greer walked. That brought up Gonzalez, who lined a wicked drive just inside the left-field foul pole for a three-run homer. Clark then singled, and one out later, Palmer deposited a hanging slider into the seats in left to make it 5–1.

Burkett made good use of the early lead and went all the way to win 6–2, scattering 10 hits, as he struck out seven and walked only one. "I was just going at every hitter," the Game 1 hero explained. "I was just trying to be as aggressive as possible."

Despite receiving the usual vocal abuse from the Bronx fans and a shower of projectiles hurled at Gonzalez in right field, the Rangers were unfazed by the hostile environment. "It's really exciting, because I was unsure how we would respond," beamed Oates. "But we responded on the road, in this ballpark, against one of the best pitchers in the game. I thought our guys did themselves proud."

Ranger fans were willing to wait in long lines for playoff tickets. Some even brought their own overnight accommodations. (Texas Rangers Archives)

GAME 2—A GIFT TO THE YANKEES

Having waited twenty-five years for their first taste of playoff action, Ranger fans now envisioned their team returning to The Ballpark with a 2–0 lead in the series. Those prospects improved when Gonzalez again opened the scoring with another home run. The Texas right fielder laced a second-inning shot down the left-field line off Yankee southpaw Andy Pettitte, who had led the league with 21 victories.

The Rangers, however, uncharacteristically allowed the Yankees to tie the game with a pair of defensive misplays in the bottom of the inning, as both Palmer and Hill made poor throws on potential double-play grounders.

With the score tied, 1–1, in the third, Gonzalez delivered again with a three-run bomb to left field that stunned and silenced the once-deafening Yankee faithful. Leading 4–1 with Hill on the mound, the Rangers had an opportunity to sweep the two games in New York. But the Yankees, of course, had other ideas.

The entire series might have turned out differently had the Texas offense not shut down at that point. But that's exactly what happened, as most of the Rangers remained in the collective slump that had plagued the team for the last three weeks of the regular season. Texas failed to score in the last nine innings of what would be a 12-inning marathon and then managed a total of just six runs in the subsequent two games at The Ballpark.

The Yankees rallied to win Game 2, 5–4, tying the score when Russell gave up an eighth-inning RBI single to Cecil Fielder. Texas squandered scoring chances with two on and two outs in the 10th when Clark flied out and again in the 12th when Palmer flied out with the bases loaded to end the inning against Brian Boehringer—the seventh Yankee pitcher of the night.

With a drizzle falling, Jeter singled, and Raines walked to start the bottom of the 12th. Henneman, the Rangers' fifth pitcher of the night, came in to

Fans file into The Ballpark for Game Three of the Division Series. (Texas Rangers Archives)

Inside The Ballpark, the atmosphere was electric during the first Red October. (*Fort Worth Star-Telegram*)

pitch to pinch-hitter Charlie Hayes, who laid down a bunt toward Palmer. The third baseman's throw to McLemore covering at first was low and wide, bouncing down the rightfield line as Jeter scampered home from second with the winning run.

Although Palmer's error ended the game, the Rangers had given it away earlier, gifting the Yankees their second-inning run and going 1-for-9 with men in scoring position. Still, Palmer attracted most of the postgame attention in the Ranger clubhouse.

The man who had starred in Game 1 with a two-run homer and a sparkling play in the field was called upon to comment from a different perspective on this night. "That's baseball," Palmer observed. "You can come through one night and not do the job the next. It was a little wet, and I didn't have a good grip, but it was a routine play."

The Yankees had won a near must-win game for them, and the teams headed for Texas tied at one victory apiece.

"SEÑOR OCTUBRE" NOT ENOUGH IN GAME 3

After a day off, both teams had their bullpens ready for Game 3, a matchup of lefties—Oliver for the Rangers and veteran Jimmy Key for New York. The Yankees had lost five out of six at The Ballpark during the regular season and were 3–10 there since it opened. And although Key had handled the Rangers over the years in his home parks, the lefty was 2–6 lifetime in Texas and had been hit hard in two losses in Arlington in '96.

The Rangers' first home playoff game was played before an energized crowd of 50,860, a large percentage of whom wore red in support of the home team. Soon after the

Managers Joe Torre (left) and Johnny Oates (right) approach home plate as their teams lined up prior to Game Three. (Texas Rangers Archives)

ceremonial first pitch was thrown out by former and current Arlington Mayors Tom Vandergriff and Richard Greene, Bernie Williams sliced a home run down the right-field line, and the Yankees had a 1–0 lead.

Williams then made a spectacular leaping catch in the bottom of the first to rob Greer of a home run. Quite an inning for the Yankee center fielder, whose personal two-day highlight film was just getting underway.

The Rangers turned in a defensive gem of their own with one out in the top of the fourth. With Williams at first and Raines at third, Oliver's pickoff move caught Williams in a rundown. Elster ran Williams back to first and pegged to Clark, who tagged out Williams and then fired to the plate to nail Raines and complete the unusual double play.

The crowd was still going crazy as the hot-hitting Gonzalez led off the fourth with Texas trailing, 1–0. The Ranger cleanup hitter, who had been dubbed "Señor Octubre" by Jim Reeves on his KRLD radio show, jumped on a 2–2 pitch and unloaded a tremendous blast down the line in left. While everyone waited for umpire Drew Coble's ruling on whether the ball was fair or foul, a celebratory fireworks display was prematurely set off.

Coble then ruled the long drive foul, setting up an almost Ruthian feat by Gonzalez. With smoke still lingering above The Ballpark from the premature pyrotechnics, the Ranger slugger launched Key's 3–2 pitch into the lower right-field porch to tie the game, 1–1, and ignite another round of fireworks.

In the Rangers' fifth, Rodriguez laced a two-out double just inside the bag at first to score Elster, who had walked, stolen second, and gone to third on an overthrow, giving the

Rangers a 2–1 lead. But once again, Texas's offensive production ended in the middle innings.

Reliever Jeff Nelson blanked the Rangers on just one hit over the next three frames. Oliver was equal to the task, retiring eight batters in a row in the sixth, seventh, and eighth, and went to the mound for the ninth still protecting a 2–1 lead.

Jeter led off the ninth with a sharp single between third and short. Raines followed with a single through the hole at shortstop, sending Jeter around to third. Oates then called for Henneman, who gave up a game-tying sacrifice fly to Williams, then induced a weak roller to third off the bat of Fielder, which moved Raines into scoring position.

Oates elected to stick with Henneman and walk Tino Martinez. Duncan then made Oates pay for that decision with a line-drive single to center, easily scoring Raines with the go-ahead run.

American League save leader John Wetteland came on to pitch the bottom of the ninth and walked Tettleton to start the inning. McLemore bunted the tying run to second. But pinch-hitter Newson was thrown out by Wetteland on a high chop behind the mound, and Hamilton struck out swinging to end the game.

"We've got to help Juan out," admitted Hamilton after the game. "It's ridiculous. Our bats have gone south completely."

Postgame analyses focused on the success of the Yankee bullpen and the lack of same on the Ranger side. But much of the locker room conversation centered around the spirit-

An attempted Yankee double steal turned into a double play in the fourth inning of Game Three. Rodriguez celebrates the tag of Tim Raines which completed the rare twin-killing. (*Fort Worth Star-Telegram*)

Darren Oliver, who went 14–6 in the regular season, leaves the mound with a 2–1 lead in the ninth inning of Game Three. (Texas Rangers Archives)

ed atmosphere of The Ballpark. "It was electric," said Yankee hero Williams, an observation that came from a man who had played postseason games in New York and Seattle.

GAME 4—PENNED IN AGAIN

The Rangers and their fans had just fourteen hours to recover before the start of Game 4, scheduled for 12:05 P.M. Saturday. Although many questioned if the Rangers could bounce back from another discouraging defeat, others wondered if the fifty thousand fans could rock The Ballpark in the same fashion after standing and screaming for over three hours the night before.

Those doubts were erased before the game even started. Former Ranger Jim Sundberg,

Juan Gonzalez carried a heavy offensive load for a slumping offense. "We've got to help Juan out," said Darryl Hamilton after Game Three. (Texas Rangers Archives)

Dean Palmer pulls up at second base with a double to start a second-inning rally in Game Four. (*Fort Worth Star-Telegram*)

accompanied by ex-teammates Tom Grieve, Pete O'Brien, and Steve Buechele, received a huge ovation when introduced for the first-pitch ceremony. That reception was then overshadowed by the crowd response to the most stirring rendition of the national anthem ever heard at The Ballpark. Nine-year-old Mikaila Enriquez of Edmond, Oklahoma, who had awed the crowd while singing the anthem in August, drew the fifty thousand out of their seats demanding a curtain call.

Yes, the crowd was again ready to roar, and it had a perfect target at which to aim. Former Ranger Kenny Rogers, who had spurned the Rangers' offer to sign with the Yankees in the off-season, would pitch against Witt. The Ranger right-hander mowed the Yankees down on just one hit for the first three innings while the Rangers and their fans got to Rogers.

Texas missed a chance to score in the first, stranding two runners, but Palmer led off the second with a double to right-center. Tettleton followed with a screaming line single to give the Rangers a 1–0 lead. After a force out, an Elster single, and a pop out, Rodriguez singled home McLemore to make it 2–0 as the crowd taunted Rogers with a chant of "Ken-ny, Ken-ny." Greer flied to deep left to end the inning, but Torre had seen enough of Rogers.

When the Rangers came up in the bottom of the third, right-hander Boehringer was on the hill. The winning pitcher in Game 2, Boehringer was less fortunate this time. His first pitch to Gonzalez leading off the inning traveled 416 feet over the out-of-town scoreboard in left, upping the lead to 3–0.

Mark McLemore nearly turned a double play over the sliding Joe Girardi in the fourth inning of Game Four, but Derek Jeter beat the relay to first base as the Yankees' third run came in to score. (*Fort Worth Star-Telegram*)

The home run put Juan in select company, as he joined Jeffrey Leonard as the only men to homer in four straight playoff games. Gonzalez also tied Ken Griffey Jr. and Reggie Jackson as the only players to hit five home runs in one postseason series.

One out later, Jeter booted a Palmer ground ball, and McLemore drove in the fourth Ranger run with a single. But staked to a 4–0 lead, Witt suddenly lost his command in a three-run Yankee fourth inning, allowing three singles and a walk before leaving with one out.

Rookie Danny Patterson came on to allow a bunt single and a run on an infield out before Cook put out the fire.

In what had become an all-too-familiar scenario, the Rangers' bats went silent. Leading 4–3, Texas had runners at first and second with nobody out in the bottom of the fourth when Torre brought on righty David Weathers to face Gonzalez. Ahead in the count, 3 and 1, Juan chased a pair of low-and-away sliders, striking out for the first out. Clark then grounded into an inning-ending double play, and the threat died.

When Williams began the Yankee fifth with a homer off Pavlik to tie the game, the game's momentum was totally on the Yankees' side. The score remained tied until the seventh, when Fielder came up with two outs and runners at the corners. The burly slugger, who had driven home the tying run in Game 2, ripped a single between third and short to give the Yankees a 5–4 lead, which Mariano Rivera protected by pitching hitless ball in the seventh and eighth.

In the ninth, Williams homered off Stanton—an insurance run that proved crucial as

Wetteland walked Rodriguez to start the bottom of the ninth. Greer flied out, and Wetteland pitched around Gonzalez, walking the tying run aboard. Clark then cracked a deep shot to the alley in left-center that was caught by Raines as he raced onto the warning track, leaving Palmer as the Rangers' last hope. On a 1–2 slider, Palmer swung and missed, the Yankees had won the game, 6–4, and the Rangers' season was over.

Once again, the Yankee bullpen had slammed the door, as it would do repeatedly on the way to winning the World Series. The Rangers scored just one run in the series against the Yankee relievers, who pitched 17 2/3 innings and collected all three New York wins. The Rangers did not score after the fifth inning in any of their three defeats. And the Ranger hitters batted a combined .218 in the series, only .206 with men in scoring position.

Gonzalez had been magnificent in defeat, batting .438, belting five HRs, and driving in nine of his team's 16 runs. Rodriguez and Elster also batted over .300, but no other Ranger hit more than .211 for the series.

Clark, who had just two hits in the series, summed it up perfectly, saying, "They pitched well, and we didn't do the job offensively."

Palmer said, "It's so disappointing, because every one of the games was so close, and every one could have gone either way."

Oates was able to look at the larger picture. "We set out to go farther," the skipper said. "But I told them to walk out of here with their heads up."

Many in the exhausted crowd stayed and cheered the Rangers as they headed off the

Will Clark's diving stop in the seventh inning kept the scored tied, 4–4, but Cecil Fielder followed with a single to drive in the winning run. (*Fort Worth Star-Telegram*)

McLemore consoles Rodriguez in the dugout after the final game. (*Fort Worth Star-Telegram*)

field, despite having been denied the thrill of a home victory. They had, however, shared in a feeling of joy and communal spirit unprecedented at a baseball game in Arlington.

A new era in Ranger history had begun. The next quarter-century would take off from the springboard of a division title and an unforgettable playoff experience.

Twenty-five years earlier, the first Ranger team had inherited a far different legacy.

4

Good-bye, Washington

In the beginning, they were the Washington Senators.

No, not the Senators of legendary pitching great Walter Johnson, who were one of the American League's charter franchises in 1901. Those Senators, who had sprinkled in three pennants and one world championship along with fifty-seven years of also-ran status, moved to Minnesota in 1961 and became the Twins.

Replacing those original Senators in Washington in 1961 were the expansion Senators, who more than kept alive the popular slogan, "Washington—first in war, first in peace, and last in the American League."

Only once in eleven years did the new Senators post a winning record. In 1969, their 86–76 mark was good enough for fourth place in the American League East, their highest standing ever, and earned first-year manager Ted Williams American League Manager of the Year honors.

A Hall of Famer and the last man to hit .400, Williams was regarded by many as the best hitter ever to play the game. But he was unable to duplicate his first-year success as a manager. The Senators fell to 70–92 the next year, with their already-mediocre attendance figures at RFK Stadium suffering a similar decline.

The club was owned by Bob Short, a Minneapolis attorney who had enjoyed success in the trucking and hotel industries. Short made millions by buying the NBA Minneapolis Lakers in 1961 and selling the franchise four years later after moving to Los Angeles. Then in 1968 he purchased controlling interest in the Senators, hiring Williams to a five-year contract as field manager the following season.

By the end of the 1970 season, Short was struggling financially and was under pressure to relocate from some other team owners, who earned very little money from their share of the meager gate receipts when their teams played at RFK. Well aware of Short's predicament was the mayor of Arlington, Texas, Tom Vandergriff.

Arlington Stadium. (National Baseball Library and Archive)

"I'VE NEVER SEEN A MAN MORE DEDICATED TO A PROJECT IN MY LIFE."

Washington Senators owner Bob Short, discussing Tom Vandergriff's efforts to move the team to Texas, September 21, 1971

51

Bob Short (center) gets acquainted with Senators' general manager George Selkirk (left) and manager Jim Lemon (right) after purchasing the club, December 3, 1968. Short would soon replace Lemon with Ted Williams. (Texas Rangers Archives)

Since 1958, Vandergriff had spearheaded a campaign to win a major league baseball franchise for the Dallas-Fort Worth area. Having been rebuffed twice by the American League and once by the National League in trying to land an expansion team and having failed to lure the Kansas City and Seattle franchises when they relocated, Vandergriff had set his sights on the Senators.

Tipped off about Short's predicament by Cleveland Indians President Gabe Paul and Angels owner Gene Autry, Vandergriff visited every American League spring training camp in 1971, lobbying club owners for their support in his goal of persuading Short to move his team to Texas.

While the '71 Senators were on their way to a 63–96 season in which they drew a total of only 655,156 fans, Short unsuccessfully attempted to sell the team to Washington interests, then had no alternative but to seriously entertain Vandergriff's proposal.

That proposal included a financial package in which ten banks in Dallas, Fort Worth, and Arlington cooperated to provide Short with $7.5 million in low-interest loans. Short would receive another $7.5 million from the sale of the team's broadcast rights for the next

Under manager Ted Williams, the Senators won 86 games in 1969, then fell to 70 wins in 1970 and 63 wins in 1971. (© *Washington Post*: Reprinted by permission of D.C. Public Library)

Arlington mayor Tom Vandergriff is welcomed back to Dallas on September 23, 1971, after securing approval of the Senators' move to Texas at an A.L. meeting in Boston, and displays a copy of a Washington newspaper reporting the franchise shift. (Courtesy of *Boston Herald*)

Dick Bosman pitching for the Senators in their final game at RFK Stadium, September 30, 1971, under the backdrop created by irate fans. (Photo by Richard Darcey, *Washington Post*)

ten years to the city of Arlington. The club would play in Turnpike Stadium, the twenty-one thousand-seat home of the Texas League's Dallas-Fort Worth Spurs. The stadium would be expanded to a seating capacity of thirty-five thousand by the start of the 1972 season.

By early summer, Short had agreed to move the team to Texas, causing Vandergriff to step up his lobbying efforts among the other A.L. owners. "We had to keep news of the pending move absolutely confidential," recalls the former mayor. "I was so thrilled that the five daily newspapers in our area, along with the radio and television people, fully cooperated with us in that effort, during the months in which we had to make sure that we had the necessary votes. I don't think we could have gotten that sort of cooperation in this day and age."

By mid-September, the mayor felt that he had the nine votes necessary to approve the franchise shift. A special league meeting was called for September 20 in Boston, at which Vandergriff was accompanied by an eight-man contingent of area business and civic leaders, including the mayors of Dallas and Fort Worth. The entourage was "a symbolic ges-

Fans stream onto the playing field in the ninth inning of the Senators' last game, causing the umpires to forfeit the game to the Yankees. It was the last major league forfeit until 1974, when the Rangers were awarded a forfeit win in Cleveland—a game in which Bosman also pitched. (© *Washington Post*. Reprinted by permission of D.C. Public Library)

ture, as this was a regionwide effort," explains Vandergriff, who expected to receive the support of ten of the twelve league owners.

Unfortunately, Autry had taken ill upon arriving in Boston and was hospitalized. On the first vote, and each vote thereafter, only eight clubs voted to approve the move. As expected, Baltimore and Chicago voted against it. The absent Autry was officially abstaining, as was Oakland owner Charlie Finley, who was present but not cooperating.

Finley, who had been counted as a supporter, was now withholding his approval, telling Short that he would trade his vote in exchange for the Senators' best young player, Jeff Burroughs. Short adamantly refused to cave in to Finley's demands, leaving the vote deadlocked at 8–2–2.

Finally, American League President Joe Cronin decided to break the deadlock by visiting Autry in his Boston hospital room, where the "Singing Cowboy" signed a proxy allowing Cronin to register his vote in favor of the move. Autry's vote decided the matter, causing Finley to give in and make the final margin 10–2.

While sports fans in Texas rejoiced, it was a time of mourning in Washington. For the first time in seventy-two years, the nation's capital would be without a major league team.

President Richard Nixon and Baseball Commissioner Bowie Kuhn had openly opposed the move. And more importantly, after the move was approved, Washington's star slugger, the six-foot-nine Frank Howard, was throwing all of his 280 pounds into resisting the move, threatening to retire.

Good-bye, Washington

When the Senators played their final home game at RFK Stadium on September 30, 1971, an extra fifty police officers were on duty to keep the peace. A crowd of 14,460 fans paid its way in, and an additional four thousand or so crashed the turnstiles without paying.

Banners defiling club owner Short were everywhere. Those containing profanity were removed by the police, and one large banner reading "Bob Short Stinks" was also taken down, causing resourceful fans to quickly manufacture another sign that proclaimed, "Bob Short Still Stinks." Other fans hung and burned in effigy a dummy resembling Short.

When Howard blasted a sixth-inning homer with the Senators trailing the Yankees, 5–1, the crowd demanded that its hero take two curtain calls. When Howard returned to the dugout the second time, he blew the crowd a kiss as tears began to stream down his cheeks.

"It's the biggest thrill I've ever had," said the gentle giant who had won a world championship with the Dodgers in 1963. "I'll take it to my grave."

Known as "The Washington Monument" and "The Capital Punisher," 280-pound Frank Howard was the darling of the Washington fans. (Texas Rangers Archives)

Howard's homer helped ignite a Senators comeback in which the home team took a 7–5 lead into the ninth inning. Senator pitcher Dick Bosman, who had been removed from the game, was watching from the Senators dugout.

Bosman recalls, "With one out, Bobby Murcer hit a comebacker to Joe Grzenda. By the time the pitcher's throw arrived at first base, the field was covered with people, and it was like a scavenger hunt out there."

Hordes of fans were swarming the playing field, looking for souvenirs of the final game. They swiped the bases and home plate, pulled lights and letters off the scoreboard, and tore chunks of sod from the playing field.

Judging the field conditions to be unsafe and unplayable, the umpires forfeited the game to the Yankees, turning what looked like a certain Senators victory into one last defeat.

On November 23, 1971, Short announced that manager Ted Williams would accompany the club to Texas. And although Short had planned to have a contest to name the team, he had decided that there just was not enough time. "We decided on the name 'Texas Rangers' because it was the overwhelming choice of the fans who wrote me and Mayor Vandergriff," he explained. "In effect, the fans held their own contest."

Turnpike Stadium, the home of the Texas League's Dallas-Fort Worth Spurs, was enlarged from 21,000 to 35,000 seats and renamed Arlington Stadium. (*The Sporting News*)

Good-bye, Washington

(Texas Rangers Archives)

As the Rangers' new fans followed the team's off-season activity, they learned that Howard had experienced a change of heart and would be joining his teammates in their new surroundings. Although there was widespread public sentiment in favor of naming the stadium after Vandergriff, the mayor resisted the idea and was successful in his effort to have the stadium renamed Arlington Stadium.

And as they would during every spring from that point on, the fans began thinking that this season, their Rangers just might make them proud.

Vandergriff, Rangers General Manager Joe Burke and A.L. President Joe Cronin, prior to the opening of Arlington Stadium in 1972. Despite having played for and managed the original Senators, Cronin was a valuable supporter of the Senators' move to Texas. (Texas/Dallas History Division, Dallas Public Library)

5

Hello, Texas

If Bob Short's prediction had come true and the Rangers had finished in the top half of their division, they would have accomplished something that the Senators never had. But Ted Williams expected to have a competitive club, guaranteeing what he termed "respectable baseball."

Perhaps things would have been different had the season not started nine days late due to the first-ever players' strike. Because right from the beginning, nothing went exactly as planned for the Rangers.

After posting an 11–14 record in spring training at Pompano Beach, Florida, the Rangers flew west for their scheduled home opener on Thursday, April 6, only to have the players' association vote to strike over the size of the owners' contribution to the players' pension fund. About half of the team worked out each morning at a school field in Euless, then took part in workouts with the college team at the University of Texas at Arlington in the afternoon.

One of those players was third baseman Davey Nelson, who recalled the last week of spring training, saying, "I felt we were playing sound ball, our personnel was in great condition, and mentally, we all were eager to get to Arlington and start the season."

Instead, the first nine games of the season were canceled, including the Rangers' inaugural home opener, which could be considered the first ominous sign that things would not come easily for this franchise. Instead of opening at home on April 6, the Rangers played their first four games on the road. By the time the transplanted Senators played in Arlington for the first time, Williams's squad was 1–3.

The Rangers' initiation to the American League in Anaheim on April 15 provided a sign of things to come. Starting pitcher Dick Bosman, whom Williams predicted "can be an 18- or 20-game winner with any batting sup-

Christi Hall of Arlington and the bullpen buggy had to wait out the first players' strike along with everyone else. The buggy was not around for long, as relief pitchers refused to wait for the cart to arrive from its parking place beyond the center field fence. (Courtesy *Fort Worth Star-Telegram*, Special Collections Division, University of Texas at Arlington Libraries.)

"I THINK WE'LL BE A FIRST-DIVISION TEAM THIS YEAR AFTER FINISHING FIFTH IN LAST YEAR'S EASTERN DIVISION RACE."
Ranger owner Bob Short, speaking before the 1972 season to the Dallas Assembly at the Fairmont Hotel

"I THINK THE PEOPLE DOWN IN TEXAS ARE GOING TO BE SURPRISED BY OUR CLUB. ... WE'RE CLOSE TO BEING A PRETTY GOOD BASEBALL TEAM."
Ranger manager Ted Williams, speaking to the press at the winter meetings in Phoenix, December, 1971

Texas' battery for the home opener—pitcher Dick Bosman (left) and catcher Rich Billings (right), pose with manager Ted Williams the day before the game. Texas beat California, 7–6. (Courtesy *Fort Worth Star-Telegram*, Special Collections Division, University of Texas at Arlington Libraries.)

port," indeed received no batting support at all. Bosman blanked the Angels for eight innings, left the game with a man aboard in the ninth, and watched from the dugout as reliever Paul Lindblad's wild pitch allowed the only run of the game to score.

The home opener on Friday, April 21 brought a much happier ending for Bosman and his teammates. The twenty-eight-year-old right-hander defeated the Angels, 7–6, before a crowd of 20,105. The first hit at Arlington Stadium was a mammoth two-run homer by Frank Howard in the bottom of the first inning off Clyde Wright. That was the 361st career home run for the man they used to call "the Washington Monument," but one of only nine that he would hit for the Rangers before being sold to the Tigers in August. Nelson also homered, one of only two he would hit all season.

Shortstop Toby Harrah delivered three hits, as did second baseman Lenny Randle. And left fielder Tom Grieve, the No. 1 overall pick in the 1966 amateur draft out of Pittsfield, Massachusetts, High School, chipped in with a pair of hits. Each of these three players would go on to imprint his own personal stamp on the pages of Ranger history.

Staked to an early lead, Bosman ran into trouble in the sixth and was relieved by Casey Cox. A thirty-year-old right-hander who had gone 36–36 in six years with the Senators, Cox had been the first Senator player to establish residence in Arlington and had spent the winter selling Ranger season tickets. Casey's customers watched him protect the lead for $3\frac{1}{3}$ innings before handing the ball to Lindblad with two outs and a runner at first in the ninth.

Lindblad struck out Billy Cowan to end the game, and the Rangers' first winning streak was underway. (As for Cox, he would be packing up and moving again soon, toting a 3–5 record to New York in a September trade to the Yankees. No figures are available regarding Cox's impact on Yankee season tickets for 1973.)

Bosman, who nearly twenty-five years later would take part in the club's first championship as pitching coach, remembered the first home game for more than the usual reasons. His wife, Pam, was expecting their first child and decided during the game that it was time to go to the hospital. After collecting the club's first home win, Bosman sprinted out to the sidewalk behind the right-field stands to a car in which his wife was waiting. A police escort accompanied the Bosmans to Harris Hospital in Fort Worth, where their daughter, Michelle, was born.

A sparse Saturday afternoon crowd of 5,517 turned out the next day to see hard-throwing righty Pete Broberg, a former first-round draft choice from Dartmouth College. The Ivy Leaguer hurled Texas's first shutout, a 5–0 win, fueling the already-high expectations for the twenty-two-year-old who had come right off the college campus to join the Senators the year before.

Victories the next two days provided the Rangers with a 5–3 record, a four-game winning streak, and a share of second place only percentage points off the division lead. The sweep of the Angels in the first series ever at Arlington Stadium sparked spectator interest somewhat, prompting 10,213 to show up on Tuesday night, April 25 as the Rangers went for their fifth straight win and a possible shot at the top spot in the West. The streak ended, however, as the Tigers defeated lefty Mike Paul, 4–1. Only 4,283 turned out the next night as Bosman lost to Detroit, 8–1.

The remaining five games of the home stand would each attract fewer than ten thousand fans. By the time the Rangers went back on the road, they were under .500 at 7–8 and would never rise above sea level again. They did get back to even at 15–15 by sweeping a doubleheader from the Twins on May 21, only to lose 11 of their next 13 games as they plummeted into the division cellar. From there, they never emerged, finishing 38½ games behind Oakland with only 54 wins and 100 losses.

Publicly, Short had anticipated home attendance of one million, which would have generated, in his words, "enough cash flow to build a championship team." Another prediction unfulfilled, Short failed to reach his stated break-even point of eight hundred thou-

Manager Ted Williams receives cowboy boot spikes on Opening Night, Friday, April 21, 1972. Also in foreground are club owner Bob Short (left) and Katy Corbin, Miss Arlington (right). (Courtesy *Fort Worth Star-Telegram*, Special Collections Division, University of Texas at Arlington Libraries.)

Rangers line up with their new cowboy hats for the inaugural home opener, Friday, April 21, 1972. From left: Ted Williams, Lenny Randle, Davey Nelson, Frank Howard, Rich Billings, Tom Grieve, Elliott Maddox, Joe Lovitto. (Courtesy *Fort Worth Star-Telegram*, Special Collections Division, University of Texas at Arlington Libraries.)

sand as home attendance totaled only 662,974, a meager average of 8,840.

As their batters grumbled about the difficulty of hitting home runs into the prevailing wind blowing in from right and right-center, the Rangers managed a major league low of 56 homers.

Outfielder Ted Ford, described by team publicist Burt Hawkins in the first Rangers media guide as "effervescent...a refreshing fellow with an infectious laugh," produced one-fourth of those homers, leading the team with 14.

Other than its use in describing Ford, the word effervescent did not come to mind often in characterizing the Ranger offense. Harrah and first baseman Larry Biittner shared the club lead in batting at .259. The club, whose manager had posted a lifetime batting average of .344, hit just .217 collectively.

Catcher Rich Billings led the club in RBI with 58. Perhaps the first modern-day player to wear the type of mustache and goatee combination favored by so many players today, Billings dubbed his facial hair "a Maynard," after the beatnik character Maynard G. Krebs on the television show *Dobie Gillis*. Billings's beard was the subject of no small amount of ridicule from opposing players and fans, but he had broken out of a slump as soon as he started growing it and superstitiously resisted shaving it off.

Surprisingly, manager Williams did not object, at least not vocally, to his catcher's new look, and Billings told the press that owner Short "told me he didn't care if I played in hot pants as long as I continued to hit."

Williams did, however, object to much of what he saw from his players and was not reluctant to tell them so. His lack of patience with his young and frequently inept team did not sit well with many of them. The former hitting star was especially tough on his pitchers, regularly yanking his starter at the first sign of trouble. Williams was often heard to say that "pitchers are the dumbest human beings on the face of the earth."

Frank "Hondo" Howard slams the first home run at Arlington Stadium, a two-run bomb to center field in the bottom of the first on Opening Night. (Courtesy *Fort Worth Star-Telegram*, Special Collections Division, University of Texas at Arlington Libraries.)

A graduate of Dartmouth College, Pete Broberg pitched the Rangers' first shutout. (Courtesy *Fort Worth Star-Telegram*, Special Collections Division, University of Texas at Arlington Libraries.)

Hitters were also subjected to harsh criticism from their manager. "Williams couldn't tolerate a mistake in the batting cage … everyone got gun-shy," remembered catcher Ken Suarez.

Billings recalls an incident during batting practice one day in Baltimore. While he was stepping out of the dugout for batting practice, he heard Williams say to a group of reporters, "Take Billings, for example. I bet he didn't even look at my book on hitting, no less read it."

Billings shot back, "As a matter of fact I did, cover to cover. But I could read a medical book, too, and that wouldn't make me a surgeon, would it?" An infuriated Williams removed Billings from that day's lineup and ordered him to spend the game in the bullpen.

Although not denying Williams's tendency to be sarcastic, Grieve is quick to add, "Although he could be impatient and negative, it was because he had thought he could get better results from what was a group of mediocre hitters at best. And I don't think he really liked to manage. I think Short talked him into it, and his heart really wasn't in it. But he

Outfielder Ted Ford, shown here after upending Cleveland second baseman Jack Brohamer, led the club with 14 homers, then failed to make the team in '73. (Courtesy *Fort Worth Star-Telegram*, Special Collections Division, University of Texas at Arlington Libraries.)

First baseman/outfielder Larry Biittner tied Toby Harrah for the team batting lead, despite hitting just .259. Graig Nettles is the Cleveland third baseman. (Courtesy *Fort Worth Star-Telegram*, Special Collections Division, University of Texas at Arlington Libraries.)

Having a ball is outfielder Joe Lovitto, who was a member of the first five Ranger teams. (Kids, don't try this at home.) (Linda Kaye)

Shortstop Toby Harrah slides home against the Twins, as on-deck hitter Don Mincher looks on. (Courtesy *Fort Worth Star-Telegram*, Special Collections Division, University of Texas at Arlington Libraries.)

Hello, Texas

liked to coach hitting. And he was a fascinating guy to talk to, about hitting or any other subject in which he had an interest."

Lacking the threat of the long ball, Williams played an aggressive running game. The Rangers led the league in stolen bases with 126, which was 26 more than their nearest rival. Nelson led the way with 51, finishing just one behind league leader Bert Campaneris.

In the last American League season before the adoption of the designated hitter rule, the Rangers' ERA was 3.53—more than a run lower than the 1996 championship team would compile. But in 1972, a 3.53 ERA left Texas dead last in the league. Bosman missed almost a month of the season after taking a line drive off his leg in July and won only eight games. The wildly inconsistent Broberg finished 5–12.

Mike Paul ranked ninth in the league in ERA (2.17) but had a losing record (8–9). Paul later served as Texas' advance scout in the 1996 championship season. (Courtesy *Fort Worth Star-Telegram*, Special Collections Division, University of Texas at Arlington Libraries.)

The bullpen was anchored by the thirty-year-old righty Lindblad, who led the majors with 66 appearances, and "Happy Horacio" Pina, a veteran Mexican right-hander who saved 15 of the club's 54 victories. The pen got plenty of work as the starters threw a league-low 11 complete games, a pitifully low figure compared with the 61 route-going outings hurled against the Rangers. In appreciation of their top relievers' tireless efforts, the Rangers traded away both men after the season.

Paul was the most effective pitcher on the staff, starting and relieving while compiling a club-best ERA of 2.17, ninth in the league. Yet, he, too, finished with a losing record at 8–9. Among his no-decisions was a scoreless duel with Cy Young Award winner Gaylord Perry, in which Paul was pulled after 11 innings while Perry went all the way to win in 14 innings, 2–0.

Right-hander Rich Hand led the club in wins with 10. After being farmed out to Denver in spring training, Hand returned in May to experience even less support than Bosman and Paul were receiving. Hand did not enjoy the luxury of seeing a Texas run on the scoreboard during his first 22 innings on the mound, as he lost his first three decisions on the way to a 10–14 mark.

The Rangers did not back up their pitchers with their gloves any better than they did with their bats. Texas committed a league-high 166 errors.

(Clockwise from upper left): The Rangers' first hispanic player, "Happy Horacio" Piña posted 15 saves to lead the '72 club. (Texas Rangers Archives)

Rich Hand was only twenty-three years old when he went 10–14 to lead the club in wins. (Texas Rangers Archives)

Lefty Paul Lindblad led the majors in appearances (66) in 1972, then was traded to Oakland, but returned to the Rangers in 1977. (Texas Rangers Archives)

In the last week of the season, Williams announced that he would not be returning in 1973. Perhaps he was driven to retire by his team's 17–48 record in games decided by one or two runs. As Paul recalled, "We killed ourselves with basic mental errors…throwing to the wrong base or missing the cutoff man. The good teams do these things right and beat you."

The Rangers were far from a good team. They were not even "close to being a pretty good baseball team," as Williams had suggested they would be. And they certainly did not play what Williams or anyone else this side of the '62 Mets would consider "respectable baseball."

Their next manager was well aware of these facts when he took the job.

6

Whitey, We Hardly Knew You

Dorrel Norman Elvert "Whitey" Herzog knew what he was getting into when he was hired by Short and General Manager Joe Burke on November 2, 1972, to be the Rangers' second manager. He just didn't know for how long.

A former major league outfielder, Herzog had just spent five years as director of player development for the talent-rich New York Mets. He had seen many recent Ranger draft choices in the Florida Instructional League and rated the Texas talent highly. Armed with a two-year contract and ten former first-round draft choices in spring training, Herzog felt he had the luxury of experimenting with some prospects at the major league level while leaving others in the minors to receive needed seasoning.

Although he tried to put a competitive team on the field, the Rangers still could not win. Herzog ran a widely praised spring training that was heavy in fundamentals and had a lineup bolstered by the acquisitions of veteran sluggers Mike Epstein, Rico Carty, and former batting champ Alex Johnson. But even with these additions, the Rangers scored fewer runs than any other team in the league. They also had the highest ERA. As a result of this deadly combination, the Rangers led the league in losses.

The forty-one-year-old Herzog and his young coaching staff employed a positive approach designed to instill confidence in his young players. Although the players voiced appreciation for the new regime, they didn't show it on the field. Epstein, a total bust, was traded to the Angels in May after batting .188 with one home run while waging a one-man campaign to have the Arlington Stadium fences moved in.

Also going to California in the deal was Hand, the club's top winner in '72. In exchange, the Rangers received slick-fielding first baseman Jim Spencer and twenty-three-year-old right-hander Lloyd Allen, who had been described by California G.M. Harry Dalton as "a potential 20-game winner."

With Texas, Allen fell exactly 20 wins short of living

David Clyde and Whitey Herzog in the Ranger dugout. (Linda Kaye)

"One of the worst clubs I ever saw."

Texas manager Whitey Herzog, assessing the 1972 Rangers after a series he watched in Kansas City

Manager Whitey Herzog (center) talks things over with general manager Joe Burke (left) and club owner Bob Short (right), perhaps asking Short where he purchased that sport jacket. (Linda Kaye)

up to that potential. In two seasons with the Rangers before being sold to the White Sox, he went 0–7 with an 8.29 ERA.

Carty also failed to live up to expectations. Entering the season with a lifetime .317 batting average, the thirty-two-year-old "Beeeg Boy" would hit just .232 with three homers. Carty had been, in Herzog's opinion, "the perfect guy" for the new designated hitter spot. But on June 1, Carty and Herzog almost came to blows in the dugout after the DH complained about a called third strike. In August, "the Beeeg Boy" was sold to the Cubs for what was termed "a minimal cash payment."

Not everyone had a bad year, though. Johnson led the team in batting (.287) and was

Mike Epstein was only in Texas for two months, but his frequent complaints made many people aware of how tough Arlington Stadium could be on home run hitters. (Linda Kaye)

Whitey, We Hardly Knew You

fifth in the league in hits. Nelson made the switch from third base to second, stole 43 bases, and played in the All-Star Game. And a new star surfaced in outfielder Jeff Burroughs.

The nation's No. 1 draft choice in 1969, Burroughs belted 30 home runs in his first full big league season, tying Frank Robinson for second in the league behind Reggie Jackson (32). Burroughs hit 22 of his long balls in the second half, including the first three grand slams in club history. The three slams came in an incredible span of ten days from July 26 to August 4.

Although Herzog saw considerable potential in his offense, he was quickly disenchanted with the pitching staff. Thinking that he would have a period of years to develop a corps of strong arms, Herzog began acquiring young power pitchers from clubs that did not have the time or patience that Herzog believed Ranger management had afforded him.

Ford, the first-season home run leader who had been cut by Herzog in spring training, was traded with Bosman to Cleveland for heat-throwing Steve Dunning. After playing behind Dunning for the first time, Johnson dubbed the right-hander "LTD," as in "Long Tater Dunning."

While "LTD" was going 2–6, Herzog uncovered one of the greatest finds in Ranger history. Best known as the older brother of pro basketball player Henry Bibby, twenty-eight-year-old Jim Bibby had just one big league win under his belt when the Rangers stole him from St. Louis in June by giving up two minor leaguers.

Whereas Herzog had swung and missed on the deals for Allen and Dunning, he hit the jackpot with Bibby. Within a month, the six-foot-five, 230-pound smoke-thrower

Rico Carty, who called himself "The Beeeg Boy," was acquired to be the Rangers' first DH, a role which suited one of his eccentricities. According to Harrah, Carty didn't trust anybody and played with a wad of cash in the back pocket of his uniform pants. (Texas Rangers Archives)

Alex Johnson, shown sliding in at the plate, led the '73 club in hitting (.287), and hit .291 in '74 before being traded to the Yankees. (Texas/Dallas History Division, Dallas Public Library)

Jim Bibby threw the Rangers' first no-hitter, then won 19 games in '74. When he returned to the Rangers briefly in 1984, manager Doug Rader chose him to start on an incredibly windy day in Toronto, because, in Rader's words, "He is the heaviest man on the planet, and would be unaffected by the wind." (Texas/Dallas History Division, Dallas Public Library)

On June 25, 1973, two days before his big league debut, eighteen-year-old David Clyde takes the line-up card to home plate to get acquainted with the umpires. From left: Ron Luciano, Clyde, Dave Phillips, Oakland coach Jerry Adair, Bill Haller. (Linda Kaye)

became the No. 1 starter. On June 29, he threw a one-hitter against the Royals, allowing only a sixth-inning single to Fran Healy. He also struck out 13 Red Sox in Boston, prompting Carl Yastrzemski to say, "He throws harder than Vida Blue."

Bibby's crowning moment came on July 31 in Oakland when he pitched the Rangers' first no-hitter. Bibby was given a 5–0 lead before he took the mound for the bottom of the first, and he proceeded to strike out 13 with an overpowering fastball and occasional slider. From the fifth inning on, his battery mate Billings called almost exclusively for fastballs.

Bibby fired one of those pitches past a swinging Reggie Jackson in the ninth, causing Jackson to remark, "That's the fastest ball I ever saw. Actually I didn't see it. I just heard it."

The massive right-hander walked six and was helped by three fine defensive plays. Shortstop Jim Fregosi, recently acquired from the Mets, went far to his left on a third-inning grounder. Center fielder Vic Harris made a running catch in the sixth. And shortstop Pete Mackanin, a late-inning defensive replacement, made the play of the game in the eighth on a one-hop smash off the bat of Bill North.

Owner Short rewarded Bibby with a retroactive $5,000 raise. A former Army truck driver in Vietnam who had been discarded by both the Mets and the Cardinals, Bibby finished the season with a 9–10 record, providing a strong hint of the brilliance he would demonstrate the following year.

Although Short referred to Bibby's gem as "my biggest thrill in sports," the game for which Short will be most remembered had occurred a month earlier.

DAVID VS. GOLIATH

By June 5, the day of baseball's amateur draft, the Rangers were buried hopelessly in last place, drawing an average crowd of only nine thousand and none greater than twenty thousand since Opening Day. However, by virtue of their last-place finish the year

Texas Rangers

before, they did possess the No. 1 pick in the draft. And Short decided to use it to his financial advantage.

Eighteen-year-old right-hander David Clyde of Westchester High School in Houston was the consensus pick as the best pitching prospect in the draft. After winning all 18 starts in his senior year with an ERA of 0.18, Clyde was certain to be the Rangers' selection. What Herzog did not know was that Clyde would be in his starting rotation barely three weeks later.

Herzog watched Clyde pitch in Austin in the state 4A championship game and expected the kid to be signed and shipped to rookie ball. Instead, Short gave Clyde a huge bonus and brought him immediately to the big leagues. The bonus was reported at the time to be $125,000 but was actually $65,000. The immensity of Short's gamble, however, could not be disputed.

In desperate need of funds to sustain his ailing franchise,

Bill Gogolewski pitched the last four innings of Clyde's debut to pick up the save, one of his six for the season. (Linda Kaye)

Short was willing to risk the arm and psyche of the kid who was envisioned to be the cornerstone of the Ranger future. Short assessed correctly the impact that Clyde's presence would have at the gate and was willing to live with the potential consequences.

Clyde's debut at Arlington Stadium on Wednesday, June 27 came just twenty days after his final high school game. In the days leading up to his first start, Clyde had joined the team for road games in Minnesota and Kansas City, had been sent by Herzog to home plate for the exchange of lineup cards—"to get to know the umpires," Herzog explained—and had been issued uniform No. 32 in honor of his hero, Sandy Koufax.

Before going to the mound, Clyde received a telegram from his idol, that read, "Go get them, Number 32." Koufax was hardly the only one eager to see how Clyde would fare.

For the first time ever, 35,698-seat Arlington Stadium was filled to capacity, with the last of two thousand available general admission seats scooped up the morning of the game. Between five and ten thousand potential ticket buyers were turned away. The Arlington Police Department assigned eighteen officers to control traffic around the stadium and urged motorists to leave early and bring exact change for the toll booths on the Dallas-Fort

Worth Turnpike. Stadium gates would open a half-hour earlier than usual, at 5 P.M. for the 7:30 P.M. game.

Despite the warnings, many of those holding tickets were still in their cars at 7:30 in an unprecedented traffic tie-up, competely missing the pregame spectacular, which included lion cubs and hula dancers. Many ticket buyers managed to see the first pitch only because Herzog decided that the game should be held up fifteen minutes to let the fans see what they had paid for.

At first it appeared that late arrivals might miss Clyde completely. Although he later claimed that he "was never really that nervous," the teenager dropped his cap when he removed it for the national anthem, then walked the first two batters of the game. Recovering magnificently, in storybook fashion he struck out the next three hitters, all of them swinging.

In the second, Clyde walked four and surrendered a two-run homer to Mike Adams but got out of the inning trailing only 2–0. The Rangers tied it on a single by Nelson in the second, and Clyde responded with three shutout innings. He retired nine of his final 10 batters and left with a 4–2 lead.

Clyde had received a total of four standing ovations, the last timed at just over four minutes. The kid had walked seven, fanned eight, and allowed only one hit, throwing 112 pitches. Only once did Herzog venture to the mound, checking to make sure that Clyde was not hurt after bouncing two pitches in the dirt.

Reliever Bill Gogolewski worked the final four innings for a hard-earned save in a 4–3 victory. A grateful Short treated Gogolewski to dinner for two at the restaurant of his choice. Meanwhile, Clyde was totally at ease in dealing with the media crush that had arrived from all directions.

"I got away with a lot of pitches tonight," said the franchise savior. "Like the high fastballs. I really didn't get my curve working until the third inning. I expected to get hit much harder than I was."

Clyde would be victimized by more than his share of hard-hitting in the years to come. But for the moment, he was the toast of the town. "It couldn't have been better," beamed Short. "For once everything we planned and hoped for went right." Later, Short added, "It's going to take someone like him and ultimately a winning team for us to stay in business."

Clyde took his regular turn the rest of the year and was amazingly effective, posting a 4–4 record before running out of gas and finishing 4–8 with a 5.01 ERA. The crowds loved him, and the turnstiles reflected that

Jim Merritt won only five games in '73 but drew national attention when he announced that he had thrown a greaseball while shutting out the Indians, calling it "my Gaylord Perry slider." Merritt was fined by A.L. president Joe Cronin, and was unable to duplicate Perry's slippery long-term success. (Linda Kaye)

Texas Rangers

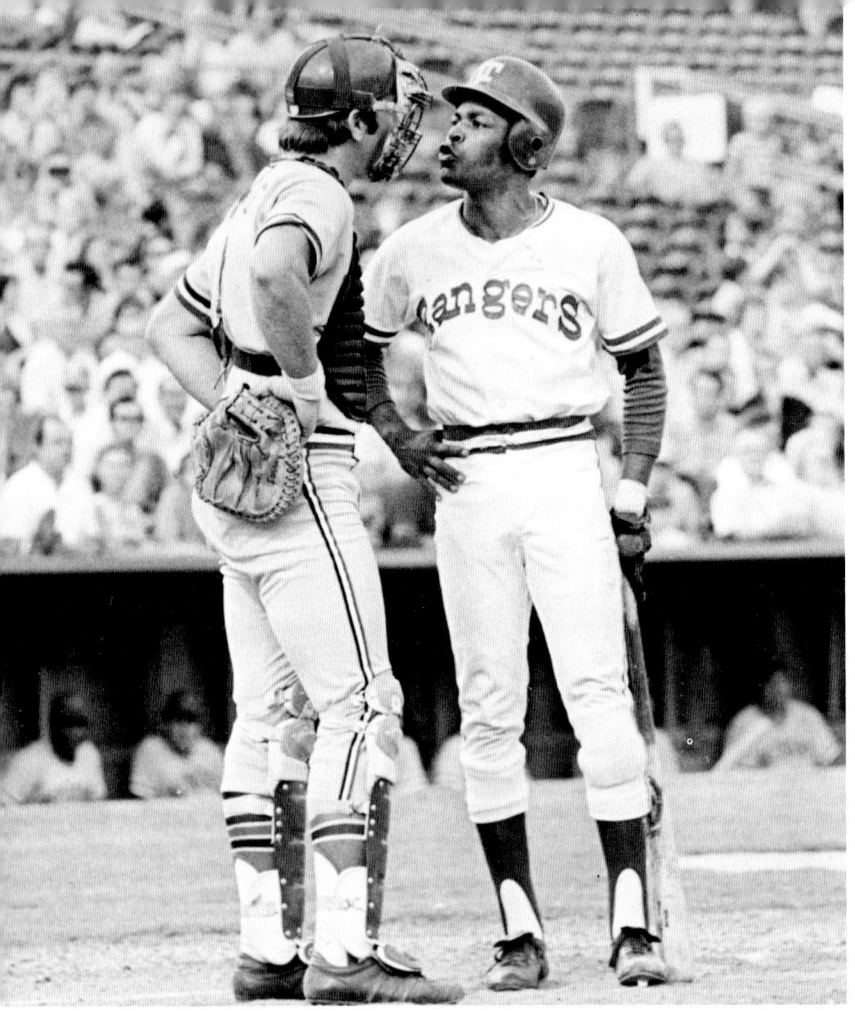

Third baseman Davey Nelson argues with Cleveland catcher Ray Fosse after being called out at the plate. Nelson led the club in stolen bases in '72 and '73, and stole second, third, and home in one inning in '74. (Courtesy *Fort Worth Star-Telegram*, Special Collections Division, University of Texas at Arlington Libraries.)

affection. On days when Clyde started, the Rangers averaged 18,187, whereas on the other days the average draw was 7,546.

Despite the promise shown by Clyde and Bibby, Herzog's pitching staff continued to struggle as a whole, and it seemed that everything and everyone was working against them. Even an opposing mascot, Milwaukee's fun-loving beer jester, Bernie Brewer, was apparently involved in a diabolical plot to foil the Ranger staff.

During a weekend series in early July in which Milwaukee hitters had thoroughly dominated Ranger pitching, Herzog alleged that the endearing Brewer mascot was tipping pitches from the center-field bleachers. According to the Ranger skipper, who actually dispatched Bibby in street clothes on a spy mission to the bleachers, Bernie was receiving signals from a mysterious man with binoculars. In turn, the mascot would clap his hands twice before Ranger pitchers would deliver a breaking ball.

"They haven't taken a bad cut all weekend, and those guys aren't that good a hitting team," claimed Herzog. "They never lunged at a breaking pitch, even against Clyde, as wild as he was. It didn't make sense."

Herzog finally complained to the umpires during the second game of a Sunday doubleheader, and the binoculared fellow was evicted from County Stadium. After the game, Whitey summed up the situation by stating the obvious. "I don't see why they think they have to cheat to beat us."

Total attendance at Arlington Stadium was only 686,974, just slightly higher than it had been in 1972. And with Herzog building for the future, the team was no bet-

Jackie Brown, "The Oklahoma Curveballer," tied for third on the club with five wins in '73, then won 13 games in '74. Brown was the Rangers' pitching coach from '79 to '82. (Linda Kaye)

A six-time A.L. All-Star, Jim Fregosi spent four years with Texas late in his career. He once complained to a sportswriter who had written that Fregosi had booted a routine grounder, "Don't you realize that when it's hit to me, there's no such thing as a routine grounder?" (Linda Kaye)

ter, setting a club record for losses with a season record of 57–105. Herzog felt that the club had taken major strides in the right direction, but the journey ended abruptly for Whitey. On September 2, with a record of 47–91, Herzog was fired.

Not coincidentally, Billy Martin had just been released from his contract by the Detroit Tigers.

Some fans obviously didn't care that the '73 Rangers had the worst record in baseball, enjoying other aspects of a day at the ballyard. (Texas Rangers Archives)

Sign of the times—pitcher Don Stanhouse flashes the peace sign. Stanhouse had control trouble in three years with Texas, then blossomed into a top bullpen closer with Baltimore. (Linda Kaye)

The bullpen phone rang often for Steve "Phone Call" Foucault, who led the club for three straight years in appearances and three straight years in saves as well. (Linda Kaye)

Outfielder Tom Grieve, who became the general manager in '84, was the No. 1 draft choice in the nation when he was taken by the Senators in '66. He played for Texas from '72 to '77 and was the Ranger Player of the Year in 1976. (Linda Kaye)

7

Billy the Kid

The uproar over the firing of the popular Herzog subsided considerably the next day when Short introduced forty-five-year-old Billy Martin as the Rangers' new manager. The fiery Martin had achieved dramatic turnarounds in Detroit and Minnesota, transforming both teams from also-rans into division winners.

"I'm not sure that anybody could have done better than Herzog did," Short said. "But this franchise is in financial trouble because we are not drawing. If we don't produce a winner here fast, chances for baseball's success in this area are slim."

Not many believed that even Martin could produce a contender in Texas in 1974 from the squad that finished the previous season with the worst record in baseball. But Martin maintained that he could, saying at the end of the 1973 season, "People are laughing at this team, and they will laugh when I say we'll be a contending team next season. Let's see who is laughing then."

The chances of Martin's prophecy being realized increased immeasurably on October 26, when new General Manager Dan O'Brien completed a trade with the Chicago Cubs that Herzog had been working on before being fired. Joining the Rangers would be six-time 20-game winner Ferguson Jenkins, who had just struggled through a 14–16 season at the age of twenty-nine. In exchange for the Canadian-born right-hander, the Rangers had to part with two of their best young prospects, Bill Madlock and Vic Harris.

Madlock had been called up in September and impressed everyone by hitting .351 in 21 games, and Martin had penciled him in as his starting third baseman for '74. Madlock went on to win four National League batting titles, but the acquisition of Jenkins was

"IF MY MOTHER WAS MANAGING THE RANGERS, AND I HAD THE OPPORTUNITY TO HIRE BILLY MARTIN, I'D FIRE MY MOTHER."

Ranger owner Bob Short, announcing the hiring of Billy Martin, September 8, 1973

Of Billy Martin, Toby Harrah said, "He hated losing more than anyone I ever knew." The combative Martin vented his anger at umpires and players alike. (Texas Rangers Archives/Courtesy *Fort Worth Star-Telegram*)

Martin is obviously displeased as he removes David Clyde from a game after the young lefty surrendered two home runs. Jim Fregosi is between Clyde and Martin, while catcher Rich Billings (left) and reliever Jackie Brown (right) look on. (Courtesy *Fort Worth Star-Telegram*, Special Colections Division, University of Texas at Arlington Libraries.)

the most significant move in enabling the Rangers to become the Cinderella team of 1974.

The Rangers also traded for two other veterans who would play major roles in the turnaround—pitcher Steve Hargan, who won 12 games, and outfielder Cesar Tovar, who hit .292.

The bulk of the Rangers' offensive improvement, however, came from their youngsters. The team batting average jumped from .255 to .272, led by Burroughs, who batted .301 in a career year. Despite losing 10 to 15 homers to the prairie winds, the twenty-three-year-old right fielder hit 25 roundtrippers, led the league with 118 RBI, and won the American League Most Valuable Player Award.

The Arlington Stadium fences were moved in ten feet in the alleys from 380 to 370 feet away, but that move had little impact. In fact, the Rangers' home run total, and that of Burroughs, decreased.

In spring training, Martin took a chance on two raw rookies whom he had watched in the Instructional League. Both first baseman Mike Hargrove and catcher Jim Sundberg seized the opportunity provided by Marin and won starting jobs.

Dudley Michael Hargrove, from the Texas Panhandle town of Perryton, became the first native Texan ever to play for the Rangers. The patient left-handed hitter made the jump all the way from Class-A Gastonia and batted .323 to win the American League Rookie of the Year Award. Out in the Panhandle, the local radio station in Perryton joined the Rangers Radio Network and had to make just eighteen phone calls to fill the eighteen sponsorship openings on the broadcasts.

The strong-armed Sundberg, who had played only 91 minor league games at Class-AA Pittsfield, batted .247, led the team in sacrifice bunts, and provided the best defense the Rangers had ever enjoyed behind the plate.

Martin's Rangers were daring on the bases, with five players stealing 13 bases or

1974 American League MVP Jeff Burroughs led the league with 118 RBI while battling the Arlington Stadium winds which blew in from right-center field. (Courtesy *Fort Worth Star-Telegram*, Special Collections Division, University of Texas at Arlington Libraries.)

The first native Texan to play for the Rangers, Perryton's Mike Hargrove, jumped from Class-A Gastonia to win the 1974 A.L. Rookie of the Year Award. (Courtesy *Fort Worth Star-Telegram*, Special Collections Division, University of Texas at Arlington Libraries.)

TEXAS RANGERS

Fittingly, Ferguson Jenkins was on the mound when the Rangers drew a million fans for the first time ever. Jenkins won a club-record 25 games, pitched 328 innings and won the Comeback Player of the Year Award. (Courtesy *Fort Worth Star-Telegram*, Special Collections Division, University of Texas at Arlington Libraries.)

more. And despite finishing only tenth in the league in home runs, the Rangers were second in runs scored.

The lack of pitching depth was a more difficult problem for Martin to solve. Jenkins and Bibby were the only two starters he knew he could count on. So he leaned on them heavily—so heavily that the pair started 82 of the 162 games and completed 40 of them. (Jenkins led the league with 29 complete games.) Together, they won 44 games, more than half of the team's 84 victories.

Clyde was a disappointment at age nineteen, going 3–9, but Hargan and a curveballing Oklahoman named Jackie Brown provided respectable starters in the third and fourth slots.

Second-year reliever Steve Foucault carried a heavy load in the bullpen, notching eight wins, all 12 of the team's saves, and appearing in 69 games, third-most in the league. But the lack of any reliable assistance for Foucault proved costly.

And where did all these fine individual performances leave the Rangers? Exactly where Martin had said they would be—right smack in the middle of the West Division race.

As a matter of fact, the Rangers led the defending world champion Oakland A's for over two weeks, holding first place from April 24 until May 9. Taking advantage of several off-days early in the season, Martin pitched Jenkins and Bibby every fourth day, using a third and fourth starter only when necessary.

Martin's strategy paid off as Texas streaked to a 15–9 start with Jenkins and Bibby posting 11 of the wins. Jenkins's American League debut was a masterful one-hitter against

Club president Dr. Bobby Brown (left) enjoys a night at Arlington Stadium with Commissioner Bowie Kuhn. (Courtesy *Fort Worth Star-Telegram*, Special Collections Division, University of Texas at Arlington Libraries.)

TEN-CENT BEER NIGHT GAME FORFEITED TO RANGERS

One of the Rangers' many achievements in 1974 was surviving Ten-Cent Beer Night in Cleveland on June 4. Scheduled less than a week after the Rangers and Indians had brawled in a game in Texas, the promotion drew a crowd of twenty-three thousand. Several spectators raced onto the field during the game, and Ranger outfielders were bombarded with various projectiles throughout the evening.

With the score tied, 5–5, in the bottom of the ninth, the Indians had the bases loaded with two outs when a fan ran out toward Texas right fielder Jeff Burroughs. The rowdy fan attempted to grab Burroughs's cap and glove, then tried to shove the Ranger player. Burroughs shoved back and started chasing the trespasser across the field.

A full-scale melee soon erupted, in which the Rangers, led by manager Billy Martin and armed with bats, charged from their dugout toward right field to come to the aid of Burroughs while several hundred fans poured onto the field. Cleveland players streamed onto the field as well, initially helping to protect the Rangers and subsequently fighting to protect themselves.

In the midst of the chaos, chief umpire Nestor Chylak phoned the public address announcer, who informed the crowd that the game had been for-

The Rangers charge from their dugout to aid right fielder Jeff Burroughs. From left: Don Stanhouse, Jim Shellenback, Rich Billings (in jacket), Jim Fregosi, coach Art Fowler, coach Charlie Silvera, Jim Spencer, Steve Hargan, David Clyde (in jacket). (Paul Tepley)

Burroughs receives an escort from coach Charlie Silvera (left) and Joe Lovitto (right) as he leaves the field. Behind Silvera is Jim Sundberg. Behind Burroughs' left shoulder is manager Billy Martin. (Paul Tepley)

feited to the Rangers. There had not been a forfeit in the major leagues since unruly spectators had forced the Senators to forfeit their final game ever at RFK Stadium in 1971.

The only serious casualty among the players was Cleveland pitcher Tom Hilgendorf, who was smacked over the head with a chair and had to be helped off the field.

"We're damn lucky we didn't get killed out there," said Ranger manager Billy Martin after his team had safely reached the clubhouse.

Texas and Cleveland players encounter the fans in right field. From left: David Clyde, Mike Hargrove (#21), Billy Martin, Jim Shellenback. To the right of the policeman are Cleveland players Dave Duncan and Tom Hilgendorf (#40), Jim Sundberg, Cleveland's Gaylord Perry (#36). (Paul Tepley)

The Rangers deal with one of the intruders. From left: Jim Merritt, Jim Bibby, trespasser, Alex Johnson, Mike Hargrove, Tom Grieve. (Paul Tepley)

According to Jim Sundberg, this bloodied fan, being held by umpire Joe Brinkman (left) is the one who ignited the riot by trying to grab Jeff Burroughs' glove in right field. Sundberg recalls that, "Burroughs, Hargrove, and Toby Harrah each hit this guy before he finally stayed down." Sundberg says that he stood back-to-back with Lenny Randle so that no one could hit them from behind. (Paul Tepley)

Opening Night, 1975, drew 28,797, the best crowd ever for Opening Day in Arlington, and a band played in the stands. Jenkins, however, was hit hard, and the Rangers lost to the Twins, 11–4, a sign of things to come. (Texas/Dallas History Division, Dallas Public Library)

Center fielder Willie Davis (left) chats with Martin during his brief stay in Texas. (Texas/Dallas History Division, Dallas Public Library)

the A's that left Reggie Jackson muttering, "He made it look so ridiculously easy that I wondered if he was even sweating. The guy that got rid of him in Chicago ought to be fired."

Plenty of American League hitters agreed, as the leader of the Ranger staff posted a 2.83 ERA in an astounding 328 innings and went 25–12, tying eventual Cy Young Award winner Catfish Hunter as the league's winningest pitcher. Jenkins won the United Press International Comeback Player of the Year Award with what remains the greatest season ever by a Ranger pitcher.

The Rangers stayed within three games of the lead for most of the first half, then slumped in July to fall nine games out. They rallied in September, however, and trailed Oakland by only six games when the A's came to town for a three-game series beginning September 13.

Defeating the A's for the fifth time in as many tries, Jenkins outpitched Hunter, 3–1, in the series opener. Then Brown beat Vida Blue, 8–3, to cut the lead to four games. But the Rangers never inched any closer as Bibby lost the finale, 4–1. Texas could not close the gap the rest of the way and finished in second place, five games behind at 84–76.

The "Turnaround Gang," as Martin's team was dubbed, had captured the attention of the Metroplex. An average of almost twenty-three thousand turned out for the series with Oakland, and the season's total attendance soared past the million mark, leaping 74 percent to 1,193,902.

No, they weren't laughing at Martin's prediction anymore. The worst team in baseball had improved by 27 wins and gone from 37 games behind to only five games behind in just one season. Martin was an easy choice for American League Manager of the Year.

"Farm and Ranch Night" was a popular promotion in the '70s. Over 20,000 fans turned out on June 27, 1977, for a doubleheader split with Minnesota. Between games, Tennesseean Clyde Wright drew the cow-milking honors while Hargrove displayed his best West Texas hog call. (Texas/Dallas History Division, Dallas Public Library)

Club owner Brad Corbett (right) and general manager Dan O'Brien (left) announce the firing of Billy Martin on July 20, 1975. Seated between them is Mervin Snyder, a member of the club's board of directors. "Hell, we were working for him," said one of the club's owners of Martin. (Texas/Dallas History Division, Dallas Public Library)

CORBETT TAKES OVER

The Rangers' success on the field and at the box office came too late for Bob Short to enjoy. Two days before Opening Day, the man who had brought the Rangers to Texas sold the club to a group of investors headed by Fort Worth resident Bradford G. Corbett. President and C.E.O. of Robintech, a plastic pipe company, Corbett assembled an ownership group that included Fort Worth publisher Amon Carter Jr., Dallas developer Raymond Nasher, and Dallas insurance executive Bill Seay.

One of Corbett's first moves was to persuade one of the investors to take a leave of absence from his medical practice to serve as president of the Rangers. Thus, former Yankee third baseman Bobby Brown became club president, a position he held for just one season.

Corbett loved the spotlight and relished associating with the players. He delighted in trading and signing players, often making moves that left his front-office personnel shaking their heads. At the winter meetings in December, the Rangers beefed up for 1975 by trading for aging veterans Willie Davis and Clyde Wright, giving up on Broberg, Mackanin, and pitcher Don Stanhouse.

The tempestuous thirty-five-year-old Davis hit just .249 in a 42-game Texas career. His antics included removing his glove for a couple of pitches and squatting down in center field in a game against Boston in late May, an act of protest precipitated by Ranger pitcher Hargan's failing to retaliate after Davis had been knocked down by a pitch. When Davis failed to show up in Baltimore the following week for the start of a road trip, protesting the Rangers' refusal to grant him an advance on his salary, the lanky center fielder was traded to St. Louis.

Wright, a thirty-two-year-old lefty who had lost 20 games for Milwaukee the year before, went 4–6 in his one season with the Rangers. Like Davis, Wright was a player well past his prime whose career came to an end in 1975.

The Davis and Wright deals epitomized the Rangers' 1975 season. Not a whole lot worked.

Frank Lucchesi meets with the media for the first time as Ranger manager. "He loved his players and his players loved him," recalls Tom Grieve of Lucchesi. (Texas/Dallas History Division, Dallas Public Library)

Martin went to spring training again hoping to convince his players that they could win—only this time he was shooting for the moon. "We are now a team that thinks like a winner and is a winner," Martin declared. "I believe we can win the American League West, win the playoff, and win the World Series."

And they would attempt to do all of that without David Clyde, who was sent to the minors in spring training, just a few weeks before his twentieth birthday.

Needing Jenkins and Bibby to repeat their ironman heroics, the Rangers lost any realistic chance of contending when both right-handers pitched far below their 1974 standards. Jenkins's ERA rose a full run to 3.83 as his record dropped to 17–18. Bibby, no longer able to get by on his fastball alone, was 2–6 when the Rangers traded him along with Jackie Brown and minor leaguer Rick Waits to the Indians on June 13.

That trade, completed with the Rangers floundering in fifth place with a 28–29 record, was an attempted quick fix. In return for the three young pitchers, the Rangers picked up thirty-six-year-old Gaylord Perry, who had won over 200 big league games, including 21 the previous year. Headed by Jenkins and Perry, the Ranger staff now boasted two future Hall of Famers. And Perry pitched well, going 12–8 for Texas, but his efforts were hardly enough.

The team batting average fell to .256, with Burroughs suffering the most severe drop. Determined to pull the ball more frequently to avoid the wind blowing in from right field, Burroughs increased his home run total from 25 to 29, but his average plummeted 75 points to .226, and his strikeout total leaped from 104 to 155.

Harrah and Randle had strong seasons, and Hargrove hit .303, but no one else could approach their 1974 performance. As General Manager O'Brien said years later, looking back at '74, "It was a very fragile sort of success. A lot of players had great years. And it was unlikely that any of those players would be able to repeat those years."

Nor was the manager capable of repeating the year in which everything he touched turned to gold. By early July, the Rangers were 13 games out, and Martin was regularly second-guessing his players. With Martin and the front office in frequent disagreement on personnel moves, Corbett traveled to Boston with the team and visited with several of his young players. The owner then decided that Martin had to go.

On July 21, with the Rangers' record at 44–51, Martin was fired, replaced by his third-base coach, Frank Lucchesi. "It had become a country club," complained Martin. "I couldn't maintain control of the players." Asked about managing again, Martin replied, "I don't think I can come back to it. I don't know about my future." Less than two weeks later, Martin was hired to manage the New York Yankees.

GENTLEMAN FRANK

The warm and gregarious forty-nine-year-old Lucchesi, who managed 20 seasons in the minors before a 2½-year stint piloting the Phillies, provided a stark contrast to Martin's abrasiveness. The players responded to Lucchesi's genial manner, going 35–32 the rest of the way while earning the new manager a contract for 1976.

The Rangers finished third, 19 games behind Oakland with a 79–83 record. The coming off-season would be the first of a series of eventful winters for the Corbett regime.

Before Christmas, the Rangers traded for a pair of veteran right-handed starting pitchers, thirty-three-year-old Nelson Briles and former 20-game winner Bill Singer, who was only thirty-one but was coming off elbow surgery. The duo would have some large shoes to fill because Jenkins was traded to Boston for center fielder Juan Beniquez, a couple of pitching prospects, and $200,000.

To bolster the bench, two more trades brought backup catcher John Ellis and outfielder Gene Clines to Texas. In order to acquire Clines, the Rangers gave up outfielder Joe Lovitto, a former first-round draft choice who had failed to hit as one of Martin's pet projects.

Lucchesi was happy with his new starting rotation of Perry, Singer, Briles, and young lefty Jim Umbarger. And thirty-nine-year-old southpaw Joe Hoerner was signed to take Umbarger's place in the bullpen.

Beniquez would be flanked by Randle and Burroughs in the outfield. Highly touted

With Harrah (throwing) at shortstop and former No. 1 draft pick Roy Smalley (behind Harrah) at second, the Rangers had a promising double play combination until Smalley was traded to the Twins. (Courtesy *Fort Worth Star-Telegram*, Special Collections Division, University of Texas at Arlington Libraries.)

Texas Rangers

shortstop prospect Roy Smalley would be moved to second, joining Hargrove, Harrah, and second-year third baseman Roy Howell in the infield, with Sundberg catching.

Lucchesi was the first manager to let Grieve play every day, usually as the DH, a move that paid off because Grieve led the team with 20 home runs, drove in 81 runs, and was named the Rangers' Player of the Year. But he had little help in producing runs.

The Rangers broke out of the gate in fine fashion, taking first place on April 18 and holding it for exactly a month. With Harrah playing well enough to win the starting shortstop spot in the All-Star Game, the Rangers were 44–38, seven games out at the break.

But the Rangers lost their first four games of the second half and 12 of their first 15 after the break, falling to fourth place, 14 games out. That's precisely where they stayed, finishing with a record of 76–86.

Unlike in many other troublesome years, Texas's pitching was not the problem.

The '76 season was a yawner for just about everyone, including starting third baseman Roy Howell. (Linda Kaye)

Perry, Briles, and Umbarger all had good years and were joined on June 1 by one of the league's premier right-handers when twenty-five-year-old Bert Blyleven came over in a blockbuster deal with the Twins.

Blyleven posted a sparkling 2.76 ERA but, plagued by low run support, had a losing record (9–11). And the price paid for him was steep—Smalley, who went on to have an outstanding career; Singer, who was 4–1 at the time of the trade; pitcher Jim Gideon, who was a No. 1 draft out of the University of Texas; and young infielder Mike Cubbage.

The Ranger offense was anemic, averaging under four runs a game and scoring almost 100 runs fewer than the year before. Hargrove slipped to .287 but still led the team in batting. And Burroughs took another giant step backward, hitting .237 with 18 homers and 86 RBI.

An early sign of trouble occurred at Fenway Park on May 9 with the team at 15–6 and in first place. Ellis, hitting .419 as the primary backup at catcher, first base, and DH, broke his left leg sliding in to second base and was lost for the season. His bat was certainly missed.

EDDIE ROBINSON JOINS CORBETT REGIME

The second straight losing season caused Corbett to make a major front-office change, hiring former big league first baseman Eddie Robinson, previously a Braves official, as executive vice president.

John Ellis hit .419 in his first 11 games as a Ranger in '76, then shattered his leg on a slide at Fenway and missed the rest of the season. Ellis spent six years with the club as a back-up catcher/first baseman. (Texas Rangers Archives)

TEXAS RANGERS

A man of many talents, Nelson Briles sings the national anthem in 1976, the year that he went 11–9 and was named Ranger Pitcher of the Year. (Linda Kaye)

Corbett and Robinson got busy in a hurry, signing the Rangers' first big-name free agents, shortstop Bert Campaneris and starting pitcher Doyle Alexander. Then came the biggest trade in club history, sending Burroughs to Atlanta for five players and cash.

The former MVP had been demoralized by the wind, which turned many of his potential home runs into outs. Grieve remembers teammates jokingly imitating Burroughs's familiar look of frustration as he rounded first base and saw his long drive caught on the warning track. Burroughs's trade value, however, was not a joking matter, having fallen so drastically that none of the five players received by the Rangers could be considered front-line personnel.

Relief pitcher Adrian Devine was the only one who made a major impact with the Rangers, leading the Texas bullpen with 11 wins and 15 saves the next year. But pitcher Carl Morton was injured and never threw a pitch in a Texas uniform. Outfielders Dave May and Ken Henderson had mediocre seasons and were moved on. And pitcher Roger Moret pitched in only 25 games over two seasons. The last image of Moret in Texas is that of the tall left-hander standing in a catatonic trance in front of his locker, holding a shower shoe in his hand, prior to a game in April 1978.

Despite his frequent complaints about the Arlington wind, Burroughs was not happy to be traded. At least that's what Braves owner Ted Turner reported to the media after his first conversation with Burroughs. Informing the media that Burroughs would be unavailable for comment, Turner said, "Jeff told me he was going to go home and rip the phone off the wall. I'd say he is in a state of shock. He loved Texas, he didn't want to leave." Playing his home games in a hitter-friendly park, Burroughs got over the shock of being traded and slammed 41 home runs the next year for the Braves.

Before the 1977 season started, the Rangers also traded Clines to the Cubs for pitcher Darold Knowles and Umbarger to Oakland for young outfielder Claudell Washington. They reacquired Lindblad in a big cash transaction when A's owner Charlie Finley decided to sell off players from what had been a championship team. But Corbett was denied a chance to purchase Oakland's star pitcher Vida Blue when Commissioner Bowie Kuhn placed a $400,000 limit on the amount that could be paid to purchase a player.

The revamped Rangers were pumped up and ready for 1977, excited about both their acquisitions and a rookie second baseman who had hit .324 with 26 homers in Triple-A ball. Elliott "Bump" Wills, the son of base-stealing great Maury Wills, was named by Lucchesi in the off-season as his starting second baseman.

Sports Illustrated pictured Wills on its cover during spring training, and Ranger fans were looking forward to seeing what Wills could do. One man who did not share those sentiments was Lenny Randle.

8

The Strangest Year of All

The winningest year in Ranger history was also the strangest. The Ranger players survived an assault on their manager by one of their own teammates and a bizarre stretch of eight days in which four different managers made out the Texas lineup card.

When the 1977 season finally ended, the Rangers had won 94 games, which remains the club record, and lost only 68. But the Kansas City Royals won 102 games, and Texas finished second, eight games behind.

Controversy dogged the club from the first day of spring training, when Wills declined to report in a contract holdout. When he did show up and received the vast majority of the playing time at second base, Randle became upset.

Claiming that he had been promised a chance to compete with Wills for the starting job at second base, Randle packed up his equipment bag one day and threatened to leave camp before teammates talked him into staying. Complaining frequently, both in public and in private, Randle eventually got under the skin of the normally mild-mannered Lucchesi, who told Texas reporters, "I'm tired of hearing $80,000-a-year punks moan and groan about not playing."

A few days later, on Monday, March 28, the Rangers were busing to Orlando when Randle posed his question to Grieve, a question that Randle also had asked Blyleven that morning. "What do you think would happen?" answered Grieve. "The player would be in a lot of trouble, and he would probably be thrown off the team."

"It never occurred to me that this was about to happen, although it was common knowledge that Lenny was very upset with Frank," recalls Grieve. But it did happen.

While the Rangers were taking batting practice, Randle approached Lucchesi near the batting cage and said he wanted to talk to the manager. What was said next remains a subject of dispute between the two. The

The demanding Billy Hunter turned the Rangers around. (Courtesy *Fort Worth Star-Telegram*, Special Collections Division, University of Texas at Arlington Libraries.)

"WHAT DO YOU THINK WOULD HAPPEN IF A PLAYER PUNCHED OUT A MANAGER?"

Lenny Randle, to teammate Tom Grieve, March 28, 1977, on the team bus going to Orlando, Florida, for a preseason game

Sports Illustrated cover boy Bump Wills was given the second base job by Lucchesi in the spring of '77. (*Sports Illustrated*)

Lenny Randle (left), shown here in happier times with teammate Joe Lovitto, was universally liked before his assault on Lucchesi. (Linda Kaye)

actions that followed are indisputable, carried out in front of dozens of eyewitnesses.

Randle suddenly punched Lucchesi in the face, dropping the manager to the ground. Randle continued to throw punches while Lucchesi was on the ground, raining lefts and rights on the fallen skipper. With blood pouring from Lucchesi's mouth and nose, Campaneris and others sprinted to Lucchesi's aid. Randle backed away, jogged to the outfield, and began running wind sprints.

Within minutes, Lucchesi was on his way to the hospital, where he would remain for seven days with a broken cheekbone that required plastic surgery and bruises to his back and kidney. Randle was ushered off the field and ordered by General Manager O'Brien to remove his uniform. Just as Grieve had foretold, it was the last time that Randle would ever wear the Texas colors.

Prior to the attack, Randle had been universally liked, intelligent and talented on and off the field. Now he was an outcast. "It was a savage attack by a finely tuned athlete against a defenseless man," says Grieve, who witnessed the incident from ten feet away. "It was the ultimate cowardly act."

Following an investigation, Randle was suspended for thirty days without pay and fined $10,000. On April 26, he was traded to the New York Mets. Randle was later fined $1,050 after pleading no contest to a charge of battery in an Orlando court. And a civil suit filed by Lucchesi was settled out of court.

Lucchesi, who still does not remember the assault, has been unable to forget its effects. Looking back, he has often said. "No one knows what I went through." And, repeating what he told Randy Galloway of the *Dallas Morning News* from his hospital bed the day of the attack, "My only wish is that I was ten years younger so I could have handled the situation myself."

Willie Horton was called out by umpire Ron Luciano on this play, but helped power the Rangers with 15 HRs, including the first three-homer game in club history. (Courtesy *Fort Worth Star-Telegram*, Special Collections Division, University of Texas at Arlington Libraries.)

FOUR MANAGERS IN EIGHT DAYS

Lucchesi returned to the club in time for Opening Day, April 7 in Baltimore, a 2–1 Blyleven win made sweeter for the skipper by Wills getting the game-winning hit in the tenth inning. The Rangers swept the three-game series and returned to Arlington for the home opener, where 25,208 saw the Rangers beat the Indians, 3–2.

The Rangers fell out of a first-place tie the next day, losing to Dennis Eckersley, 5–3. Needing another RBI man, the Rangers picked up veteran Willie Horton from the Tigers on April 13. But the club muddled along near the .500 mark, unable to put together a hot streak. Not even a fifteen-minute brawl with the Royals during a game in Arlington could ignite the squad.

On June 15, the Rangers purchased another player from Oakland—flamboyant starting pitcher Dock Ellis. One week later, with the Rangers at 31–31, Robinson took a more dramatic step—he fired Lucchesi and replaced him with former major league player and manager Eddie Stanky.

"Something had to be done," explained Robinson. "Attendance was lagging. The fans were booing Frank every time he came out of the dugout. The performance of the team was less than .500 ball, and we never put together a sustained drive. Put that all together, it's time to change managers."

Seldom has the firing of a manager been that clearly explained. Never has the hiring of a new manager worked out so poorly.

The fifty-nine-year-old Stanky had been out of pro ball since managing the White Sox from 1966–68. Since then, he had been living a quiet family life in Mobile, Alabama, coaching at the University of South Alabama.

Robinson originally favored hiring Orioles third-base coach Billy Hunter, but he was advised by sources close to Stanky that the former scrappy second baseman would love to have the job. The idea of the man who had been nicknamed "The Brat" during his play-

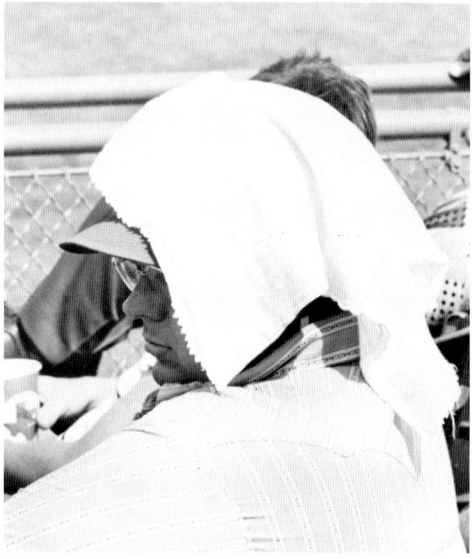

An early-season heat wave had fans seeking protection from the sun. (Courtesy *Fort Worth Star-Telegram*, Special Collections Division, University of Texas at Arlington Libraries.)

ing days breathing new life into the Rangers and into ticket sales seemed appealing.

On June 22, with the Rangers in Minnesota, Stanky was introduced as the Rangers' fifth manager at a pregame press conference at Metropolitan Stadium. Letting his coaches run the game, Stanky watched his new team come from behind to beat the Twins, 10–8. Only once did Stanky venture out of the dugout—a brief ninth-inning visit to the mound to check on reliever Mike Marshall, who went on to finish the game.

The next morning, at 8:15, the phone rang in Robinson's hotel room. It was Stanky, who had decided overnight to give up the job and return home. "I can't take the job," Stanky told Robinson. "I've never been so lonesome and homesick in my life."

Robinson offered to meet Stanky for a cup of coffee, to talk things out, but it was too late. "I'm at the airport," said Stanky. "I'm getting on an airplane."

Before boarding, Stanky also called O'Brien, Ranger coach Connie Ryan, and Harrah, encouraging Harrah to assert himself as team leader. Stanky intended to call some other players, too, but having run out of time, or dimes, he got on the plane to Mobile, where he arrived to a hero's welcome.

"The attitude of the ballplayers was great," explained Stanky. "I would have stayed if I didn't have to go to my room alone each night… I just feel my place is with my family back home."

Before Stanky had taken off for Minnesota, University of South Alabama President Frederick Whiddon had asked him, "How long is it going to take to get this out of your system?" The next day, Whiddon had his answer—and his coach back.

The Rangers, on the other hand, had two ex-managers, one in Mobile and the other

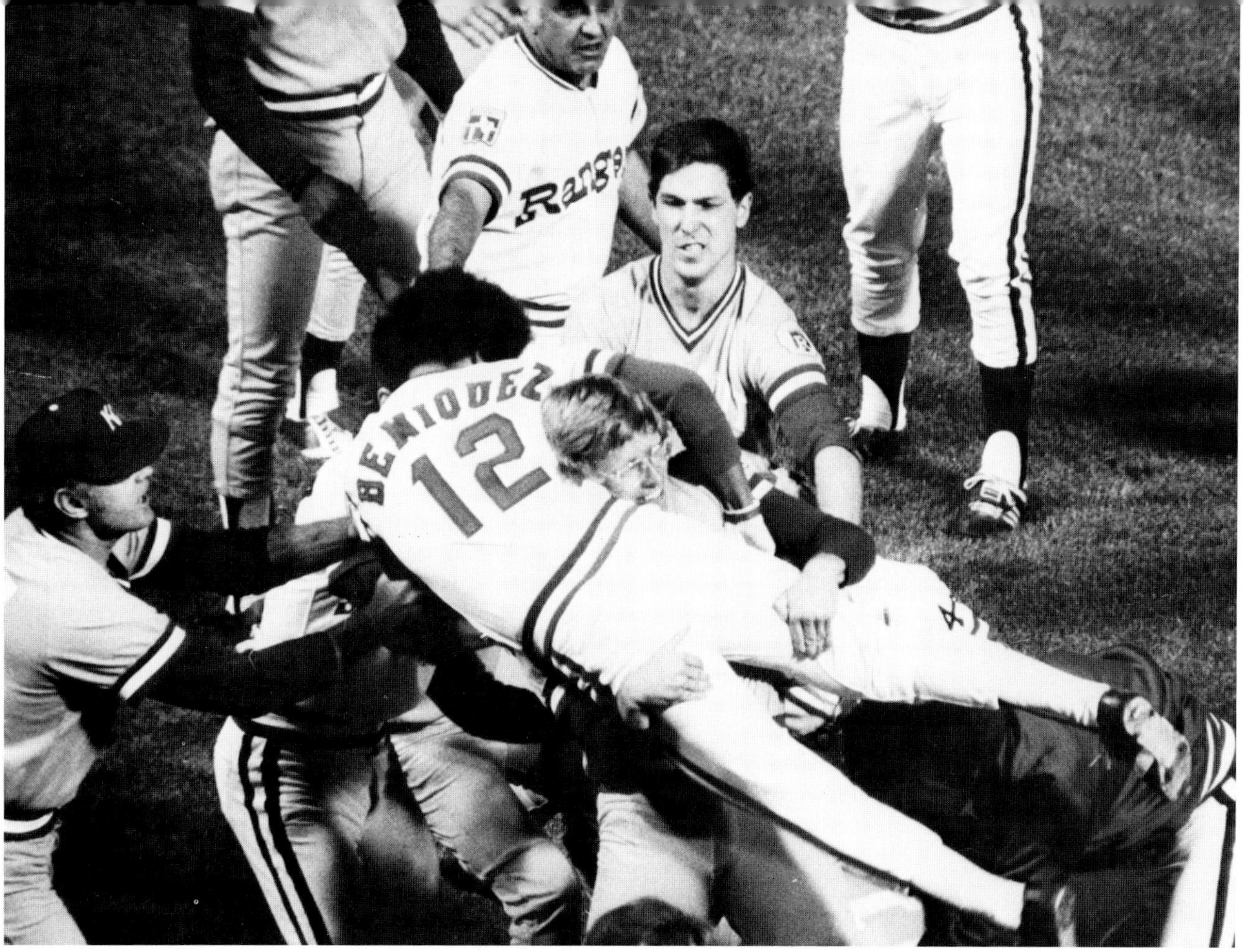

Things really got hot when the Royals came to town. Juan Beniquez lands on top of the pile during a 15-minute brawl. (*Dallas Morning News*/AP)

This is one of the few photos taken of Eddie Stanky during his one-game stay as Ranger manager. (*St. Paul Pioneer Press*)

Claudell Washington tips his cap to the Arlington crowd after slugging a three-run homer on August 14, a win that drew the Rangers within a game of first place. (Courtesy *Fort Worth Star-Telegram*, Special Collections Division, University of Texas at Arlington Libraries.)

still in Minneapolis. As Sam Blair quipped in the *Dallas Morning News*, "If Stanky hadn't been in such a hurry, he and Lucchesi could have shared a cab to the airport."

For the most part, the Ranger players also treated Stanky's rapid departure facetiously, wondering what he would have done had the Rangers lost that night. More seriously, Briles pointed out, "Stanky's leaving could be a real blow, but it might have a reverse effect. This could pull us together." Briles, as it turned out, was correct. But it took a while.

Ryan was named interim manager while Robinson, Corbett, and O'Brien decided on a course of action. First they offered the job to Ryan on a full-time basis, but the fifty-seven year old Ryan turned it down. Under Ryan, the Rangers went 2–4 in a five-day stretch before welcoming their fourth manager in eight days.

LITTLE HITLER

"If you put Billy Martin and Frank Lucchesi in a can and shook it up, Bill Hunter is what you'd get. He has Martin's baseball instinct and Frank Lucchesi's honesty and straightforwardness. He is the best of both."

Mike Hargrove, September 1977

On Monday, June 27, exactly one tumultuous week after Lucchesi's last game as Texas manager, Robinson finally hired the man he originally intended to hire—forty-nine-year-old Billy Hunter, who had been the Orioles' third-base coach for thirteen years. But a day earlier, Corbett almost hired retired slugger Harmon Killebrew, who decided he did not want to spend that much time away from his family. (Apparently, there was quite a bit of that sentiment going around.)

Hunter, who had turned down other managerial offers before, was unfazed at being the fourth man to be offered the job. "Not being the first choice doesn't make me feel bad at all," said Hunter as he was introduced to the press before a game in Oakland. "I'm the fella who has the job. Sparky Anderson is very successful at Cincinnati, and the Reds offered that job to me first."

Nicknamed "Little Hitler" by Frank Robinson after a series of exhausting spring training drills with the Orioles, Hunter wasted no time in living up to his reputation as a taskmaster. The new skipper put the Rangers through a two-week seminar in fundamen-

The Strangest Year of All

tals that required the players to report to the stadium forty-five minutes earlier than usual each day.

Despite his strict adherence to fundamentals, however, Hunter was not without humor. After Beniquez and Washington let a fly ball fall between them, Hunter approached the two outfielders in the dugout and offered an introduction. "Juan, I'd like you to meet Claudell Washington. Claudell, this is Juan Beniquez. Now that you know each other, you might chat for a while about how to catch fly balls."

"I'm not knocking anybody," Hunter had remarked on his first day on the job. "But for a team with this talent to be 33–35 means something is wrong." Something remained wrong in Hunter's first ten days as the Rangers lost five out of nine. The last of those losses, a 1–0 defeat to the Royals before

(Top right): Hall-of-Famer Gaylord Perry, who was known to throw a variety of funny stuff on the mound, tries something new while loosening up during batting practice. (Courtesy *Fort Worth Star-Telegram*, Special Collections Division, University of Texas at Arlington Libraries.)
(Above): An intense competitor, Perry would do anything he could to beat you, including throwing from his knees. (Texas/Dallas History Division, Dallas Public Library)

TEXAS RANGERS

Bert Blyleven won 14 games and hurled five shutouts in '77, including a no-hitter in Anaheim. (Courtesy *Fort Worth Star-Telegram*, Special Collections Division, University of Texas at Arlington Libraries.)

a Fourth of July crowd of 34,660 in Texas, prompted one of the more memorable quotes in Ranger history.

An obviously depressed Corbett departed his suite after the game and told reporters that he would be selling the team, ripping his players with the now-famous words, "Some of them are dogs on the field and off the field. It's not worth it anymore. It's killing me."

Five weeks later, Corbett changed his mind as the Rangers had become the hottest team in baseball. Beginning on July 6, the Rangers reeled off seven straight victories and won 31 of their next 40 games.

Under Hunter, the Rangers ran and bunted more. Despite his lack of speed, Hargrove was moved to the leadoff spot to take advantage of his .424 on-base percentage. The team batting average jumped almost 10 points, led by Sundberg, who hit .343 in the second half. With five players (Beniquez, Campaneris, Harrah, Washington, and Wills) stealing over 20 bases, the Rangers made the most of their chances to score, improving their run total by 151 over 1976.

The solid starting rotation of Alexander (17–11), Perry (15–12), Blyleven (14–12), and Ellis (10–6), kept the Rangers in almost every game. And the Ranger defense was much improved as Beniquez and Sundberg won Gold Gloves.

On August 17 at Arlington Stadium, Sundberg's tenth-inning single scored Harrah from second to give the Rangers a 6–5 win over the Blue Jays and a half-game lead in the West. Ellis shut out Toronto the next night to retain the lead.

Harrah, who had been in Texas from the beginning, may have enjoyed the Rangers' lofty status more than anyone. The two-time All-Star shortstop, who was playing third base in '77, proudly told

Acquired in the trade for Burroughs, Adrian Devine led the club with 15 saves in '77. (Texas Rangers Archives)

reporters, "Being in first place...it's the best feeling in the world."

That feeling disappeared the next day, never to be be felt again in that storybook season. Until 1996, August 18 remained as the latest date on which the Rangers had ever held first place. You can blame the New York Yankees for the end of the Rangers' fun.

Invading Arlington Stadium for a three-game series that attracted an average of over thirty thousand fans, the Yankees won all three games to knock the Rangers out of first place. Texas recovered, going 26–15 the rest of the way, but fell steadily behind the Royals, who won 102 games that season.

The Rangers had gone 60–33 under Hunter, posting the best winning percentage (.645) in the majors during that span. But their 94–68 finish, although a club record, was not nearly good enough to catch George Brett and the Royals.

Harrah led the club in homers (27) and RBI (87) and was the only Ranger to surpass 20 homers and 75 RBI. Looking ahead to 1978, Hunter expressed his desire for another big bat, preferably a power-hitting outfielder. He also longed for a top-notch left-handed starting pitcher.

By the time spring training rolled around, Hunter was granted both of those wishes—and more.

1977 ODDITIES

- **FIRST TRIPLE PLAY**—On August 8, with Roger Moret pitching against Oakland at Arlington Stadium, the Rangers turned the only triple play in their history. Manny Sanguillen, batting with runners at first and second in the fifth inning, hit a grounder to third baseman Toby Harrah, who stepped on third, then threw to Bump Wills at second for the second out. Wills relayed to Mike Hargrove at first to get Sanguillen. The Rangers won the game, 3–0.
- **BACK-TO-BACK INSIDE-THE-PARK HOME RUNS**—On August 27 at Yankee Stadium, Harrah blasted a shot off the right-field wall. Yankee right fielder Lou Piniella crashed into the wall and slumped on the warning track as Harrah circled the bases with a three-run homer. On the very next pitch from Ken Clay, Bump Wills belted a deep fly to center that deflected off the glove of center fielder Mickey Rivers. Wills sped all the way around the bases, giving the Rangers back-to-back inside-the-park home runs. The feat had been accomplished only one other time in major league history, by the 1946 Chicago Cubs.
- **BLYLEVEN NO-HITTER**—On September 23 in Anaheim, Bert Blyleven pitched the second no-hitter in Ranger history, blanking the Angels, 6–0. Blyleven was nursing a pulled groin muscle and had not pitched in sixteen days. Born in Holland, Blyleven was raised just a few miles from Anaheim Stadium and was an Angels fan. A crowd of 8,031 gave Blyleven a standing ovation when he took the mound for the ninth inning and again when the game ended.
- **COLBORN NO-HITTER**—The first no-hitter ever thrown against the Rangers was pitched by Jim Colborn of the Royals at Kansas City on May 14. It remains one of only two no-hitters ever pitched against the Rangers and the only one in a Ranger road game. K.C. won, 6–0.
- **HORTON'S THREE-HOME RUN GAME**—On May 15, the day after Colborn's no-hitter, Willie Horton became the first Ranger to hit three home runs in a game. The Rangers won, 7–3, at Royals Stadium.

The Rangers pulled out all the stops to win. Harrah (left), seated in the front row, went into the stands to catch this foul pop, while Hargrove (right) landed on his head in eluding the tag of Minnesota catcher Butch Wynegar. Umpire Mike Reilly makes the call. (Courtesy *Fort Worth Star-Telegram*, Special Collections Division, University of Texas at Arlington Libraries.)

Jim Sundberg was the Ranger Player of the Year in '77, hitting a career-high .291 and playing through injuries to both of his shoulders, as this photo indicates. (Courtesy *Fort Worth Star-Telegram*, Special Collections Division, University of Texas at Arlington Libraries.)

One of the Rangers' first big-name free agents, shortstop Bert Campaneris, tags Bobby Bonds. (Texas/Dallas History Division, Dallas Public Library)

The first time the Rangers appeared on ABC Monday Night Baseball in '77, ball boy Rich Thompson shouted disparaging remarks about Howard Cosell into a crowd-noise microphone. When the ABC crew returned to Texas, Ranger players made sure there would be no repeat performance. (Courtesy *Fort Worth Star-Telegram*, Special Collections Division, University of Texas at Arlington Libraries.)

9

Wheeling and Dealing with Brad

By the time the 1978 season began, Hunter had his power-hitting outfielder, his left-handed starting pitcher, and seven other players who had been obtained via trade or free agent signing.

In a three-day span in early November, Corbett inked two big-name free agents—outfielder Richie Zisk, who had produced 30 homers and 101 RBI the previous year for the White Sox, and right-handed starting pitcher Doc Medich. And the Ranger owner was just getting warmed up.

At baseball's winter meetings in December, Corbett engineered a spectacular four-team trade in which the Rangers exchanged players with the Mets, Pirates, and Braves. Joining the Rangers would be a left-handed starter as Hunter had requested—Jon Matlack, who had slipped to a 7–15 record with the Mets, as well as line drive-hitting outfielder Al Oliver and highly touted shortstop prospect Nelson Norman.

The price paid by Corbett included no-hit man Blyleven, bullpen stopper Adrian Devine, and original Ranger Grieve.

The trading frenzy continued the next week. With Corbett traveling in Europe, Robinson learned that the Red Sox were looking to deal former Ranger Ferguson Jenkins. Unable to reach the Ranger owner, Robinson made a deal anyway, reacquiring Jenkins for cash and a minor leaguer.

After the new year, the Rangers shipped Perry to San Diego for pitcher Dave Tomlin, who subsequently was traded away in spring training. They also signed first baseman Mike Jorgensen. And in a historic move, they traded Clyde, the former franchise savior, along with Willie Horton to the Indians for outfielder John Lowenstein and pitcher Tom Buskey.

Hunter was overjoyed with the off-season overhaul, confidently crowing, "With this material, if we don't win it will be my

Club owner Brad Corbett loved hanging out with his players, offering several of them off-season jobs with his plastic pipe company. Here he warms up with the club in spring training. (Linda Kaye)

"WALKING INTO OUR CLUBHOUSE IS LIKE WALKING INTO A HOTEL LOBBY. IT'S JUST A LOT OF STRANGE FACES."

Toby Harrah, shortly before being traded in December 1978

"Rootin' Tootin' Ranger" was the team mascot in the late '70's. (Linda Kaye)

fault." Those words would come back to haunt him.

Arlington Stadium was also revamped, sporting a new five thousand-seat upper deck behind home plate. Seating capacity was raised to 41,097, and all of the extra seats were needed on Opening Day on Saturday, April 8.

Playing against Billy Martin's Yankees in front of a full house and on national television, Hunter's prized acquisitions came up big. Matlack pitched nine brilliant innings in a duel with Yankee lefty Ron Guidry, carrying the Rangers to the bottom of the ninth in a 1–1 tie. With flame-throwing Goose Gossage on in relief for New York, Zisk belted an 0-2 slider over the wall in the left-field corner to win it, 2–1.

Oliver, wearing the number 0, was an instant hit with the fans in left field and received an ovation the first time he ran out to his position. Sufficiently proud of his batting prowess to have "AL HITS" imprinted on his personalized license plate, Oliver lived up to that billing early and was the hitting star in the season's third game. The Rangers took two out of three from New York before heading out on the road for what would be a disastrous trip.

Betrayed by poor pitching, the Rangers dropped eight games in a row to fall seven games out of first place. Without an experienced bullpen stopper, Hunter experimented unsuccessfully with fireballing rookie Len Barker in that role. Having traded the previous year's stopper, Devine, the Rangers went looking for bullpen help and purchased veteran right-hander Reggie Cleveland from the Red Sox.

Cleveland went on to save 12 games but lost seven others. The Ranger bullpen continued to be a liability, one that was compounded by poor infield defense.

The new-look offense sputtered, leading to another big trade on May 16 in which the Rangers acquired the vast offensive talents of outfielder Bobby Bonds. That trade cost

The Rangers had a new look in 1978.... as did Arlington Stadium, which had been expanded through the addition of an upper deck behind home plate. (Courtesy of Joe Macko)

Wheeling and Dealing with Brad

them Washington, the young outfielder who was off to a slow start.

The combination of Bonds, Oliver, and Zisk was a potent trio in the middle of the lineup. Sundberg put together a club-record 22-game hitting streak, and Wills set a club record with 52 stolen bases. But Harrah and Hargrove had off years. Campaneris hit just .186, feuded with Hunter, and was benched. The outspoken Dock Ellis also engaged in a verbal battle with the manager, whose strict rules and authoritarian style began to wear on the players.

Despite the obvious friction between the players and their manager, the club got hot in June and held first place for a few days into early July. Then a horrendous stretch after the All-Star break, in which they lost 15 out of 20, dropped the Rangers out of the race by the end of August.

September was the Rangers' best month. Without any pennant race pressure, Texas reeled off 18 wins in its last 22 games to finish at 87–75, tied with California for second place behind Kansas City.

Starting pitching was the strength of the team. Jenkins (18–8) and Matlack (15–13, 2.30 ERA) were outstanding. Medich and Alexander each won nine games, and unheralded rookie Steve Comer, an undrafted soft thrower who had been signed off a Minnesota construction crew in 1976, moved into the rotation and went 11–5.

In every other area, the Rangers had not played up to expectations. The standings showed the Rangers only five games behind the Royals, but Corbett was not satisfied by his team's late charge into second place. Despite being the Rangers' winningest manager ever, with a two-year record of 146–108, Hunter was fired before the final game of the season.

Without blaming Hunter for the team's failures, several players cited a lack of communication between the manager and players. Oliver, who finished second to Rod Carew for the A.L. batting title and set a club record by hitting .324, claimed to be one of the

Richie Zisk was more of a hero than the Lone Ranger after his ninth-inning homer gave the Rangers a 2–1 win over the Yankees on Opening Day in '78. (Linda Kaye)

Al Oliver hit over .300 in each of his four seasons as a Ranger, leading the club in hitting three times. (Courtesy *Fort Worth Star-Telegram*, Special Collections Division, University of Texas at Arlington Libraries.)

Hall-of-Famer Fergie Jenkins returned in '78 and was the Ranger Pitcher of the Year, going 18–8, then won 16 games in '79. Jenkins won 93 games as a Ranger, second in club annals to Charlie Hough's 139. (Courtesy *Fort Worth Star-Telegram*, Special Collections Division, University of Texas at Arlington Libraries.)

few Rangers who was not disgruntled. Perhaps he put it best, saying, "One way or another a manager must keep his players happy. A lot of his moves were being questioned because the players were dissatisfied and no longer respected him."

After sounding out many of his players in the final weeks of the season, Corbett turned to one of Hunter's coaches, former big league catcher Pat Corrales, as the Rangers' new manager. "I wanted a hard-nosed guy in there," said Corbett. "But also a guy who can offer a kind word when it is merited."

Born and raised in California, Corrales became the first Mexican-American to manage a major league team. Known for his toughness, Corrales told the team, "I only have two rules. Be on time and hustle on the field."

When asked what the club needed to become a division winner, Corrales replied, "A quality relief pitcher and, if possible, a strong third baseman."

NO STANDING PAT WITH CORRALES

The dust from the managerial shift had hardly settled when Corrales's first wish was granted.

Just two days after the 1978 season ended, the Rangers landed former All-Star reliever Jim Kern in a deal with the Indians. The deal sent Bonds and Barker to Cleveland, giving up the former's 29 homers and 37 stolen bases, along with the latter's unfulfilled mound potential. But it also relieved Corbett of Bonds's big salary.

Most importantly, the Kern trade gave the Rangers their first proven bullpen stopper. Five weeks later, Corbett would trade for another one.

Bobby Bonds, shown diving back into first base, hit 29 homers and stole 37 bases in his one season with Texas before going to Cleveland in the deal for Jim Kern. (Courtesy *Fort Worth Star-Telegram*, Special Collections Division, University of Texas at Arlington Libraries.)

Wheeling and Dealing with Brad

In a blockbuster ten-player deal with the Yankees on November 10, Corbett acquired southpaw reliever Sparky Lyle. In 1977, Lyle became the first reliever to win the A.L. Cy Young Award, but the thirty-four-year-old southpaw had lost his job as the Yankees' closer to Goose Gossage.

Three of the five players going to New York were minor leaguers, but one of them, pitcher Dave Righetti, was considered the Rangers' best pitching prospect. Righetti went on to greatness, whereas Lyle saved a total of only 21 games in two years with Texas.

Corbett also received $400,000 from the Yankees in the deal, an infusion of cash that was much-needed because Corbett's chemical and plastic pipe business had fallen on hard times. That was not the only one of his deals motivated by financial considerations.

First baseman Mike Hargrove, still a fan favorite despite an off year, was one of three players sent to San Diego for outfielder Oscar Gamble and utility man Dave Roberts. Corbett received a reported $300,000 in that deal and then sold John Lowenstein to Baltimore. He also received cash in a trade that sent Reggie Cleveland to Milwaukee for pitcher Ed Farmer and a minor leaguer.

One deal that finances did not enter into brought the Rangers a new third baseman. Saying good-bye to the last remaining original Ranger, Texas sent Harrah to the Indians for Cleveland third baseman Buddy Bell.

An outstanding fielder, Bell did not possess the speed or power of Harrah, but Corrales was delighted with the deal. "It's a trade that gives us a bona fide third baseman for the first time since the team moved to Texas," gushed the new manager. "With Nelson Norman at shortstop and Bell at third, we'll be extremely strong defensively on the left side, which has been our problem area."

Harrah, a rags-to-riches figure who had risen from poverty in Sissonville, West Virginia, was the Rangers' all-time leader in every major offensive category except batting average. He had played 999 games in a Ranger uniform in the club's seven-year history, 273 more than Hargrove. Now both were gone. The Rangers' ties to the Senators, at least between the white lines, had finally been cut.

Harrah and Hargrove were among ten players from the 1978 Rangers who were traded or sold before the start of the 1979 season. The free-wheeling Corbett had outdone even his own performance of the previous off-season.

Outspoken pitcher Dock Ellis, who won 10 games in '77 and nine in '78, challenged Hunter's authority, leading to the manager's demise. (Texas/Dallas History Division, Dallas Public Library)

DEALING CONTINUES, RESULTS THE SAME

The never-ending series of transactions continued throughout the 1979 season. The Rangers got off to their best start ever, winning their first six games, then fell to fourth

TEXAS RANGERS

Jon Matlack, "The Senator," posted a 2.30 ERA in '78, which was second-best in the league. His elbow injury in '79 may have cost the Rangers a division title. (Courtesy *Fort Worth Star-Telegram*, Special Collections Division, University of Texas at Arlington Libraries.)

place in mid-June. Just before the trading deadline on June 15, the Rangers made three deals involving nine players. In the most significant of the three, Corbett and A's owner Charlie Finley negotiated a swap of left-handed starter John Henry Johnson to the Rangers for bench players Dave Chalk and Mike Heath, plus a large sum of cash.

The deal for Johnson was necessitated by an arm injury sustained by Matlack in spring training. The Rangers' top left-hander tried to pitch despite bone chips in his elbow, made only 13 starts, and was largely ineffective before submitting to surgery and missing the rest of the season.

The twenty-two-year-old Johnson had won 11 games for Oakland as a rookie in '78 but was struggling with a 2–8 record at the time of the trade. To make room for him in the starting rotation, the Rangers traded Dock Ellis to the Mets for two minor leaguers. Then, because the Rangers were struggling against lefties, they acquired a right-handed hitter, first baseman-designated hitter Eric Soderholm, from the White Sox. Going to Chicago in that deal was Farmer, who went on to become an outstanding bullpen stopper for the White Sox and Phillies.

Johnson had a brilliant Texas debut, striking out 10 in five innings. The lefty won his first two starts and keyed an eight-game winning streak that vaulted the Rangers into first place at the end of June. But Johnson went 0–6 the rest of the way, and most of his teammates followed suit.

Trailing by just two games at the All-Star break, the club lost 10 of its first 12 in the second half, leading to yet another trade in which the Rangers picked up speedy center fielder Mickey Rivers from the Yankees for Gamble and three minor leaguers. Rivers ignited the Texas offense, batting .300, but could not prevent the team from sliding further in the standings.

By late August, the Rangers had lost 31 of their last 41 games, falling nine games off the lead. As it had in '78, the club closed strongly with the pressure off, going 19–8 in September to finish five games out. This time their 83–79 record left them in third place behind California and Kansas City.

Statistically, the Rangers had a lot to be proud of. They set club records in hits, home runs, RBI, and batting average. The pitching staff ranked fourth in the league in ERA. But a stretch of three straight doubleheaders in July exposed the lack of depth on the staff. And defense continued to be a problem, especially at shortstop and second base.

There were some tremendous individual performances. First baseman Pat Putnam took Hargrove's place and won *The Sporting News* American League Rookie of the Year Award, slugging 18 homers to share the club lead with Bell and Zisk. Outfielder Johnny Grubb put together a 21-game hitting streak, which equaled the longest in the league. Rookie left fielder Billy Sample hit .292, and Wills was fifth in the league with 35 stolen bases.

Wheeling and Dealing with Brad

Bell became the first Ranger ever to play all 162 games, the first to amass 200 hits, and the first Texas infielder to win a Gold Glove. His 101 RBI represented the second-highest total in club history. And his often-acrobatic defensive wizardry made the blond third baseman the new darling of the crowds at Arlington Stadium.

Kern was even more dazzling as the gangly, scraggly bearded reliever captured the Rolaids Relief Pitcher of the Year Award. Nicknamed "the Great Emu" after the large, nonflying bird, the eccentric Kern was as entertaining off the mound as he was on it, playfully tormenting teammates and media with a host of practical jokes.

On one team flight, Kern noticed *Fort Worth Star-Telegram* writer Jim Reeves reading John Dean's book, *Blind Ambition*. Kern grabbed the book and ripped out the last four pages, which he proceeded to place into his mouth and eat. "You're lucky I just wanted a snack," he informed the startled writer. "If I'd been really hungry I would've eaten the whole last chapter."

On the mound, however, Kern was a tough customer, throwing an incredible 143 relief innings, going 13–5 with a club-record 29 saves. Mixing in curves and palm balls with his occasionally errant 95-mph fastball, Kern held opposing batters to a .199 average and

Promising southpaw Roger Moret lapsed into a catatonic trance in front of his locker in April, 1978, and never appeared in another major league game. (Texas Rangers Archives)

Unheralded Steve Comer, who went 28–17 in '78–'79, confers with battery mate Jim Sundberg. (Texas Rangers Archives)

posted a glittering 1.57 ERA. "I can throw the ball through a cement wall," Kern was fond of saying. "If I can hit the wall."

Lyle was effective as a left-handed complement to Kern, appearing in 67 games and notching 13 saves. Together, the wacky duo provided Texas with the best late-inning relief work in the league.

But not even the accomplishments of Bell, Kern, and Lyle could keep the Rangers in the race.

Corrales had no easy explanation, saying, "There's no way you can blame any one thing. It was a combination of everything." However, when asked what it would take to win in 1980, Corrales quickly shot back, "A healthy Jon Matlack." And who knows where the Rangers would have finished had their ace lefty been able to repeat his 1978 performance.

"It's hard to believe this team finished just four games over .500," lamented Bell. "If they keep this club together, I think we can win."

Juan Beniquez is caught in a rundown by California's Ron Jackson. Note the pukka-shell necklace worn by Beniquez, who won a Gold Glove in center field in '77. (Courtesy *Fort Worth Star-Telegram*, Special Collections Division, University of Texas at Arlington Libraries.)

Pat Corrales (left) replaced Billy Hunter as manager and brought back Frank Lucchesi (right) as his third base coach. Here the two show off their new cowboy boots. (Texas/Dallas History Division, Dallas Public Library)

The revolving door at third base stopped with the arrival of Buddy Bell, who won six straight Gold Gloves. (Texas/Dallas History Division, Dallas Public Library)

First baseman Pat Putnam, shown here alongside California base runner Bobby Grich, succeeded Mike Hargrove at first base and became *The Sporting News* A.L. Rookie of the Year in '79. (Texas Rangers Archives)

Oscar Gamble hit .335 in half a season with the Rangers, but was shipped to the Yankees in the deal for Mickey Rivers. (Texas Rangers Archives)

Outfielder Johnny Grubb was the first Ranger to collect four extra-base hits in one game. (Texas Rangers Archives)

Outfielder Billy Sample played six years with the Rangers. Here he knocks off Brian Downing's helmet as he scores against the Angels. (Courtesy *Fort Worth Star-Telegram*, Special Collections Division, University of Texas at Arlington Libraries.)

Doyle Alexander, the Ranger Pitcher of the Year in '77 when he won 17 games, won just five games in '79 and was traded to Atlanta. (Texas/Dallas History Division, Dallas Public Library)

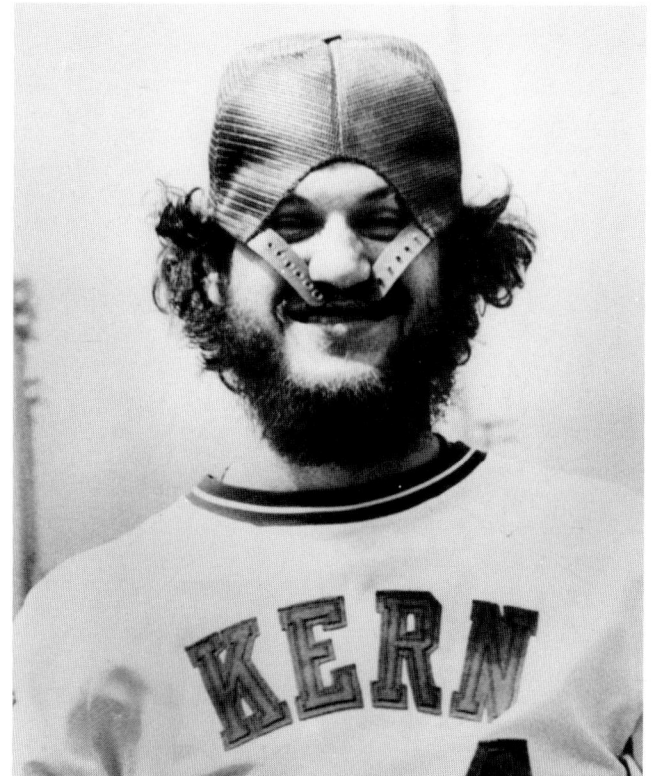

While always looking their best, Jim Kern—"The Great Emu" (left) and Albert "Sparky" Lyle combined for 42 saves in '79. Kern captured the Rolaids Relief Pitcher of the Year Award while cultivating his image as a flake—a reputation that Lyle had established long before. (*Fort Worth Star-Telegram*/Linda Kaye)

10

Mad Eddie

Corbett and Robinson apparently agreed with Bell's assessment of the Rangers' talent and made remarkably few changes for 1980. But the dealing duo was not completely idle.

Still undecided on twenty-two-year-old Nelson Norman's readiness to be an everyday shortstop, the Ranger brain trust traded for veteran Pepe Frias in a deal that also brought back reliever Adrian Devine from Atlanta. Texas also reacquired David Clyde, now twenty-four years old, after two lackluster years with the Indians.

Seeking a left-handed bat, the Rangers added thirty-six-year-old outfielder Rusty Staub. "Le Grand Orange" still had enough left to hit .300 in a part-time role, but the other off-season deals did not meet expectations.

Clyde was released in spring training, ending his once-promising big league career with a lifetime record of 18–33. Devine hurt his shoulder and pitched in only 13 games, an unfortunate development magnified by the disappointing performances of vaunted stoppers Kern and Lyle, whose combined save total dropped from 42 to 10.

Kern's demise was brought on by a series of injuries that included a sore elbow, a pinched nerve in his neck, and a more unconventional malady. While warming up in the bullpen on August 9, Kern threw a pitch, then turned to watch the action on the field. The return throw from the catcher drilled Kern right in the mouth, opening a nine-stitch gash. Even worse, the blow caused the six-foot-five reliever to keel over backward, a fall that left him with a concussion and temporary amnesia.

Forgetting the 1980 season may not have been a bad idea for Kern, who finished with a 3–11 record, two saves, and a 4.83 ERA. Lyle was not much better, with eight saves and a 4.69 ERA before he was traded in September to the Phillies.

Late in the season, the lefty-righty tandem of John

Despite bad knees, Richie Zisk scored here against the Brewers and brought a bundle of players to Texas in the trade which sent him to Seattle. (Courtesy *Fort Worth Star-Telegram*, Special Collections Division, University of Texas at Arlington Libraries.)

"I'VE SEEN GUYS PITCH BAD, AND I'VE SEEN GUYS PITCH IN BAD LUCK, BUT YOU'VE DONE AN OUTSTANDING JOB OF PUTTING IT ALL TOGETHER."
Sparky Lyle to bullpen mate Jim Kern, late in the 1980 season

TEXAS RANGERS

Rusty Staub, "Le Grand Orange," hit .300 for the Rangers in 1980 and provided Gaylord Perry with a place to set down his drink. (Linda Kaye)

Henry Johnson and Danny Darwin was impressive in replacing Kern and Lyle. Darwin, an undrafted fireballer from nearby Bonham, Texas, set a club record by winning eight straight decisions from May 22 to August 9. Unfortunately, the fearless right-hander was forced to take a four-week vacation during his winning streak after breaking a knuckle on his pitching hand. Darwin sustained the injury while punching out a fan who was hassling teammate Rivers outside Comiskey Park.

The Ranger starting rotation struggled. Perry won just six games and was traded in August. Matlack (10–10) and Jenkins (12–12) were .500 pitchers, and Comer fell victim to a sore arm, winning just two games. Veteran Ed Figueroa, acquired from the Yankees in July, went 0–7. Medich was the club's leading winner at 14–11.

The shortstop position proved to be a revolving door. Norman was sent down two weeks into the season, replaced by Frias, who quickly played his way out of the line-up. But the colorful shortstop did leave behind one of the classic quotes.

A former Brave and Expo playing in his initial American League campaign, Frias complained about many of the cities he was visiting for the first time. Finally, the thirty-one-year-old Dominican found a locale to his liking when the Rangers made their first trip to Toronto. Arising from his seat near the back of the team bus, Frias happily declared, "This is my kind of city…Canada!"

Former Met star Bud Harrelson, in semiretirement, was recruited from a Philadelphia softball league to fill the shortstop void. In amazing fashion, Harrelson did a fine job at the age of thirty-five. But a bruised thigh, suffered in a collision while chasing a pop-up, landed him on the disabled list for two months.

Danny Darwin, "The Bonham Bullet," won eight straight decisions in 1980 and led the team in saves in '80 and '82. Here he visits with catcher Jim Sundberg. (Texas Rangers Archives)

(From left): Gaylord Perry, Jim Kern, Fergie Jenkins, and Sparky Lyle all had off-years in 1980, but that certainly did not prevent them from having a good time. (Linda Kaye)

Offensively, the Rangers set club records in batting average (.284), hits, and RBI, led by the inimitable John Milton "Mickey" Rivers. "Mick the Quick" set new Texas standards by hitting .333, with 210 hits and a 24-game hitting streak. Bell missed 34 games with injuries but hit .329, and Zisk batted .290 and shared the club lead in home runs (19).

Oliver carried his game to a new dimension, setting club records for homers (19) and RBI (117) by a left-handed batter. He played in every game, highlighted by an August 17 doubleheader in Detroit in which he tied an American League record with four home runs. Going deep in each of his last three at-bats in the nightcap, Oliver drew a pair of standing ovations from the fans at Tiger Stadium.

Another former National Leaguer made a significant late-season contribution. Purchased from the Dodgers on July 11, thirty-two-year-old Charlie Hough baffled opposing hitters (and Ranger catchers) with his fluttering knuckleball. Used primarily in relief, Hough pitched complete games in both of his starting assignments, foreshadowing a Texas career that would make him the club's all-time winningest pitcher.

Hough's performance brightened an otherwise dismal September in which the Rangers staggered to a 76–85 finish. Manager Corrales might have survived for another year had Corbett, the man who hired him, still been running the show. The unlucky Corrales, however, had to answer to a new boss.

Eddie Chiles, spry and aggressive at the age of seventy, had assumed command on April 29 when Corbett's mounting financial problems forced him to sell the club. Chiles was already a celebrity throughout the Southwest, voicing unforgettable commercials for his oil-field service business, the Western Company.

"I'm Eddie Chiles, and I'm mad," he would bark on radio and television, complain-

Gaylord Perry never got hot in his last season with the Rangers, going 6–9 at the age of 41 before being traded to the Yankees. (Texas Rangers Archives)

ing about "big government," often closing his spots with the slogan, "If you don't own an oil well, get one."

Chiles was a self-made success, having hitchhiked from his family home in Itasca, Texas, to the University of Oklahoma. Working in oil fields and on a grain-hauling freighter, Chiles earned enough money to complete college with a degree in petroleum engineering. He started the Western Company in 1939 with three employees, building the firm into a $500 million-a-year corporation.

Obviously, the Rangers' new chairman of the board was not accustomed to losing. It was hardly surprising that the 1980 disaster did not sit well with Chiles and his partners in the Ranger ownership group.

"It's not Corrales's fault and not the coaches' fault," offered Staub, a veteran of eighteen major league seasons. "I've never been with people who worked any harder."

Kern, whose bad year was the single biggest reason for the team's collapse, agreed with Staub. "If anyone should be fired, it should be me."

Firing the players is easier said than done, of course. Catching on quickly to the time-honored baseball tradition, on the last day of the 1980 season Chiles fired manager Pat Corrales.

Before deciding on Corrales's replacement, Chiles and Robinson were subjected to a barrage of criticism from the fans, the media, and the players. Bell was particularly incensed, demanding to be traded. "I know how to win. A lot of guys here don't," the popular third baseman exploded to the press. "And changing managers isn't going to change that. They're going to make some changes this winter, and I hope I'm one of them."

Bell's wish was not granted. The popular third baseman was back in 1981, playing for a manager whom he would come to love.

On November 12, 1980, following a six-week search, forty-nine-year-old Don Zimmer was named manager of the Rangers. A former big league infielder, Zimmer had just been fired after his fifth season managing the Red Sox, with whom he posted a winning record every year.

Twice during his playing days, Zimmer had recovered from serious beanings to resume his career. His ability to bounce back, it was hoped, would be passed on to his new team.

George "Doc" Medich, the last physician to pitch in the majors, led the Rangers in wins in '80 and in ERA in '81. (Courtesy *Fort Worth Star-Telegram*, Special Collections Division, University of Texas at Arlington Libraries.)

Shortstop Pepe Frias came from the Braves and hit just .242 but had his teammates in stitches. (Texas Rangers Archives)

Former Met star Bud Harrelson came out of semi-retirement to help out at shortstop, hitting .275, but spent almost half his time on the disabled list. (Texas Rangers Archives)

"I could fall out of bed and hit line drives," claimed Al "Scoop" Oliver, who tied an A.L. record by blasting four home runs in a doubleheader. (Texas Rangers Archives)

ONE STRIKE AND YOU'RE OUT

After they had hired a new manager, Robinson and company turned their attention to solving the shortstop problem and improving the pitching. They were able to achieve both ends in an eleven-player megadeal with the Seattle Mariners in which the Rangers gave up Zisk, four young pitchers, and a minor league shortstop. In return, Texas received five players, including left-handed pitcher Rick Honeycutt, slick-fielding shortstop Mario Mendoza, and outfielder Leon Roberts.

The Rangers also traded for Tiger back-up shortstop Mark Wagner. And they signed versatile Bill Stein as a utility man.

The acquisition of knuckleballer Charlie Hough for the $20,000 waiver price was the best bargain in Ranger history. Hough is the club's career leader in wins, innings, and strikeouts and had something funny to say about everything. (Texas Rangers Archives)

Rangers' owner Eddie Chiles (right) appears to have tickled the funny bone of Yankees' owner George Steinbrenner (left). Brad Corbett, who sold the club to Chiles, is in the background. (*Times-Herald*, courtesy of *The Dallas Morning News*.)

When the Rangers arrived in Pompano Beach for spring training, they found a full-time conditioning instructor, Mike Fitzsimmons, waiting to drill them into shape—a novel concept in a sport whose teams had previously placed little emphasis on fitness.

Zimmer's thirty-third spring training, his first with the Rangers, went smoothly. The club went 15-12 in exhibition play and responded positively to the new conditioning program. Robinson declared the Rangers to be "the best-conditioned baseball squad I've ever seen," a feeling that was shared by most of the players.

One of the few dissenters was Rivers, who complained, "I ran $2\frac{1}{2}$ miles every day and gained two pounds. My stomach got smaller, but my butt got bigger."

It was Zimmer's plan to have the club run more, pitch better, and play better defense. In keeping with that philosophy, the Arlington Stadium outfield fences were moved back to their original locations.

Honeycutt joined Matlack, Jenkins, Medich, and Darwin in the starting rotation. Johnson and Comer would handle late-inning relief along with Kern, provided that "the Great Emu" could recover from another unusual ailment—an injured left shoulder that hampered the right-hander's delivery.

Optimism abounded as the season began, despite a dark cloud looming. The players' union and the owners were at odds over the issue of free agent compensation, with the players threatening to strike in late May if the dispute were not resolved by then.

The Rangers were 6–7 on April 27 when their starting pitchers turned things around with an unprecedented stretch of dominance. Medich tossed his second shutout of the young season, a 10–0 blanking of the Red Sox in Arlington. Jenkins, Comer, and rookie Bob Babcock combined on a five-hit shutout the next night. The Red Sox were blanked for the third straight night when Darwin fired a one-hitter, allowing only a soft looping single to Rick Miller in the sixth inning. And Honeycutt followed with Texas's fourth straight whitewash, a five-hit shutout of the Royals.

The Rangers were one shutout away from the American League record, a streak that

Never without his chew while in uniform, Don Zimmer almost managed the Rangers to a first-half title in the strike-divided 1981 season. (Texas Rangers Archives)

ended the next night. Filling in for Matlack, who had a throat infection, Comer lost to the Royals, 4–0. The scoreless string ended after a club-record 39 innings, but that string ignited a 20–11 run that catapulted the Rangers above Oakland into first place on May 30.

In the midst of that stretch, the Rangers enjoyed an incredible chain of success by Stein in his pinch-hitting role. Wearing the lucky No. 13, the thirty-four-year-old veteran came off the bench to deliver hits in seven consecutive pinch-hit at-bats, setting an American League record. The record-breaking seventh consecutive pinch-hit, a ninth-inning single off Minnesota's Doug Corbett on May 25, gave the Rangers a dramatic come-from-behind victory.

In the meantime, the players' union had moved its strike deadline to June 12, the date on which it vowed that no games would be played without an agreement. On June 11, the Rangers trailed Oakland by one game. The Athletics did not play that day, meaning that a Texas win at Milwaukee would have lifted the Rangers into first place by one percentage point over Oakland.

The Rangers jumped out to an early 3–1 lead with Jenkins on the mound, but Milwaukee rallied to tie the game, 3–3. Former Ranger Roy Howell homered in the seventh inning to put the Brewers in front to stay as the Rangers did not score again against Pete Vuckovich and Rollie Fingers.

The final score—Milwaukee 6, Texas 3—is a score that lives in infamy as the one that denied the Rangers their first postseason berth. As scheduled, the players went on strike the next day and stayed out for fifty days.

As part of the strike settlement, teams leading their division on June 12 were declared first-half champions and earned a spot in a new miniseries that would open the playoffs.

Utility man Bill Stein, "The Amazing Mr. Stein," set an A.L. record with seven consecutive pinch hits in 1981. (Texas Rangers Archives)

Lee Mazzilli, who complained that left field was "an idiot's position," was acquired in one of the Rangers' worst trades ever and hit just .241 in '82. (Texas Rangers Archives)

The A.L. West standings on June 12 looked like this:

	W	L	PCT.
Oakland	37	23	.617
Texas	33	22	.600

Had the Rangers won on June 11, the standings would have looked like this:

	W	L	PCT.
Texas	34	21	.618
Oakland	37	23	.617

Back in June, there was no way for the Rangers to know that leading on June 12 would guarantee a playoff spot. When play resumed on August 10, however, they were quite aware that they could still reach postseason play by winning the 50-game "second half."

But the Rangers did not take advantage of the second-half opportunity. Texas's second-half record, 24–26, left them in third place, 4½ games behind Kansas City, as their bats never got back on track after the long layoff.

Overall, the Rangers were nine games over .500 at 57–48. They had dramatically improved their pitching and defense. Ranger fans dreamed of what might have been had the strike not intervened and felt better than usual while waiting for next year.

JUST ONE PLAYER AWAY?

The Rangers came to camp in 1982 bolstered by two free agent signees, left-handed starter Frank Tanana and designated hitter Lamar Johnson. They also had a new second baseman—former N.L. Gold Glove winner Doug Flynn, who had been obtained in a trade

TEXAS RANGERS

Center fielder George Wright, who jumped from Double-A ball in the spring of '82, makes a sensational catch as Billy Sample backs up the play. (Texas Rangers Archives)

for Kern. To make room for Flynn, the Rangers shipped Wills to the Cubs late in spring training for reliever Paul Mirabella.

Surprisingly, the trade of Wills was one of the lesser happenings in a tumultuous spring. The Ranger camp was marked by trouble right from the start when Medich, the club's top starter in '80 and '81, came down with hepatitis and was quarantined. Then Rivers came up lame in an early exhibition game and missed most of the year.

Spring sensation George Wright hit safely in 17 straight exhibition games, jumping from Double-A ball to replace Rivers in center field, but there were question marks both in left and right field.

Oliver, complaining about his contract, created the problem in left by demanding to be traded. On March 31, Robinson complied, sending Oliver to Montreal for third baseman Larry Parrish and minor league first baseman Dave Hostetler. Zimmer would take advantage of Parrish's cannon-like arm by moving the slugger to right field.

The left-field vacancy was filled the next day. Parting with two of the best pitching prospects in the organization, Robinson traded Ron Darling and Walt Terrell to the Mets for center fielder Lee Mazzilli.

Telling the press that Mazzilli was "the final piece of the puzzle," Robinson explained trading the two prized young arms, saying, "We're trading young talent for a twenty-seven-year-old who's going to play for us for a long time, a player that we all agree could be a big key for this team."

Unfortunately, Mazzilli did not share Robinson's enthusiasm. Unhappy about moving to Texas, the native New Yorker balked at playing left field, calling it "an idiot's position." His play in left field fit his description of the position, but only until August, when Mazzilli returned to New York in a trade with the Yankees for shortstop Bucky Dent.

Darling and Terrell went on to long and successful careers, serving as a constant reminder that if the Rangers were one player away from a 1982 title, that player was certainly not Mazzilli. Nor could any mere mortal have turned that team into a champion.

The Rangers' first two regular season games were snowed out in New York, but the eventual opener provided cause for optimism. Hough, finally granted his wish to be a starter, went all the way to beat the Indians in Cleveland, 8–3. The rookie Wright had three hits, including a home run, in his major league debut.

Texas had a 6–4 record on April 22 when the club hit a tailspin unlike anything the

Rangers had experienced since dropping 15 straight back in 1972. An ugly 12-game losing streak, in which the Rangers had a chance to win almost every game but played just badly enough to lose, spoiled any hope of the team contending.

On June 10, Chiles responded by firing Eddie Robinson, the executive vice president, leaving the organization without a baseball man in charge. Chiles would do the job himself, aided by Robinson's assistant, baseball sage Paul Richards.

The Ranger offense just was not producing many runs, despite Hostetler bursting upon the scene in a big way. The rangy first baseman was called up 40 games into the season and proceeded to belt an incredible 22 roundtrippers in his first 76 games. His 10 home runs in June established a club record for one month. But as quickly as Hostetler ignited, he went cold, failing to go deep in the last 46 games.

Parrish, meanwhile, had a disastrous first half. Failing miserably to adjust to a new league, a new position, and new contact lenses, the easygoing strongman from Haines City, Florida, had a .186 average and just one home run through June. Then on July 4, big Larry caught fire, smacking a grand slam and driving in a club-record seven runs in Oakland. "L.P." hit another slam on July 7 and topped off an unbelievable week on July 10 with his third grand slam, tying the major league record for slams in one week.

Parrish went on to have a big second half. Also, part-time outfielder Billy Sample compiled an 18-game hitting streak, and Bell hit .296. But Texas's offensive achievements were infrequent. Somehow the new No. 1 starter, Hough, won 16 games. But he was the only starter with a winning record. Darwin and rookie Dave Schmidt were effective in relief, but there were few save opportunities.

On July 28, after a 3–2 loss to Milwaukee, Chiles announced that Zimmer had been fired, a move that had actually been made two days earlier, when Zimmer had somehow been persuaded to continue managing the club until a replacement had been hired.

The Rangers were 38–58 when former Boston and Seattle manager Darrell Johnson took over as interim manager. Johnson, who had been a coach under Zimmer, guided the club to a 64–98 finish. Although the team's results remained pretty much the same, many of its faces changed.

Looking to the future, the Rangers took a look at some of their young talent. Auditioning successfully for future roles were first baseman-outfielder Pete O'Brien, infielder Wayne Tolleson, second baseman Mike Richardt, and pitchers Mike Smithson, John Butcher, and Tom Henke.

Evaluating those young prospects would be easy for the man selected to oversee the baseball operation. Because on October 4, 1982, Chiles named his own director of player development as the new general manager.

Forty-year-old Joe Klein had been a minor league first baseman for seven years and a minor league manager for ten years before taking over the Ranger farm system in 1980. His first task as general manager was to hire the Rangers' eighth full-time manager in twelve years.

First baseman Dave Hostetler burst upon the scene with 10 HRs in June of '82 before flaming out in August. "Hoss" is greeted here by hitting coach Merv Rettenmund after a 1983 home run. (Texas Rangers Archives)

Three grand slams in one week tied a major league record and earned Larry Parrish a silver tray as A.L. Player of the Week in July, 1982. (Texas Rangers Archives)

THE WIT AND WISDOM OF MICK THE QUICK

Known as "Gozzlehead" to his teammates because that's what he called so many of them, Mickey Rivers left a legacy of memorable quotes from his six seasons with the Rangers.

These are some of the favorites:

To his teammates telling dirty jokes—"Get your minds out of the ghetto."

On his goals for the season—"To hit .300, score 100 runs, and stay injury-prone."

On how the team will do—"We'll do all right if we can capitalize on our mistakes."

On the harsh weather conditions in Milwaukee—"the wind was blowing 100 degrees."

On the Rangers' abundance of outfielders—"I may have to commute. You know, left field, designated hitter, whatever they want."

On the ugliest player he had seen—"The scariest guy I ever saw was Danny Napoleon. When you walked by Napoleon, your clothes would wrinkle. Not only that, when someone hit a fly ball at him, it would curve away from him—turn right around."

His advice to youngsters on how to play center field—"The first thing you do is check the wind-chill factor."

His definition of his favorite nickname, "Gozzlehead"—"Just, you know, like a bullfrog face."

His outlook on life—"Ain't no sense worrying about things you got control over, 'cause if you got control over them, ain't no sense worrying. And there ain't no sense worrying about things you got no control over, 'cause if you got no control over them, ain't no sense worrying."

"Gozzlehead" Rivers was usually smiling. (Texas Rangers Archives)

Rivers, the Ranger Player of the Year in 1980, enjoys a light moment with Bump Wills and Jim Sundberg after hitting a home run. Rivers considered Sundberg and other seasoned veterans to be members of a group he called, "The Knowledge Brothers." (Courtesy *Fort Worth Star-Telegram*, Special Collections Division, University of Texas at Arlington Libraries.)

11

The Rooster

Joe Klein, a newcomer to the general manager's position, had no reluctance to hire a rookie manager. In fact, he narrowed his list of contenders to three—Jim Leyland, Bobby Valentine, and Doug Rader, none of whom had ever managed in the major leagues.

Klein's choice, the thirty-eight-year-old Rader, was announced on November 1, 1982. A former Gold Glove third baseman who was dubbed "The Rooster" in his playing days with the Astros, the six-foot-three, 230-pounder was known as a fun-loving prankster. Although he had mellowed somewhat during three years as manager of the Triple-A Hawaii Islanders, Rader retained his boisterous exuberance.

Impressed by Rader's intelligence, aggressiveness, and ability to motivate, Klein decided that Rader was the ideal sort to turn around a team that had lost 98 games in 1982. Rader's style would be far different from that of his predecessors.

"I plan to stay as close to my players as I possibly can," stated Rader in his first spring training. "I think those days when managers stayed aloof are over."

Although wanting to be close to his players, Rader could also be intimidating. A black belt in karate, Rader had a persona that included what Klein described as a "hint of unsteadiness," which would serve to keep his players in line.

Klein was not shy about making changes, but Rader would start 1983 with almost the same team that finished 29 games out in 1982. The new general manager was bold enough to engineer a deal with the Dodgers in which six-time Gold Glove catcher Sundberg would go to Los Angeles for four players—including young pitchers Orel Hershiser and Dave Stewart.

But Sundberg, who had a no-trade clause in his Texas contract, vetoed the deal when the Dodgers tried to unfavorably renegotiate the terms of his contract. The question

Doug Rader, "The Rooster," crowing at spring training. "I refuse to be miserable," Rader said. "People tell you there is supposed to be a certain amount of misery in life, but I won't buy it." (*Times-Herald*, courtesy of *The Dallas Morning News*.)

"DOUG RADER IS THE TYPE OF GUY WHO DOES THINGS THAT EVERYONE ELSE WOULD LOVE TO DO BUT DOESN'T HAVE THE GUTS TO TRY."
Rangers coach Rich Donnelly, March 1983

Odell Jones led the Rangers with 10 saves in '83, then tried unsuccessfully to become a submarine-baller in '84. (Texas Rangers Archives)

of how Ranger history would have differed had the trade gone through has been debated ever since.

Klein was successful in adding two valuable arms to the Rangers' bullpen. Journeyman right-hander Odell Jones was drafted from Pittsburgh and became the Rangers' bullpen stopper. Another veteran, Dave Tobik, came over from Detroit in a trade for outfielder Johnny Grubb.

Spring training was definitely more fun for everyone with Rader around, despite his rule that prohibited fraternizing with the opposition—"No sucky-facing" is how Rader put it. Upon arriving at the ballpark in Pompano, Rader, as his first act each day, drove his car into a tree. Yes, the same tree every day.

Rader's players contributed to the merriment. When pitcher Dan Boitano struck and killed a flying seagull with a practice pickoff throw, Hough quickly cracked, "That's what you get when you don't wear a helmet."

Spirits remained high despite misfortunes that cost Rader his top two starting pitchers, Hough and Darwin. The former would miss the first week of the season after undergoing knee surgery, while the latter would miss two weeks with an intestinal ailment.

Rader chose Mike Smithson as his Opening Day starter, and the six-foot-eight rookie combined with John Butcher on a 5–3 win over the White Sox. Back-to-back 4–1 wins behind Matlack and Honeycutt completed a three-game sweep over the eventual division champions. Those three low-scoring games served notice that this Ranger team did not have to outslug its opponents to win.

The fun-loving '83 Rangers jam with The Chicken. From left: Mike Smithson, John Butcher, Bill Stein, Dave Hostetler, Bobby Jones. Pete O'Brien looks on in background. (Texas Rangers Archives)

Shortstop Bucky Dent led the A.L. in fielding percentage in '83, anchoring the Rangers' league-leading defense. (Texas Rangers Archives)

Rick Honeycutt led the A.L. in ERA in '83, even though he was traded to the Dodgers in August. (Texas Rangers Archives)

Charlie Hough authored a club-record 36 ⅔ innings shutout string in '83 and led the team in wins, as he did for seven consecutive seasons. (Texas Rangers Archives)

Arlington Stadium received a face-lift in '84, including new scoreboards and billboards above the bleachers, and fifty-two luxury suites. (Texas Rangers Archives)

Mike Stone became club president in '84 and emphasized winning through internal development. (Texas Rangers Archives)

Under new pitching coach Dick Such, the Texas staff was outstanding. Leading the way was Honeycutt, who had endured a 5–17 nightmare in '82. While working with Such in the off-season, the affable southpaw had rediscovered his sinker and his confidence. Starters Hough, Darwin, Smithson, and Tanana all would post ERAs under 4.00, while Butcher, Schmidt, Jones, and Tobik were getting the job done out of the bullpen.

Not even the loss of starting second baseman Mike Richardt to a knee injury in April could derail Rader's team early in the year. Wayne Tolleson took over at second base, played solid defense, and became the team sparkplug with a feisty attitude and 33 stolen bases.

The sure-handed O'Brien became the regular first baseman and teamed with Bell, Dent, and Tolleson to provide the tightest infield defense in club history.

Having only Parrish as a steady long-ball threat, Rader encouraged aggressiveness on the bases. Left fielder Sample responded by stealing 44 bases in his first year as an everyday player.

Struggling to score runs, the Rangers lost eight out of nine in late May to fall five games behind California before rebounding to take first place during a six-game winning streak in late June.

The Rangers went into Anaheim on June 27 with a one-game lead, split a four-game series, then took three of four in Oakland to lead by two games at the All-Star break. Their final triumph before the break was a 15-inning marathon in which the Rangers scored an

Both of the Rangers' newcomers struggled in 1984. Catcher Ned Yost (left) hit .182 and had problems defensively—bothered by "eyelid tension," according to Rader. Outfielder Gary Ward batted .230 in the first half, then hit well after the Rangers dropped out of the race. (Texas Rangers Archives)

Dave Stewart went 12–22 in three years with Texas before achieving stardom in Oakland. (Texas Rangers Archives)

Shortstop Curtis Wilkerson (left) beat out Dent in spring training '84, then was moved to second base in July when Jeff Kunkel (right) was rushed to the big leagues. (Texas Rangers Archives)

amazing 12 runs in the 15th inning to win, 16–4. Establishing a major league record for runs in an extra inning, the 12-run outburst featured 16 batters, eight hits, four walks, and one error. Part-time outfielder Bobby Jones, who had just 16 hits all year, delivered a pair of doubles in the remarkable frame.

The White Sox were making a strong bid to catch the Rangers and Angels as the first half closed. But Rader dismissed Chicago's climb toward the top by saying, "They're winning ugly," a statement that would come back to haunt the Ranger skipper.

The Rangers' magic disappeared abruptly after the break, beginning with three straight losses at Toronto's Exhibition Stadium, which Rader dubbed "the Voodoo Palace." Texas lost 20 of its first 25 second-half contests, falling out of first for the last time on July 25 when Dave Winfield's two-out, two-run triple off Jones in the ninth inning gave the Yankees a nationally televised victory.

That crushing loss was the first of eight straight defeats that left the Rangers six games behind the White Sox and falling fast. On August 19, with the Rangers eight games out, the Texas front office conceded.

Fearing that they would lose staff ace Honeycutt, who could have become a free agent after the season, the Rangers dealt the lefty to the Dodgers for unproven pitchers Dave Stewart and Ricky Wright. Honeycutt was 14–8 with a league-leading 2.42 ERA, and his 174 innings pitched were enough to make him the A.L. ERA champion at the end of the season.

Stewart arrived the next day and pitched no-hit ball for the first four innings in beating the White Sox, 6–1. A hard-throwing right-hander who welcomed the chance to pitch regularly, Stewart took advantage of the opportunity. Posting Honeycutt-type numbers, Stewart went 5–2 the rest of the way with a 2.14 ERA, prompting Such to remark, "He has the stuff to be a No. 1 starter for any team."

Stewart was one of two shining stars as the rest of the club continued to crumble. The other bright spot was Hough, who tossed three consecutive shutouts in compiling a string of 36 2/3 consecutive scoreless innings.

The final team record, 77–85, represented an improvement of 13 wins over 1982. The Rangers led the league in pitching and defense, but lacking firepower, lost 56 games by a margin of one or two runs. Texas ended up 22 games behind the "winning ugly" White

Larry Parrish (left) and Buddy Bell (right) carried the Rangers in the early '80s. Parrish was the Ranger Player of the Year twice. Bell won the award three times, made the All-Star team in four straight seasons, and captured six consecutive Gold Glove awards. (Texas Rangers Archives)

Sox, but by the time spring training began in 1984, Rader would predict a division title for the Rangers.

TOO MANY HOLES

Nineteen eighty-four would be a landmark year for the Rangers—off the field.

Mike Stone, a Western Company executive, was brought in by Chiles to serve as club president.

Arlington Stadium underwent a major face-lift, with the addition of luxury suites, an instant replay screen, and new scoreboards. Billboards rising thirty feet above the back of the bleachers would serve to curb the strong wind from right field, creating a swirling effect.

New uniforms and a new logo were unveiled.

On the field, however, the Rangers took a step back, due in part to a pair of ill-advised trades.

Believing their league-leading pitching staff to be sufficiently deep, Klein and Rader were willing to trade Smithson and Butcher—who had combined for 16 wins—for hard-hitting outfielder Gary Ward.

The very next day, December 8, the Rangers said good-bye to Sundberg, the Texas landmark whose personality conflict with Rader had become quite public. "I think we need a different kind of human being," said Rader. "We need a little more offense out of that position and a little more overt get-up-and-go."

Sundberg defended himself, telling Tim Kurkjian of the *Dallas Morning News* that Rader "just works through intimidation...he wants to be totally in control. He wants to be the top dog."

In return for the fans' beloved "Sunny," Texas received Milwaukee back-up catcher Ned Yost and a minor league pitcher. "We made the deal because Yost is a better player. Period. That's it," Rader claimed. "I would have traded him even up."

Both trades proved to be major miscalculations. The Ranger pitching staff could not sustain the loss of two of its stalwarts. And both newcomers got off to terrible starts at the plate. Yost was also a disaster behind it.

The new catcher hit just .182 and threw out only nine of 70 baserunners. Right fielder Ward rebounded in the second half to hit .284 with 21 homers, but his slow start let the club down.

"The G-Man," George Wright, was the Ranger Player of the Year in '83 before wrecking his shoulder crashing into a wall the following season. (*Times-Herald*, courtesy of *The Dallas Morning News*.)

Texas never recovered from a 9–19 start. After spending forty-eight days of 1983 in first place, the Rangers spent all but thirty-three days of 1984 in the division cellar.

Stewart, who had said that he expected to win 20 games or more, went 7–14. Darwin slumped to 8–12, and the Rangers fell to sixth in the league in ERA.

The thirty-two-year-old Dent was released in spring training in favor of rookie Curtis Wilkerson, who was moved to second base in July when No. 1 draft choice Jeff Kunkel was called up to play shortstop. The duo combined to make 44 errors at shortstop—33 more than Dent had committed the previous year.

The offense was as unproductive as it had been in '83, despite a banner year by Parrish, whose 22 home runs and 101 RBI led the club. Parrish's hot streaks became legendary, including an 11-game RBI streak in June that was just two games shy of the league record.

Bell batted .315 and won his sixth straight Gold Glove. O'Brien came into his own, socking 18 homers and 80 RBI. Hough and Tanana combined to win 31 games, and Schmidt saved 12, the most since Kern in '79.

But ranking thirteenth in the league in runs scored was the club's downfall. Center fielder Wright, who had been the Ranger Player of the Year in '83, started slowly, then injured his shoulder crashing into the wall at Comiskey Park. "The G-Man" missed 60 games and hit just .243 with 48 RBI.

The Rangers could hardly afford to lose one of their big bats. The final humiliation for the Texas hitters came on the last day of the season when California right-hander Mike Witt pitched a perfect game against them at Arlington Stadium. The Angels won, 1–0, with Hough losing on an unearned run.

Wright, whose awful year ended with an 0-for-3 with three strikeouts, was heard muttering as he left the clubhouse, "I'm going to change my name and move to Africa."

Bell, who was named by Rader in September as the club's first-ever captain, bemoaned the club's lack of depth. "We just don't have enough talent right now," he frankly admitted. "We're close, but we've got to shore up some spots."

The responsibility for the shoring up now fell on new shoulders. As the club staggered to a 69–82 finish, Klein had resigned under fire on September 1. To replace him as general manager, Chiles and Stone selected Tom Grieve, the original

Frank Tanana was the Ranger Pitcher of the Year in '84 with a 15–15 record. (*Times-Herald*, courtesy of *The Dallas Morning News*.)

The Rooster

High-flying Wayne Tolleson became the starting second baseman in '83 and stole over 20 bases in three consecutive seasons. (Texas Rangers Archives)

Ranger who had been directing the club's minor league operations. At the age of thirty-six, Grieve became the youngest general manager in the game.

"Tom Grieve is the one supreme embodiment in our statement of purpose," Stone said in announcing the appointment. "Tom has made a substantial commitment to his own internal development. He has taken on new duties and performed admirably at them."

While pondering whether to accept the top position, Grieve had discussed the offer with his family. Although Tom's wife, Kathy, and children Tim and Katie were all in favor of the move, his son Ben had some reservations.

"Dad," the eight-year-old warned. "If you take that job, you're going to get fired."

Ben Grieve's advice, although demonstrating a precocious insight into the game's inner workings, proved to be overly protective. His father would hold the general manager's job for the next ten years. A new era in Ranger history had begun.

GRIEVE GOES TO WORK

Insisting that the Rangers upgrade their scouting system, Grieve made a front-office acquisition as his first off-season move, hiring San Diego Padres Scouting Director Sandy Johnson as the Rangers' new director of player personnel and scouting. Grieve and Johnson would be responsible for creating a player development system that was among the best in baseball.

Prospects for 1985, however, were not very good.

Dave Schmidt led the Rangers in saves and appearances in 1984. (Texas Rangers Archives)

Looking to fill the obvious holes, Grieve signed free agent pitchers Burt Hooton and Dave Rozema and designated hitter Cliff Johnson. He traded Darwin for catcher Don Slaught and dealt Sample for original Ranger Toby Harrah, who would return as a second baseman. Curveballing right-hander Greg Harris was purchased to help in the bullpen.

At the urging of Sandy Johnson, Grieve drafted fireballing lefty Mitch Williams from San Diego. But another hard-throwing prospect was lost when Tom Henke, left unprotected in the free agent compensation draft, was plucked away by Toronto.

Rader planned to move Stewart to short relief, using a starting rotation of Hough, Tanana, Hooton, second-year left-hander Mike Mason, and former Cub Dickie Noles.

The additions of Slaught, Harrah, and Cliff Johnson, it was hoped, would rejuvenate the offense.

Things did not look promising in spring training, however, as the club stumbled to a 10–14 record. First-year pro Oddibe McDowell, the Ranger's No. 1 pick in the 1984 draft, stole the spring show by hitting .360. A speedy and powerful outfielder, the five-foot-nine sensation was sent to Triple-A Oklahoma City at the end of spring training. But he would not remain in the minors for long.

Admitting their blunder in trading Sundberg the previous year, the Rangers released Yost. And in his most difficult decision, Rader also released Rivers, choosing instead to keep rookie Tommy Dunbar and veteran Bobby Jones. Although the loss of Rivers was mourned by fans and teammates alike, the popular center fielder did not catch on with any other club and never played another big league game.

During this spring training, no one connected with the Rangers was predicting a pennant. While looking for improvement in '85, Grieve was primarily looking further down the line.

"The image of the team is bad," admitted the general manager. "A pretty good season is not going to change that, if in fact it can be changed.... The attitude of the team itself, the fans, everybody, is something that needs to be changed. But three or four or five years from now when we've gradually gotten better, we will be respected throughout baseball, not just here."

Nothing that happened in the first month of the '85 season served to encourage an attitude adjustment. The Rangers lost their first five games and at the end of April were mired in the cellar with a 7–12 mark.

Texas's plight worsened in May. Its anemic offense, combined with mediocre pitching, caused a dismal stretch of 11 losses in 13 games. Consecutive 6–5 losses at Yankee Stadium in mid-May left the Rangers 10½ games out of first place with a 9–23 record.

That's when Chiles, Stone, and Grieve pulled the plug on Rader. The Rooster, who had managed the Rangers for two years and five weeks—longer than anyone else in the history of the Texas franchise—was fired on May 16.

Meeting the club in Chicago the following day was the man who would guide the club for the next seven years.

12

Bobby V.

There was little doubt that when given a chance to hire a manager, Grieve would select Bobby Valentine. The pair had been friends since riding the New York Mets' bench together in 1978, a time in which Grieve developed a tremendous respect for Valentine's creative mind and baseball savvy.

Valentine's lack of managerial experience at any level had cost him the Texas job when Rader was hired for 1983. But Grieve was willing to overlook that void on Valentine's resume.

The new manager, a former No. 1 draft choice of the Dodgers, had seen his promising big league playing career derailed by injuries that relegated him to the role of utility player. After retiring in 1979, Valentine became a minor league instructor and then the New York Mets' third-base coach before being picked by Grieve to pilot the Rangers.

Often described as "a Frankie Avalon look-alike," the thirty-five-year-old Valentine wore a winning smile and had an outgoing personality, possessing the ability to win over players, fans, and media. "It's a people sport, and I'm a people person," he explained in his first day on the job. "When you're dealing with twenty-five guys, the person who can deal with them the best will get the most out of them."

A disciple of Dodger manager Tommy Lasorda, Valentine brought to the job a type of charisma never before seen in Ranger circles. He brightened the clubhouse with encouraging words and good-natured ribbing. He urged his players to be aggressive, to take chances—"to express themselves," as Bobby V. put it.

As charming as Valentine could be to some, to others he was a "hot dog," perceived as loud and cocky. It did not take long for the new kid in town to ruffle the feathers of some of the league's established managers with his piercing voice, a sometimes-biting wit, and merciless bench jockeying of opposing players.

Valentine did not make friends easily among the

Valentine and the umpires often did not see eye-to-eye. (Brad Newton)

"HE COMPARES IN BASEBALL KNOWLEDGE TO ANYONE I'VE EVER KNOWN IN THE GAME. HE'S THE KIND OF GUY WHO MANAGED EVERY GAME HE EVER WATCHED."

Tom Grieve, announcing the hiring of Bobby Valentine as manager, May 17, 1985

Bobby Valentine (left) and Tom Grieve (right) have been friends since both were with the Mets in 1978 at the end of their playing careers. (Texas Rangers Archives)

Pitching coach Tom House (right), "The Professor," works with lefty Mike Mason, who was a mainstay of the rotation for three years. (*Times-Herald*, courtesy of *The Dallas Morning News*.)

umpires, either. After being ejected for the first time, Valentine said of umpire Tim McClelland, "If he's an umpire I'm a submarine pilot... their umpiring crew works with about as much intensity as a chain gang."

Undaunted by the adverse effects of his comments, the new manager was more concerned with figuring out which of the Rangers could actually play. The rest of the 1985 season quickly became something of a tryout camp in which Valentine weeded out some of the aging veterans.

First, the 1984 Ranger Pitcher of the Year, Tanana, who was struggling with a 2–7 record, was dealt to the Tigers for a prospect named Duane James. Next, Grieve accommodated Bell's request to be traded, sending the team's best player ever to Cincinnati.

Unfortunately for Texas, Bell's trade value had plummeted due to a season-long slump that left him batting .236. All that the Rangers could get in return for their four-time All-Star was backup outfielder Duane Walker and young pitcher Jeff Russell. It appeared to many that the Reds had pulled off the steal of the century, but the Rangers reaped long-term rewards as Russell developed into an All-Star under the tutelage of a new pitching coach.

Within a week after taking over, Valentine hired former big league southpaw Tom House as pitching coach. Best known for catching Hank Aaron's record-breaking 715th home run in the Atlanta bullpen, House was a doctoral candidate in psychology who had some radical ideas about how to handle a pitching staff.

Looking more like a college professor than a baseball coach, the bespectacled House instituted new running, weight-lifting, and nutrition regimens for his staff. Nicknamed "the Professor" and "the Mad Scientist," House drew attention and frequent ridicule from opposing personnel for one of his more controversial practices.

Pete O'Brien spent six years as the Rangers' starting first baseman and was the Ranger Player of the Year in '85. (Texas Rangers Archives)

Believing that the mechanics of throwing a football are greatly similar to those of pitching, House had his pitchers throw footballs to each other on the field before batting practice.

When asked if the football throwing helped the staff, Hough was quick to respond, "I don't know. But we are leading the league in third-down conversions."

While bidding adieu to Bell and Tanana, as well as to Stewart and Cliff Johnson—who both were traded in September—Valentine auditioned a multitude of new talent.

Steve Buechele, the obvious heir apparent to Bell, was called up to play third base and reminded fans of Bell defensively with his ability to make spectacular diving plays in the field.

Even more impressive was the new center fielder. Recalled from Oklahoma City on Valentine's second day as manager, McDowell was installed as the regular leadoff batter in early June. Uncoiling out of a distinctive crouch at the plate, Oddibe blasted 18 homers to lead all American League rookies and swiped 25 bases.

On July 23 at Arlington Stadium, McDowell pulled off a feat that is still unmatched in Ranger history when he hit for the cycle, homering in his last at-bat to complete the rare accomplishment.

Far less heralded than Buechele and McDowell was backup catcher Geno Petralli,

Steve Buechele replaced Bell at third base with a similar flair for the spectacular. (Texas Rangers Archives)

No. 1 draft pick Oddibe McDowell, who spent just a month in the minors, was the starting center fielder for four years in the late '80's. He returned to the Rangers for one season in 1994. (Texas Rangers Archives)

Valentine (right), looking out for catcher Geno Petralli (left), who spent nine seasons with the Rangers after being signed off the loading dock of a Dr. Pepper plant.
(Texas Rangers Archives)

Outfielder Pete Incaviglia went straight from Oklahoma State to the majors after an impressive spring training in which his line drive knocked this hole in the outfield fence at Pompano Beach. (*Fort Worth Star-Telegram*)

who had been signed to a Triple-A contract in May. At the time he signed, Petralli was driving a forklift at a Dr Pepper plant in Sacramento. Promoted only due to a series of injuries, the former Toronto prospect would spend nine seasons with the Rangers.

Most of the Rangers' veterans had off years, and despite Valentine's daring running game, Texas scored the fewest runs in the league. Only O'Brien, with 22 homers and 92 RBI, produced runs as expected.

The pitching was equally bleak, particularly the starting rotation, which featured fourteen different participants. Hough led the club with 14 wins, with Mason (8–15) a distant second. "We have to see if we have a creditable one through five," admitted Valentine, who loved what he saw of September call-up Jose Guzman, a rookie from Puerto Rico who won three straight starts.

All but six days of the Ranger season were spent in last place, including all of Valentine's term. The club barely avoided 100 losses (62–99), but, looking forward to running the show from the first day of spring training, Valentine was somehow optimistic.

When asked his goal for 1986, Valentine responded, "To field a team that can win our division."

If anyone who witnessed the 1985 Rangers took him seriously, they certainly would not admit it.

Shortstop Scott "Scooter" Fletcher came from the White Sox and became the first million-dollar-a-year athlete in Dallas-Fort Worth. (Texas Rangers Archives)

KIDDIE CORPS COMES THROUGH

By the time he arrived in Pompano Beach, Valentine had scaled down his aspirations for the '86 season, announcing that his goal was to have "the most improved team in the majors."

Valentine's goal had not been lowered by a disappointing off-season. On the contrary, the Rangers pulled off two stunning moves. But in contrast to previous winters, this winter the Rangers were dealing to improve themselves for the long run, stocking up with young talent.

In a deal that shocked the baseball world, Grieve arranged to trade for the Expos' unsigned No. 1 draft pick, outfielder Pete Incaviglia of Oklahoma State. Baseball rules prevented the trade of an unsigned pick, but nothing prevented Grieve from agreeing to a contract with Incaviglia and his agent, then having the Expos sign him to that contract and trade him to Texas.

The Rangers gave up only young pitcher Bob Sebra and utility man Jim Anderson in return for the burly power-hitter who had been the

Pitcher Bobby Witt on the day he signed with the Rangers in 1985 at the age of twenty-one. Ten months later he was in the majors, despite never winning a minor league game. (Texas Rangers Archives)

TEXAS RANGERS

eighth player selected in the June draft. Grieve announced that Incaviglia would be given an honest opportunity to make the team in spring training—a disclosure at which many in baseball scoffed.

In late November, Grieve pulled off another deal, trading Tolleson and Schmidt to the White Sox for twenty-seven-year-old shortstop Scott Fletcher and pitching sensation Edwin Correa—a nineteen-year-old Puerto Rican right-hander considered to be among the top young pitchers in the minors.

Valentine was ecstatic, saying, "In getting Ed Correa, I think we may have the finest stable of young arms of any major league team."

Not even Valentine expected to see the entire stable pitching in the major leagues in '86, but that's what happened. Correa and Guzman both made the team in spring training and were joined in the starting rotation by 1985 No. 1 draft pick Bobby Witt, who earned a spot despite having gone 0–6 at Double-A Tulsa the previous summer. Not only had Witt never won a big league game—he had never won a professional game at any level.

Delaware high school sensation Dwayne Henry showed flashes of brilliance but never developed enough consistency to stay in the big leagues. (Texas Rangers Archives)

A Puerto Rican Treasure Chest—twenty-year-old pitcher Edwin Correa (left), twenty-one-year-old outfielder Ruben Sierra (center), and twenty-three-year-old pitcher Jose Guzman in 1986. Correa and Sierra were the two youngest players in the majors. (Texas Rangers Archives)

Bobby V.

Two more rookie flame-throwers, Dwayne Henry and Mitch Williams, won spots in the bullpen as Valentine gambled with five first-year pitchers to start the season.

In the outfield, Valentine was willing to take an even bigger gamble, choosing as his right fielder and cleanup hitter the kid who had never played even a day in the minors.

Before Incaviglia played his first exhibition, the NCAA home run record-holder caused jaws to drop. In his first day of batting practice, "the Ink Man" drilled a 380-foot line drive that ripped a baseball-sized hole in the wooden fence in left-center. "That's one-inch plywood. Awesome," marveled Valentine. "The fat kid is something, isn't he?" And thus was born the legend of the new Texas strongman, whose drives could bore holes through the outfield fence.

Valentine hoped that a pair of veteran hitters signed as free agents, Tom Paciorek and Darrell Porter, would help steady his young lineup. Hough and Mason were to anchor the starting rotation, a plan that was derailed briefly in spring training when Hough broke his right pinky finger while shaking hands with an old friend.

"The Horse," Dale Mohorcic, tied a major-league record by pitching in 13 straight games in '86, then led the Rangers with 16 saves in '87. (Texas Rangers Archives)

With Hough unavailable, Guzman received the Opening Day assignment at Arlington Stadium.

As a sellout crowd of forty thousand welcomed the young team, Texas beat the Blue Jays, 6–3. Incaviglia doubled for his first professional hit, Guzman collected the win, and Greg Harris picked up the save.

Playing .500 ball for the first six weeks, the Rangers stayed close to the front-running Angels, then grabbed and held first place for a month, beginning on May 24. Texas maintained the top spot until June 25 with help from two call-ups whose career paths were drastically different.

On May 30, an elbow injury to Henry caused the Rangers to summon thirty-year-old rookie reliever Dale Mohorcic, who was toiling in his ninth minor league season without ever having reached the big leagues. The right-handed sinkerballer went on to post a 2.51 ERA while carrying a staggering workload. In August, Valentine called on Mohoric to pitch in 13 straight games, tying a major league record and setting an American League record.

On the first of June, with Parrish and Ward injured, the Rangers turned to their brightest prospect, twenty-year-old outfielder Ruben Sierra. Dubbed "the Franchise" by hitting instructor Tom Robson, Sierra had been expected to spend one full season at Triple-A before reaching the majors. But as in the cases of McDowell and Incaviglia, the future came early for Sierra.

The switch-hitting right fielder, who was younger than every other major league player except teammate Correa, went 3-for-4 in his major league debut, hammering a three-run homer in his second at-bat. Sierra's promotion was designed to be a short-term stint until the veteran outfielders healed. Instead, the phenom from Rio Piedras, Puerto Rico, stayed with the club for the next seven seasons, becoming the Rangers' all-time leader in home runs and RBI.

The Rangers withstood the loss of their regular catcher when Slaught was hit in the face by a pitch from Boston's "Oil Can" Boyd, suffering a fractured nose and cheekbone.

Catcher Don Slaught missed seven weeks in '86 after being beaned by "Oil Can" Boyd, returning with a plastic faceguard attached to his batting helmet. (*Fort Worth Star-Telegram*)

During his absence, the catching was shared by Porter, Petralli, and call-up Orlando Mercado.

On June 16 in Anaheim, Mercado played a major role in perhaps the most heartbreaking loss in Ranger history. Hough had a 1–0 lead with a no-hitter going in the ninth, struck out the first batter, then allowed a high, twisting fly ball down the left-field line. Defensive replacement George Wright ran a long way into the corner, then dropped the ball for a three-base error. Wally Joyner followed with a clean single up the middle, ending the no-hitter and tying the game.

Joyner advanced to second on a passed ball and, one out later, was still at second base with a full count on George Hendrick, who swung and missed on the 3-2 pitch. The knuckleball danced away from Mercado for another passed ball, and when Hough failed to cover home, Joyner raced all the way around from second base to score the winning run.

Texas lost all six games against the Angels in June, fell out of first, then regained the top spot when Hough shut out the Twins on July 1. That win improved Hough's record to 8–3, sewing up the first All-Star berth for the thirty-eight-year-old pitcher. But the Rangers lost five out of six before the break and found themselves 1½ games out as the second half began.

Texas then saw its record drop to 47–48, losing the first seven games of the second half. The losing streak was halted by yet another neophyte, right-hander Mike Loynd, who had made just five starts at Double-A Tulsa since being selected out of Florida State in the seventh round of the June draft.

In his major league debut on July 24, Loynd beat the Indians, 7–3, pitching six strong innings. His fist-pumping, animated antics on the mound antagonized opponents, but Loynd was a lifesaver for a club that badly needed a lift.

Ignited by Loynd, the Rangers stayed in the race and scored one of their more improbable wins ever on August 6 in Baltimore. Trailing 11–6 after the Orioles hit a major league-record two grand slams in the fourth inning, the Rangers rallied to win, 13–11. Harrah had five hits for Texas, including a grand slam that gave the two teams an unprecedented three slams in one game.

On August 25, the Rangers were three games out as the Red Sox came in for a nationally televised

Pitcher Mike Loynd infuriated opponents with his celebratory fist-pumping as he sparked a Ranger turnaround in '86. (*Fort Worth Star-Telegram*)

Monday night game. Boston ace Roger Clemens was going for his 20th win and had a 2–0 lead in the eighth inning when Petralli tied the game with the second home run of his career. Sierra ended the game with a bang, crushing a two-run homer off reliever Calvin Schiraldi in the bottom of the ninth.

A four-game losing streak in early September finally knocked the Rangers seven games out, and as California got hot, Texas fell 10 games out before the Angels clinched the division with nine games remaining. But along the way, there had been more fireworks.

On September 11 in Minnesota, Valentine was ejected from a game by Larry Barnett, who later claimed that the Ranger manager had questioned his integrity during the argument at home plate. Valentine, who denied Barnett's charges and believed that he had become a marked man to the men in blue, was forced to sit out a four-game suspension.

With first-base coach Art Howe managing the team, the Rangers smashed a club-record seven home runs in a morning game at the Metrodome. Both Porter and Sierra went deep twice, the latter becoming the youngest player ever to homer from both sides of the plate in one game.

Following their mathematical elimination, the Rangers reeled off seven wins in their last nine games to finish five games out, the closest to first place that a Texas team had ever finished. Their 87–75 record represented a jump of 25 wins over the previous year, fulfilling Valentine's goal of being the most improved team in baseball.

They had achieved a minor miracle with a pitching staff that set a major league record for appearances by rookies and used first-year players to start 101 games. Guzman, Correa, and Witt combined to win 32 games. Williams set a major league rookie record by appearing in 80 games, posting eight wins and eight saves.

The Rangers' ERA improved from 12th to 8th in the league despite the Rangers leading the league in walks and setting a major league record by uncorking 94 wild pitches.

Witt's 22 wild pitches set an A.L. record. His 143 walks were the most in the majors in eighteen years. In his second start, the young fireballer was pulled from a game in

Greg Harris led the Rangers in saves in '85 and '86 but lost his touch in '87, a year in which he hurt his elbow flicking sunflower seed shells in the bullpen. (Texas Rangers Archives)

Valentine set an example for his players, signing autographs every day and playing an active role in the community. (Texas Rangers Archives)

TEXAS RANGERS

"I pitch like my hair is on fire," said the excitable, unpredictable lefty Mitch Williams, who led the A.L. with a club-record 80 appearances in '86, the most ever by a major league rookie. Williams led the club in appearances three years in a row and in saves in '88. (Texas Rangers Archives)

Milwaukee despite having a no-hitter through five innings in a 2–2 tie. At the time he was lifted, Witt had struck out 10, walked eight, and thrown four wild pitches.

Williams was similarly wild, ranking fifth in the league with a team-high 11 hit batsmen, despite hurling only 98 innings. Still, the twenty-one-year-old southpaw had come a long way from the spring of '85, when Rader refused to allow Williams to pitch batting practice against left-handed hitters, fearing for their safety.

As expected, Hough led the club in wins, going 17–10. Unexpected was the emergence of Harris as bullpen stopper. The curveballer saved 20 games, won 10, and hurled an exhausting total of 111 relief innings.

The Rangers set club records for runs scored and home runs. Incaviglia became the second Ranger ever to hit 30 home runs, with Parrish (28) and O'Brien (23) each surpassing 20 homers and 90 RBI. Buechele and McDowell hit 18 apiece, and Sierra slammed 16 in just 113 games.

The success of the '86 Rangers reminded many of the '74 turnaround under Billy Martin, in which the Rangers' record improved by 27 wins. Even more substantial this time, however, were the box-office benefits.

Attendance in 1986 skyrocketed to a club record 1,692,021, an increase of almost six hundred thousand. Metroplex fans were excited by the pennant race and enthusiastic about the team's budding stars, who displayed a new attitude toward their followers.

Led by their manager, who sat atop the dugout signing autographs before every game and worked tirelessly for charitable causes, Ranger players displayed a new enthusiasm toward community involvement. Of Valentine's many contributions to the franchise, his role in improving the relationship between the Rangers and their fans is among the most important.

In a moving on-field ceremony following the season finale, Rangers players tossed their jerseys into the crowd and Valentine grabbed the public address microphone, promising, "You ain't seen nothing yet."

In the visiting dugout, manager Gene Mauch of the division champion Angels looked across the field at the young challengers. "They deserve a nose bleed," Mauch told Frank Luksa of the *Dallas Times Herald*. "That's how high they should be carrying their heads."

Valentine's role in the Rangers' reversal was well recognized. He was selected as American League Manager of the Year by United Press International and finished second to Boston's John McNamara for the Baseball Writers' version of the award.

Texas's 87 wins represented its most victories since 1978 and matched the team's second-highest win total ever. As usual, it was the glib Hough who put things into perspective in the Ranger clubhouse. "If someone had told us in spring training that we might finish 10 games over .500, we'd have danced in the street," he said.

A REPEAT OF '75?

Looking ahead to the next year and beyond, Grieve made very few moves, hoping for continued development from the team's young nucleus. But in no way did he take for granted a better year in '87. As a member of Martin's surprising 1974 team and of the '75 team that took a step backward, Grieve was hoping that the '87 Rangers could avoid suffering the same fate.

Chiles was hoping to sell the team before the next season to Gaylord Broadcasting but ran into a roadblock when the American League owners vetoed the deal. Chiles was forced to remain in charge of an operation that he no longer cared to, or could really afford to, own.

Still, hopes were high, with fan interest at a record level as the Rangers opened their first spring training at their new state-of-the-art facility in Port Charlotte, Florida. Ranger players talked openly about winning their division, and *Sports Illustrated*, among others, picked the Rangers to win the West.

Almost all the key faces were the same, except that of Harrah, who had retired to manage one of the organization's minor league teams. Rookie Jerry Browne would take over at second base. Otherwise, the '86 lineup and pitching staff returned intact.

The results, however, were drastically different. After splitting the first two games of the year in Baltimore, the Rangers lost a frightful nine games in a row, falling to 1–10. The ninth loss was an improbable come-from-ahead defeat in Milwaukee. Harris came in and blew a 4–1 ninth-inning lead, allowing a three-run homer to Rob Deer and then a two-run bomb to Dale Sveum.

The club came home from Milwaukee for the annual "Welcome Home Luncheon" and did not make it through even that event unscathed. McDowell accidentally sliced an eight-stitch gash in his right middle finger while cutting a dinner roll and was sidelined more than a week. Oddibe eventually returned to the lineup but suffered through a disappointing season, as did many of his teammates.

The Rangers' long journey back to the .500 mark took over three months, but a win on July 27 got the Rangers even at 49–49. They immediately lost their next four games and never approached a winning record again.

Offensively, the Rangers improved over

Geno Petralli (right), who usually drew the unenviable assignment of catching Hough's knuckleballs, did so successfully on this date. However, on August 22, 1987, in Detroit, Petralli tied a major league record when he was charged with six passed balls. "It's too unhittable...and too uncatchable," said Tiger manager Sparky Anderson of Hough's knuckler. (Texas Rangers Archives)

Larry Parrish, who had given up his glove for the DH role, was the Rangers' career home run leader when he was released in 1987. (Texas Rangers Archives)

1986, again setting club records for runs scored and home runs. Parrish set a club record with 32 homers and drove in 102 runs. Sierra was electrifying in his first full season, smacking 30 homers and leading the club with 109 RBI. Incaviglia had 27 HRs and 80 RBI. O'Brien, Fletcher, and Browne all had solid seasons at the plate. But the Rangers gave away far too many runs as the pitching and defense collapsed.

Correa was lost to a shoulder injury and won only three games. Mason was ineffective early and was traded. Witt and Guzman, bothered by injuries, were inconsistent. Hough was better than ever, winning a career-high 18 games, but was the only dependable starter.

The bullpen was hurt by the disappointing performance of Harris as the closer. Mohorcic led the club with 16 saves. Williams was as wild as ever but appeared in a club-record 85 games and held opposing batters to a .175 batting average.

A controversial addition helped the bullpen in the last two months. Former Dodger lefty Steve Howe, on a drug rehabilitation program, was signed to a Triple-A contract on July 12 and called up on August 6. Baseball Commissioner Peter Ueberroth objected to the call-up and fined the Rangers the staggering sum of $250,000.

Pregame football-tossing was a routine performed by Ranger pitchers, including two-time All-Star Jeff Russell, shown here at the Tokyo Dome on a post-season All-Star trip in '88. (Yomiuri Shimbun, Tokyo, Japan)

Had Howe remained with the Rangers after 1987, the fine might have been a small price to pay. But the oft-suspended southpaw violated his aftercare program during a January 1988 minicamp in Arlington and never pitched for the Rangers again.

Texas's team ERA, 4.63, was 11th in the league, a rank that was better than that turned in by its defense. The Rangers made 151 errors, the league's second-highest total, and their catchers set a major league record with 73 passed balls—65 of which were committed while Hough was pitching.

The Rangers slumped to a 75–87 finish, tying the Angels for last place. "I'm not sure we ever recovered from that 1–10 start," observed Parrish. "Making up the games wasn't the hard part. Regaining our confidence was."

STILL WAITING FOR THINGS TO HAPPEN

For the most part, the Rangers sat out the winter trading season again, making just a minor deal in which Slaught went to the Yankees for pitcher Brad Arnsberg. Grieve and Valentine still believed that the talent needed to win was already in the organization.

"We have a couple of potential No. 1 starters and a couple of potential bullpen closers," Grieve maintained. "We have guys capable of hitting in the 3-4-5 spots. We are just waiting for them to develop, for things to happen."

Not much good happened in the first month of the 1988 season. Correa was lost for the season with recurring shoulder trouble, and Witt was sent down to Oklahoma City in early May with an 0–5 record, unable to throw strikes. Oakland broke out of the gate quickly and left the Rangers in the dust, 10 games behind with a 10–16 record.

Despite putting together a club record-tying eight-game winning streak in May, the

Rangers won only 70 games, losing 91 in their worst year since 1973. Texas finished 33½ games behind the Athletics. Browne and McDowell both played their way back to the minors. And Parrish suffered an even harsher fate.

After representing the club in the All-Star Game the previous summer, Parrish was slumping at .190 with seven homers in early July when the Rangers decided to release him. On the day that Valentine was to give his veteran designated hitter the bad news, a *Dallas Times Herald* story by Phil Rogers revealed that Parrish would be released. So when Valentine, leaning against the tarp along the right-field stands in Baltimore, gave Parrish the official word, the message had already been delivered by the media.

With Parrish gone, the Rangers never found a productive DH, although they tried no fewer than 17 different players in that role. Not many other spots in the lineup were getting the job done, either. Almost every hitter had an off year, including Sierra, who led the team with 23 HRs and 93 RBI.

The Rangers' run total fell by almost 200 runs from 1987, and the home run count dropped by 82. Texas ranked 12th in runs and last in long balls.

Pitching and defense actually improved significantly, but not enough to overcome the offensive deficiencies. Witt returned from Oklahoma City in mid-July and astounded everyone by pitching nine consecutive complete games. Hough (15–16), Paul Kilgus (12–15), and Guzman (11–13) pitched well despite losing records. And Russell moved into the starting rotation, winning a spot in the All-Star Game on his way to a 10–9 record.

Williams assumed the closer role with mixed results. Still wild, the left-hander saved 18 games while his ERA soared to 4.63. Mohorcic saved just five before being traded to the Yankees for Cecilio Guante.

The Rangers' on-the-field humiliation was accompanied by an embarrassing deal made by Chiles. The nearly desperate owner agreed to sell the club to a Tampa Bay group that declined to guarantee that it would keep the Rangers in Texas.

Fortunately, minority owner Edward Gaylord stepped in and killed the Tampa deal by exercising the right of refusal that he possessed, allowing him to match any offer from outside to buy the club. Gaylord's bid was turned down by American League owners the following March—the second time they had rejected the media magnate as Ranger owner.

After the final game of 1988, many of the clubhouse postmortems centered around the lack of a winning attitude. Pointing to the team's 70–91 record, the realistic Hough was far more blunt in his assessment.

"You can have all the attitude you want, but that won't win games when you're facing teams who are better than you are," the senior Ranger noted. "This combination of players isn't working, so what has to be done is you have to change the combination."

Grieve was quick to agree with his star pitcher, stating, "It's obvious we didn't hit very well. We will do everything we can to help the offense."

And, signaling a change in philosophy, Grieve admitted, "We are no longer in a position where we can just wait for our young players to get better."

As Ranger fans would soon find out, the waiting definitely was over. Some serious action was about to begin.

13

A New Combination

The magnitude and swiftness of the Rangers' off-season transformation were absolutely stunning. Just five days after signing Scott Fletcher to a three-year, $3.5 million contract—which made the shortstop the first million-dollar-a-year athlete in Dallas-Fort Worth history—Grieve and his staff initiated a series of moves that turned the Rangers from a last-place team into a contender.

On December 5, a nine-player deal with the Cubs brought the Rangers twenty-four-year-old outfielder-first baseman Rafael Palmeiro, left-handed starter Jamie Moyer, and lefty reliever Drew Hall. The trade sent Mitch Williams, Paul Kilgus, and Curtis Wilkerson to the Cubs, along with three minor leaguers.

The following day, Grieve landed twenty-seven-year-old second baseman Julio Franco by sending Oddibe McDowell, Pete O'Brien, and Jerry Browne to the Indians.

"We've added two .300 hitters without creating a hole in our starting rotation," Valentine marveled. But the best was yet to come.

The very next day, Grieve announced the free agent signing of baseball's all-time strikeout king, Nolan Ryan. The forty-one-year-old future Hall of Famer was miffed at the Astros' attempt to cut his salary and turned down a higher offer from Angels' owner Gene Autry in order to stay in his home state.

"The Rangers have given me an opportunity to stay in Texas, play for a club that is going to be competitive, and have a family situation I think is the most workable for the Ryan family," said Ryan, whose home in Alvin, Texas, was 230 miles from Arlington.

Blood spurted from a six-stitch gash in Ryan's lower lip after he was hit by a Bo Jackson one-hopper in the second inning, September 9, 1990. Nolan went through two jerseys as he stayed in the game until the eighth inning of a 2–1 win. "I saw it, put up my glove and never saw it again. When it didn't hit my glove, I knew I was in trouble," said Ryan, who complied with Jackson's postgame request for one of his jerseys. The jersey sent over to Jackson, however, was not one of the bloodied shirts. They were laundered and worn again. (Linda Kaye)

"NOT SINCE SHERMAN HAS A MAN MARCHED THROUGH ATLANTA WITH THE IMPACT OF RANGERS GENERAL MANAGER TOM GRIEVE AT THIS WEEK'S BASEBALL WINTER MEETINGS."

Tracy Ringolsby, Dallas Morning News, December 8, 1988

Rafael Palmeiro came to Texas from the Cubs after finishing second in the N.L. batting race in '88. Palmeiro led the Rangers in hits for four straight years and was the Ranger Player of the Year in 1990. (Texas Rangers Archives)

The Rangers gave up three everyday players to acquire Julio Franco, who represented Texas in the All-Star Game three years in a row and won the A.L. batting title in 1991. (Texas Rangers Archives)

Without exaggerating, Valentine evaluated the Ryan signing by saying, "This is the one most important transaction the Texas Rangers have ever made."

Ryan, who expected to play just one year for Texas before retiring, went on to spend five unforgettable years with the Rangers, helping establish once and for all the credibility of the franchise.

Ryan and Moyer were to join Hough, Guzman, and Witt in the starting rotation. Russell would move to the bullpen and replace Williams as the closer.

Palmeiro and Franco would replace O'Brien and the Browne-Wilkerson duo on the right side of the infield. Lightning-quick center fielder Cecil Espy was given McDowell's job. And to fill the troublesome DH spot, the Rangers re-signed Buddy Bell and added left-handed-hitting free agent Rick Leach.

The uncertainty regarding the team's ownership finally ended during spring training. Eight days after American League owners rejected Gaylord's bid to buy the club, Chiles announced on March 17 that he had agreed in principle to sell the team to a Dallas-Fort Worth investor group led by George W. Bush (the son of President George Bush) and Edward W. "Rusty" Rose.

The Bush-Rose group was unanimously approved by the club owners of both leagues on April 18 and officially completed the takeover on April 21. By that time, their new property was baseball's hottest commodity.

Although a spring training rotator cuff injury sidelined Guzman for the season, former No. 1 draft pick Kevin Brown stepped in to replace him. Another rookie, southpaw Kenny Rogers, earned a bullpen position. The Rangers won 15 of their last 19 exhibitions, prompting Sundberg, who was back with the club for his final season, to declare the pitching staff to be "the best staff Texas has ever had."

In April, Sundberg's assessment appeared to be correct. The Rangers blazed to their best month ever, winning eight games in a row on the way to a 17–5 record. Witt and Moyer each went 3–0, and Russell was 2–0 with five saves.

Ryan flirted with no-hit-

Nolan Ryan (right), with manager Bobby Valentine, on the day Ryan signed with the Rangers, December 7, 1988. The acquisition of Ryan was the most important transaction in Ranger history. "When Nolan Ryan came here, he was a superstar. When he left here, he was a legend," club president Tom Schieffer stated. (*Fort Worth Star-Telegram*)

ters on two occasions, including a 4–1 win at Toronto in which Nelson Liriano spoiled the no-hit bid with a one-out triple in the ninth inning. "Big Tex" ended the month with a 3–1 record by prevailing in one of the most memorable battles ever at Arlington Stadium.

Matched up with another Texas strikeout king, Boston ace Roger Clemens, on April 30, Ryan allowed just one run in eight innings. The Rangers, however, were trailing 1–0 until the bottom of the eighth, when Palmeiro lined a two-run game-winning homer off the right-field foul pole. Russell fired a perfect ninth to complete the 2–1 win, which put the Rangers a game in front of Oakland.

Unfortunately, the Rangers' stay in first place was short-lived. The 17–5 April was followed by a 10–17 May, which left Texas 5½ games out. Never again did the Rangers reach first place.

Hough and Moyer both suffered shoulder injuries, and Witt lost his magic. Despite lefty Mike Jeffcoat emerging as a steady No. 5 starter, the Ranger staff struggled for the rest of the year.

Beset by injuries, on July 24 Texas called up nineteen-year-old lefty Wilson Alvarez to pitch against the Blue Jays. The promising Venezuelan was bombed for two home runs and failed to retire any of the five batters he faced. Five days later, Alvarez was traded to the White Sox in a deal that has haunted the Rangers ever since.

The Rangers were still not getting run production from the DH position. Bell, failing to regain his stroke after a knee injury, retired on June 24, leaving the Rangers with no power from that spot.

With the club floundering in third place, seven games out on July 29, Grieve felt the need to make a move and acquired All-Star designated hitter Harold Baines and reserve shortstop Fred Manrique from the White Sox. Describing the thirty-year-old Baines as "the best designated hitter in baseball," Grieve explained that the deal was not made only for the last two months of the season. "We think Baines can help for who knows how long—four, five, or six years," he said.

Passing The Bat On... Eddie Chiles (right) and his wife, Fran, announcing the sale of the team to Edward "Rusty" Rose (far left) and George W. Bush, March 17, 1989. (*Fort Worth Star-Telegram*)

Center fielder Cecil Espy stole 45 bases in '89 to lead the team. (Texas Rangers Archives)

The price paid for Baines was steep. The Rangers surrendered their starting shortstop, Scott Fletcher, a move that backfired when Jeff Kunkel failed to pan out as Fletcher's replacement. Even more damaging in the long run was the loss of the two young prospects sent to Chicago in the deal—twenty-year-old outfielder Sammy Sosa and the teenager, Alvarez, both of whom went on to become stars.

Bothered by bad knees, Baines drove in just 16 runs in 50 games. The Rangers never mounted a charge toward the top and settled in fourth place, finishing 16 games behind Oakland with an 83–79 mark.

An impressive array of individual achievements helped soften the team's disappointing finish. Sierra led the league with a club-record 119 RBI, joined teammates Franco, Russell, and Ryan in the All-Star Game and finished second to Robin Yount in a very close MVP vote.

Franco hit .316, and Espy ranked second in the league with 45 stolen bases. Russell led the league with a club-record 38 saves and won the Fireman of the Year Award. And Ryan continued to re-write the record book.

At the age of forty-two, Ryan was the Ranger Pitcher of the Year, going 16–10 with a league-leading 301 strikeouts. He pitched two one-hitters and carried five no-hitters into the eighth inning or later.

On August 22, the Rangers enjoyed their earliest sellout ever. Arlington Stadium had been sold out five days in advance, as Ryan was six strikeouts away from the 5,000th of his career. The magic moment arrived when Rickey Henderson, leading off for Oakland in the fifth inning, worked

Nineteen-year-old Wilson Alvarez leaves the mound after allowing two first-inning home runs in his only Texas appearance. Alvarez was traded to the White Sox five days later, along with twenty-year-old outfielder Sammy Sosa (right) and Scott Fletcher, in the deal which brought Harold Baines to the Rangers. (Texas Rangers Archives)

the count full and then swung and missed at a 96-mph fastball as thousands of flashbulbs illuminated the stadium.

Despite the historic 5,000th strikeout, Ryan lost the game, 2–0, partially due a pair of outfield miscues—a defensive weakness that plagued the Rangers all season.

Ryan was sensational but was the club's only consistent starter. "You can't compete, expect to win a division, with one starting pitcher," lamented Grieve, who at least was somewhat appeased by a record turnout at the gate.

For the first time ever, the Rangers drew over two million fans, a strong statement of acceptance by the ticket-buying public. The new owners seemed happy, agreeing with Grieve that the team was headed in the right direction.

"From where we were last year to where we are now is a step in the right direction," said the general manager. "We need to make another step, about the same size, next year."

Harold Baines, an All-Star designated hitter, was a disappointment in his one year with the Rangers, while Alvarez and Sosa became stars. The Baines trade was the Rangers' biggest mistake since the 1982 trade for Lee Mazzilli. (Texas Rangers Archives)

SAME TEAM... SAME RECORD

The Rangers' attempt to take that next step was delayed about a month, when club owners locked out the players for thirty-two days before spring training began in 1990. After the dispute over arbitration eligibility was finally settled, teams hurried through a shortened spring training. The full 162-game schedule began only six days later than originally scheduled.

Compared with the massive makeover they engineered the previous winter, the Ranger management was less aggressive following the '89 season. Actually, the organization's strategy continued to stress development from within, hoping for improvement from the abundance of young talent. Just two player moves were made, both serving to improve the team's defense up the middle.

On November 24, Gold Glove center fielder Gary Pettis was signed as a free agent to replace Espy. It was not until spring training, when it became clear that help was

Ruben Sierra, "El Caballo" (The Horse), finished second to Robin Yount in the 1989 MVP vote after leading the league in RBI (119). Sierra led the Rangers five straight seasons ('87–'91) in RBI, winning Ranger Player of the Year honors in four of those years. (Texas Rangers Archives)

needed at shortstop, that Grieve acted again, acquiring Jeff Huson from the Expos in exchange for Drew Hall.

Led by Ryan (4–0) and Brown (5–0), the Rangers had a solid first month. The club was 13–10 on May 6 when an offensive slump caused a horrible tailspin. The Rangers dropped 22 of their next 30 games, falling 15 games behind Oakland with a 21–32 mark.

Injuries were a major factor in the swoon. Buechele, swinging the team's hottest bat, suffered a broken wrist when hit by a pitch in late April and was out for a month. Sierra was hobbled by a sprained ankle and struggled at the plate. Guzman was still unable to pitch after shoulder surgery. Russell tried to pitch despite an injured elbow and finally submitted to surgery in late May.

Even the seemingly superhuman Ryan succumbed to the injury jinx and spent twenty days on the disabled list, suffering from muscle spasms in his lower back. When Nolan returned to the mound on June 6 at Arlington Stadium, still bothered by back pain, he allowed five runs in five innings and lost to the A's, 5–4.

But just five nights later in Oakland, the forty-three-year-old phenomenon avenged the defeat and was carried off the field on the shoulders of his teammates—having thrown the sixth no-hitter of his incredible career. Staked to a 3–0 lead in the first inning on home runs by Franco and catcher John Russell, Ryan steamrolled the Oakland hitters, striking out 14 and walking only two on the way to a 5–0 win.

Taking extra time between pitches to help ease the discomfort in his back, Ryan required only one tough defensive play to preserve the no-hitter. Shortstop Huson came to the rescue on a ninth-inning slow roller off the bat of Rickey Henderson, charging and throwing almost underhand to first base to nip the fleet outfielder.

Nolan's wife, Ruth, and daughter, Wendy, were in the stands, and his fourteen-year-old son Reese was in uniform in the dugout, helping to break the between-innings tension by rubbing his father's back.

When right fielder Ruben Sierra clutched a foul fly by Willie Randolph to end the game, the Ranger dugout exploded in jubilation. After flirting with a no-hitter so many times since joining the Rangers, the only man in major league history to throw five of those gems had just fired his sixth.

The dugout celebration by Ryan's teammates surpassed anything ever experienced on the Rangers' side of a ball field. Russell, the veteran catcher who had been out of baseball a month earlier after being released by the Phillies, could hardly believe the event in which he had just shared.

"This is the most exciting moment of my life," proclaimed the twenty-nine-year-old backstop. "I'm emotionally drained."

Despite having been on this stage many times before, Ryan allowed that this no-hitter stood out among the others. "This one has a special place next to my fifth no-hitter because it came so late in my career," he said. "And because the team became so emotionally involved."

The following day, another trip to the doctor revealed that the forty-three-year-old living legend, the oldest man ever to pitch a no-hitter in the big leagues, had done so with a stress fracture in his back. Not surprisingly, Ryan vowed to make his next start, received a cortisone injection, and stayed in the rotation.

Ryan's heroics clearly gave the club a spiritual lift. The next day, they rallied in the bottom of the ninth to beat Oakland's All-Star stopper, Dennis Eckersley.

Those two dramatic wins over the division leaders helped propel the Rangers to a strong three months in which they turned their season around. After June 7, when they were 11 games under .500, the Rangers went 62–47, finishing with the same 83–79 record they had posted the previous year. But with the Athletics winning 103 games, the Rangers finished 20 games back, in third place.

Most significant in the turnaround was the pitching of Witt. Having pitched so poorly early in the year that he was demoted to the bullpen for a week, the often-overpowering right-hander was undefeated over a stretch of 14 starts. Witt set a club record with 12 straight wins, finished the season 17–10, and was the Ranger Pitcher of the Year.

Ryan not only continued to pitch despite the back injury, but he also made baseball history again on July 31 by becoming the 20th man to win 300 games. Having failed in his first attempt at No. 300, Ryan gained the milestone victory in Milwaukee.

With more than forty of Nolan's friends and family, 250 members of the media, and fifty-one thousand fans at County Stadium, another 7,828 watched the game on the Diamond Vision screen at Arlington Stadium, roaring when the Rangers jumped to a 4–1 lead in the fifth inning.

The Rangers led 5–1 in the eighth inning when a pair of errors by Franco at second base led to two unearned runs. With two outs in the eighth, Valentine called to the bullpen for right-hander Brad Arnsberg. As Ryan and his manager waited on the mound for the reliever to arrive, the crowd rose and chanted, "Nolan, Nolan" for close to a minute.

Arnsberg got the final four outs to notch the save in what turned out to be an 11–3 victory. Franco, who had atoned for his errors with a ninth-inning grand slam to break the game open, was the object of ribbing in the postgame celebration. "Hey, Julio," yelled Incaviglia. "At least you drove in more than you let in."

Ryan, who had heaved 146 pitches in his 7 2/3 innings of work, appeared more relieved than ecstatic, saying, "I'm glad it's over with. The last

Jeff Russell led the A.L. in saves (38) in '89 to win the Rolaids Relief Man and Fireman of the Year awards. Here he celebrates a Ranger victory with catcher Geno Petralli. (Texas Rangers Archives)

On August 22, 1989, Ryan fanned Rickey Henderson for his historic 5,000th strikeout. At the age of forty-two, Ryan led the league that season with 301 strikeouts and was the Ranger Pitcher of the Year. (National Baseball Library and Archive)

Gary Pettis joined the Rangers as their lead-off hitter in 1990 and won a Gold Glove in center field. (Texas Rangers Archives)

A New Combination

fifteen days [since winning No. 299] emotionally have been the toughest fifteen days I've gone through. I didn't want this to be an ongoing deal."

Paced by starters Ryan, Witt, and Brown and relievers Rogers and Arnsberg, the Rangers ranked sixth in the league in pitching. But their offense failed to measure up, averaging barely four runs per game, 10th in the league.

Taking much of the heat for the club's lack of punch was Baines, for whom the Rangers had given away so much. Benched at times by Valentine against left-handed pitching, the designated hitter drove in just 44 runs in 103 games before being traded to the Athletics in late August for a pair of minor league pitchers.

"I haven't been doing the job," Baines admitted the day before the trade. "There's nothing for me to be proud of... I've got a lot of work to do. To forget the season."

The trade of Baines opened a spot in the Texas lineup for their most prized prospect, a lanky twenty-year-old center fielder from Vega Baja, Puerto Rico. Juan Gonzalez had received a record signing bonus at the age of sixteen and progressed steadily through the Texas farm system since then. After winning the American Association MVP award by leading in homers (29) and RBI (101), Gonzalez was ready to contribute immediately and hit .289 with four homers and 12 RBI in 25 games.

Shortstop Jeff Huson came from the Expos in the spring of 1990, won a starting job and saved Ryan's sixth no-hitter with a great play on a ninth-inning roller. (Texas Rangers Archives)

Palmeiro led the league in hits and finished third in the batting race (.319), but he was the only regular to hit over .300. And although Incaviglia became the first Ranger to have five 20-homer seasons, no one could produce as many as 25 HRs or 100 RBI. Sierra, for example, who had been the Ranger Player of the Year in each of the previous three seasons, hit just .280 with 16 home runs.

Franco, who hit .296, was the only Texas player on the A.L. All-Star team and made the most of the opportunity. Julio's two-run double off Rob Dibble drove in the game's only two runs and earned him the All-Star MVP award—the only Ranger ever to win the honor.

Undoubtedly the strangest day of the year was spent on a rainy Sunday in Chicago on August 12. What would have been the Rangers' final game ever at old Comiskey Park, a scheduled 1:35 P.M. start, never got underway due to heavy rains that began around 11 A.M. Wanting to avoid a makeup game in Texas the following weekend, White Sox management stubbornly refused to call the game until 8:58 P.M. Players from both teams were forced to endure the cramped quarters of Comiskey's clubhouses during the seven-hour, twenty-

Nolan Ryan pitching in the ninth inning of his sixth no-hitter (opposite page), June 11, 1990, being congratulated by catcher John Russell (left), and then being carried off the field on his teammates' shoulders (below). *San Francisco Chronicle* reporter David Bush wrote, "The A's march to a division title paused last night to let a little bit of history go by." (Texas Rangers Archives)

Julio Franco receives his trophy as MVP of the 1990 All-Star Game, in which he drove in the only two runs of the game with a double off Rob Dibble. (Texas Rangers Archives)

Nolan Ryan being congratulated by catcher Geno Petralli (left) and Mike Stanley (right) after his 300th win, an 11–3 victory on July 31, 1990, in Milwaukee. Ryan led the league again in strikeouts at age 43. (Texas Rangers Archives)

A New Combination

three-minute rain delay, which is believed to be the longest in major league history.

Despite failing to improve their standing, the Rangers drew over two million fans and broke their home attendance record again. But clearly, there would have to be some changes for the team to improve.

Included among the changes was the departure of Hough, who was allowed to leave via free agency. In saying farewell to the man who won a club-record 139 games in his eleven years in Texas, the Rangers no longer had any players remaining from the pre-Valentine days.

The biggest news of the off-season was delivered on October 24 when the Rangers and the city of Arlington announced plans to build a new ballpark. On January 19, 1991, Arlington voters set those plans in motion by approving a one-half-cent sales tax to finance the municipal bonds for ballpark construction.

The man who had spent six months coordinating the effort to design and finance the new ballpark, Tom Schieffer, was named club president on January 31. A lifelong resident of Fort Worth, Schieffer replaced Mike Stone, who had resigned after the 1990 season.

Brad Arnsberg, who came to Texas after a cup of coffee with the Yankees, recorded the save in Ryan's 300th victory. (Texas Rangers Archives)

14-GAME WIN STREAK, MOST RUNS IN MAJORS ... SAME THIRD-PLACE FINISH

The 1991 season saw the Ranger offense finally fulfill its promise. Bolstered by the addition of Gonzalez and forty-one-year-old designated hitter Brian Downing, Texas led the majors in runs scored, averaging over five runs per game.

The hitting breakthrough occurred after Valentine shocked his team in spring training by releasing Incaviglia. Attempting to put together a more team-oriented, contact-hitting attack, Valentine replaced Incaviglia with young left-handed hitter Kevin Reimer, who went on to hit 20 homers in his first full major league season.

Downing provided the Rangers a leadoff hitter with a high on-base percentage, an asset on which the Rangers capitalized with regularity. The three men following Downing in the batting order—"the Three Amigos," as Palmeiro, Sierra, and Franco were dubbed—each delivered more than 200 hits, scored over 100 runs, and hit better than .300.

Franco became the first Ranger ever to win a batting title, hitting .341 to lead the majors. Gonzalez, usually hitting after Reimer in the No. 6 spot in the order, led the club in homers (27) and joined Sierra with over 100 RBI.

Unfortunately, not only did the Rangers score the most runs in the majors, but they also allowed the most runs in the majors. The Ranger staff was decimated by injuries and plagued by a porous defense that ranked 12th in the A.L. for the second year in a row.

Ryan and Witt, the top two starters in 1990, both

Bobby Witt was the Ranger Pitcher of the Year in 1990, setting a club record with 12 straight wins. (Texas Rangers Archives)

Juan Gonzalez (left), a twenty-year-old center fielder in those days, reached the majors to stay in August, 1990, while third baseman Dean Palmer (right) was a September call-up in 1989 and returned as a regular in 1991. (Texas Rangers Archives)

Plans to build a new ballpark were announced by the Rangers and the City of Arlington, October 24, 1990. From left: Rusty Rose, Arlington Mayor Richard Greene, George W. Bush, Tom and Paul Schieffer. (*Fort Worth Star-Telegram*)

went on the disabled list twice, with Witt's record falling to 3–7. Ryan (12–6), on the other hand, was brilliant whenever his ailing shoulder allowed him to pitch. "The Express" was second on the club to 13-game-winner Guzman in victories and fifth in the league in ERA (2.91) in a sensational campaign punctuated by yet another Ryan classic.

It was Arlington Appreciation Night on May 1 when "Big Tex" thrilled the hometown crowd of 33,439 with his record seventh no-hitter, a 3–0 win over Toronto featuring 16 strikeouts and only two walks. Mixing a 96-mph fastball with a knee-buckling curve and deceptive changeup, Ryan was dominant from start to finish. Only one tough defensive play was needed, a running catch by Pettis in short center field on a sixth-inning bloop by Manuel Lee.

Veteran designated hitter Brian Downing filled the lead-off spot for two years, setting the table for the big guns hitting behind him. (Texas Rangers Archives)

"It was my most complete performance," the forty-four-year-old Ryan said—after once again being carried off the field on the shoulders of his teammates—in referring to his combination of great stuff and command of all three pitches. "This no-hitter was the most rewarding because it was in front of these hometown fans who have supported me since I have been here."

Another aging pitching star, reliever Rich "Goose" Gossage, returned from a year in Japan, signed with Texas, and won his first four decisions. The Rangers were in first place at the All-Star break, but their reliance on high run totals to win led to a roller-coaster season marked by long streaks in both directions.

Texas rolled into first place in late May with a club-record 14-game winning streak, during which the Rangers averaged over eight runs per game and scored at least five runs each day.

When the offense cooled off in early June, the Rangers lost eight in a row, falling from first place all the way to fifth. One of those losses, an 18-inning heartbreaker in Kansas City, was the longest game in franchise history. The six-hour, twenty-eight-minute marathon ended abruptly when Kenny Rogers fielded an attempted sacrifice bunt and pegged the ball past third base into the left-field corner as the winning run scored.

A four-game winning streak just before the break lifted Texas back into first place by percentage points over Minnesota. Ryan again provided heroics in the final game before the break, taking a no-hitter into the eighth inning while blanking the Angels, 7–0.

Disaster struck immediately after the break. The Rangers lost their first three games and eight of their first nine, falling to fifth place, 5½ games behind. The club made a trade with Montreal for pitcher Dennis "Oil Can" Boyd. But the flamboyant right-hander was not the answer, going 2–7 as the Rangers tumbled out of contention.

On August 30, the Rangers turned toward the future, trading Steve Buechele to the Pirates for a pair of top pitching prospects, Kurt Miller and Hector Fajardo. With Buechele gone, the hot corner belonged to rookie Dean Palmer, who had been playing out of position in left field since his call-up in June.

Also joining the Rangers in June was a nineteen-year-old catcher from Vega Baja, Puerto Rico—also the

After becoming the first Ranger to hit 20 homers in five straight seasons, Incaviglia was unceremoniously released in spring training in 1991. (Texas Rangers Archives)

Ryan's drawing power was personified by a 20' x 24' poster raised into place above the Arlington Stadium ticket office on April 5, 1991. The poster remained until the stadium's final days in 1993. (*Fort Worth Star-Telegram*)

hometown of Gonzalez. On the day he was recalled from Double-A Tulsa due to an injury to Petralli, Ivan "Pudge" Rodriguez was to have been married on the field between games of a doubleheader.

Rodriguez and his bride, Maribel, got married that morning instead, then flew to Chicago, where Pudge put on a stunning display in his major league debut. The youngest position player in club history, Rodriguez nailed two would-be base stealers and drilled a two-run single in a 7–3 victory.

"I'm going to stay in the major leagues. I'm not going back to Tulsa," Rodriguez had told the media prior to the game. He was, of course, absolutely right.

The wildly inconsistent year left Texas with a final mark of 85–77. Although the Rangers were one of only four major league teams to boast a winning record in each of the past three seasons, their record was good enough for only third place, 10 games behind the Twins.

With the arrival of Gonzalez, Rodriguez, and Palmer, the pride of the minor league system built by Grieve and Sandy Johnson had reached the majors. But as the '91 season dramatically proved, the Rangers would never take that next big step until they drastically reduced their number of runs allowed.

Ryan called his seventh no-hitter, on Arlington Appreciation Night, May 1, 1991, "my most rewarding," as reflected in his expression after striking out Roberto Alomar for the final out. (Linda Kaye)

Rich "Goose" Gossage helped pitch the Rangers into first place at the All-Star break in 1991. (Texas Rangers Archives)

Dennis "Oil Can" Boyd wore this look often in 1991, as he went 2–7 with a 6.68 ERA. (Texas Rangers Archives)

Jose Guzman pulled off a magical comeback in 1991, leading the team in wins after missing almost two full seasons because of a torn rotator cuff. (Texas Rangers Archives)

"I'm not going back to Tulsa," nineteen-year-old Pudge Rodriguez correctly predicted on the day he was called up in 1991. The catcher with the golden arm became an A.L. All-Star the very next season. (Brad Newton)

14

The End of an Era

After three straight winning seasons, wholesale changes did not seem necessary for 1992. Grieve and Valentine agreed that the club could win if it avoided the previous year's rash of injuries. Their only major off-season transaction was the signing of veteran free agent Dickie Thon to start at shortstop.

During the spring, club personnel both on and off the field spoke openly about expecting to win their first division title. Valentine said he felt better about this club than any of his previous teams, and Rogers boldly stated that the Rangers would win the division by five games. Even the normally cautious Ryan was quoted as saying, "I expect us to win the division.... It's our time to win."

Those high expectations were a contributing factor in July when Valentine's days as Ranger manager came to an end.

The season opened in Seattle with a dramatic comeback win in which Texas rallied for a nine-run eighth inning capped by Petralli's game-winning pinch-hit homer. The Rangers went on to sweep the four-game series from the Mariners, then won two out of three in Minnesota to start the year at 6–1.

The first-week success was achieved without the benefit of Franco, the defending batting champion who was on the disabled list with a knee injury. Although the second baseman was activated on April 19, he soon returned to the injured list and played only 35 games all year.

Without Franco, the Ranger lineup was without its most reliable hitter, a loss from which the club never fully recovered. The team slipped below .500 in early May, streaked into first with a seven-game winning streak at the end of the month, then fell to third place in mid-June.

Paced by Kevin Brown, who won 14 games before the All-Star break, and a healthy Guzman and Witt, the

Opening Day at The Ballpark, April 11, 1994. The national anthem was performed by Van Cliburn and the Fort Worth Symphony. (Texas Rangers Archives)

"THIS IS AN IMPORTANT YEAR FOR US. WE HAVE TO GO FROM POTENTIAL TO 'IT'S TIME TO DO IT.' IT'S TIME FOR US TO BE MORE THAN AN ENTERTAINING TEAM."

General Manager Tom Grieve, February 23, 1992

Kevin Brown was the first Ranger pitcher to start an All-Star Game, picking up the victory along with 21 wins during the regular season. (Texas Rangers Archives)

Rangers were getting good starting pitching—despite the fact that an injury-plagued Ryan did not collect his first victory until June 28.

The Rangers withstood the loss of Rodriguez to a back injury for three weeks in June and found themselves in third place, 4½ games out, at the start of an important 14-game home stand on July 1. The club was sporting a 43–37 record despite not hitting the way it had in '92—except for Gonzalez, who set a club record by blasting 11 homers in the month of June. Russell and Rogers were the only reliable relievers, and the team defense led the league in errors.

The long home stand was viewed by the Rangers as an opportunity to gain some ground. But Texas lost three of the first five games, with two of the losses directly attributable to errors. Then on July 8, three unearned runs caused the Rangers to blow a 3–1 eighth-inning lead and lose to the Brewers, 4–3.

At a meeting the following morning, Bush, Schieffer, and Grieve decided to change managers. Valentine was told of the decision at noon and promptly cleaned out his office. As the players arrived that afternoon, they saw in the lower right corner of the clubhouse blackboard a neatly printed message that read: "Good luck, guys. Bobby V."

In contrast to previous Ranger managerial firings, this one caught everyone by surprise. Valentine had been criticized in past seasons for having too strong a clubhouse presence, and he had clashed with several veteran players. But his demeanor had softened considerably in '92.

Bush, the managing general partner, explained management's decision. "We're 6½ games back and not playing very well in a season where we think we ought to be in contention," he said. "We were afraid of this pennant race getting away from us."

The man who managed the club for more than seven years had posted a record of 581–605 and had a winning record (45–41) for the fourth straight year when he departed. "I gave my heart, my soul, and every waking hour to the Texas Rangers organization," said Valentine. "If anybody wanted more than that, I didn't have it to give." For a variety of reasons, however, Bobby V.'s Rangers could never bring home a title.

Grieve, who had often defended Valentine from his detractors, reminded everyone, "When Bobby came here in 1985, we were probably the worst team in the majors. He has been a tireless worker, an excellent teacher, a person who went out of his way to promote our product, and certainly played a major role in the franchise changing its image with the public and the press."

Bench coach Toby Harrah, an original Ranger who had been a three-time All-Star during his playing days, was named interim manager. Harrah earned the job for the rest of the season when the club won four straight before the All-Star break.

The End of an Era

Brown became the first Ranger pitcher to start the midseason classic and picked up the win. Rodriguez was selected as a back-up catcher, and Sierra belted a home run. But there was not much glory for the Rangers from that point on.

Harrah was unable to lead a second-half charge for much the same reasons that the club was floundering under Valentine—an unproductive batting order and sloppy defense. The Rangers lost 14 of their first 21 games after the break to fall under .500 and out of the race.

On August 13, with the Rangers 12½ games out, Bush told Gerry Fraley of the *Dallas Morning News* that the club's second-half collapse could lead to "a shakeup...that means new players, new attitude, a different look."

Bush's remarks foreshadowed a stunning four-player trade announced on August 31 while the Rangers were playing the Royals in Kansas City. Texas was sending soon-to-be free agents Sierra and Russell, along with Witt, to Oakland in exchange for former A.L. MVP Jose Canseco.

The Rangers' most significant trade since the 1988 winter meetings sent shock waves throughout baseball, especially in the Texas and Oakland clubhouses.

Expressing the prevailing feeling among the Rangers, Jeff Huson said, "We're all in disbelief. That's as big a trade as you're ever going to see."

Whereas Canseco had worn out his welcome in Oakland, his arrival provided the Rangers with a charismatic superstar. A's manager Tony LaRussa had once said that managing Canseco "is like managing Elvis."

Grieve, who had tried before the season to sign Sierra to a long-term deal, stated his team's position. "This puts a better nucleus in place to build on," he said. "We hope this is the first of several moves to help the team next year. We don't have the team we want to go to war with."

Out in Oakland, Canseco's slugging teammate Mark McGwire wondered aloud about what the Cuban-born outfielder might achieve after escaping pitcher-friendly Oakland Coliseum. "It's going to be mind-boggling what he's going to do in that yard," said McGwire, referring to Arlington Stadium. "I'd have to say Mr. Maris's 61 is going to be gone in a year or two."

Canseco's presence could not prevent the Rangers from suffering through a losing September in which the club took a look at several candidates for future employment. Jeff Frye, who had been called up on the day Valentine was fired, played every day at second base. Speedy center fielder David Hulse batted .304, and pitchers Roger Pavlik and Matt Whiteside appeared promising.

Juan Gonzalez won the first of his back-to-back home run titles in 1992, circling the bases 43 times. (Texas Rangers Archives)

After the firing of Valentine, Toby Harrah became the Ranger manager. In his first game at the helm, Harrah exchanged lineup cards with Cleveland skipper Mike Hargrove, an old friend and former Texas teammate. (Texas Rangers Archives)

Brown continued to win games, joining Fergie Jenkins as Texas's second 20-game winner ever. On the final day of the season in Anaheim, the sinkerballer beat the Angels to finish at 21–11, helped by Gonzalez's 43rd home run of the year. That roundtripper snapped a tie with McGwire and made the twenty-two-year-old Gonzalez the major league home run champion—the first Ranger to lead the league in homers.

Overall, however, it had been a very disappointing year, as indicated by a 77–85 record and a fourth-place finish, 19 games behind Oakland.

"We didn't hit, and our weaknesses were exposed," Grieve admitted. "Maybe that's good. Now we can look at our weaknesses and do something to address them."

GUYS WHO KNOW HOW TO WIN

Beginning what would be a flurry of off-season personnel moves, Grieve was faced with the task of deciding on a new manager. He strongly considered giving the job to Harrah, listing the incumbent skipper as one of his four final candidates—along with former Seattle and Milwaukee manager Rene Lachemann, minor league manager Jerry Royster, and Montreal bench coach Kevin Kennedy.

Grieve chose the thirty-eight-year-old Kennedy, whose teams had never finished lower than second place during his eight seasons managing in the Dodger farm system. The tall, rugged, mustachioed Kennedy exuded an aura of aggressive confidence.

"I'm all about winning and expecting to win," declared Kennedy upon meeting the Texas media. "I want our players expecting to win. It's not by a hope or a prayer. It's by design... I sound confident, and I am. That's going to rub off on my players."

The 1993 season would be the final one at Arlington Stadium and the finale for Ryan, who announced prior to spring training that his record-breaking 27th major league season, his fifth as a Ranger, would be his last.

The End of an Era

Ryan would be accompanied by four newly acquired accomplished veterans—left-handed starters Charlie Leibrandt and Craig Lefferts and relievers Bob Patterson and Tom Henke, who would be returning to Texas as the bullpen stopper after an eight-year stint with Toronto.

Manuel Lee, a teammate of Henke on the world champion Blue Jays, was signed to replace Thon at shortstop. To provide more bench depth, second baseman Billy Ripken and outfielders Gary Redus and Doug Dascenzo were brought in.

Almost all of the newcomers had played for championship teams. "We wanted guys who know how to win," Kennedy explained. "These guys know what it's like to play in October."

The Rangers' chances of playing in October were jolted even before April rolled around. Frye, slated to start at second base, blew out his knee in February while jogging, and Lee pulled a rib cage muscle in spring training. The injuries left twenty-year-old rookie shortstop Benji Gil teaming with second baseman Ripken on Opening Day in what would be the first of Kennedy's fourteen double play combinations.

Still having knee problems, Franco was restricted to the designated hitter role. Canseco would be the full-time right fielder, with Hulse in center and Gonzalez moving to left.

A rib injury to Brown caused the 20-game-winner to miss the first week of the season. Lefferts replaced him as the Opening Day starter and picked up a 7–4 win in Baltimore as Gonzalez and Palmer each homered twice. Newly acquired utility man Doug Strange won the second game with an 11th-inning pinch-hit home run, and the Rangers were on their way to a 6–1 start.

The club's enthusiasm was tempered in the eighth game when Ryan tore cartilage in his right knee, the first of several injuries that would mar his farewell campaign. Fortunately, a solid start by Rogers, who had won a rotation spot in spring training, helped offset the loss of Ryan.

The Rangers were 23–19, 1½ games behind division-leading Chicago, on May 24 when they embarked on a 2–7 road trip that would prove to be one of the most notorious in club history. The calamitous journey began in Cleveland, where the Rangers managed just one hit against rookie Tom Kramer, who posted his first big league win.

Two nights later, Rogers lost to the Indians, 7–6, in part because a Carlos Martinez fly ball to deep right field bounced off Canseco's head and over the wall for a home run.

"I'll be on ESPN for a month,"

Second baseman Jeff Frye, called up on the day Valentine was fired, became the Rangers' everyday leadoff hitter, then missed the entire '93 season after injuring his knee in the offseason. (Texas Rangers Archives)

Major league home run champ Juan Gonzalez (left) teams with Rafael Palmeiro to drive in the first steel structure at The Ballpark in Arlington, October 30, 1992. Palmeiro would never play at The Ballpark in a Ranger uniform. (Texas Rangers Archives)

Ruben Sierra, who became the first Ranger to homer in the All-Star Game in '92, was traded to Oakland the next month, leaving Texas as the all-time club leader in home runs and RBI. (Texas Rangers Archives)

joked Canseco. Little did Jose know that by the end of the week, he would provide the network even more buffoonish highlight film material.

Three days later, on May 29th in Boston, Kennedy allowed Canseco to pitch the eighth inning of a 15–3 loss. Canseco, who had pitched in high school, had lobbied since spring training for a chance to take the mound and had been effective in a one-inning stint during an April exhibition game. With his pitching staff struggling, Kennedy had threatened to let his slugger take the mound the next time the Rangers were blown out of a game. Kennedy made good on his threat and has regretted it ever since.

Canseco's inning on the Fenway Park hill was a complete disaster. After throwing far too many warmup pitches in the bullpen, he had little left for the Boston hitters. Hopelessly wild, the slugger allowed three runs on two hits and three walks. Only 12 of his 33 pitches were strikes.

More damaging than the runs Canseco allowed was the torn elbow ligament he suffered, an injury that eventually required season-ending surgery. To their credit, both Canseco and Kennedy were willing to accept the blame for the fiasco.

"We had him prepared," noted Kennedy. "He had thrown on the side many times…I did it to save the bullpen. I'll take any heat you want to throw my way." Kennedy would later add, "There was some goodwill involved, a lot of things behind it that nobody realized."

Kennedy was much less calm after another defeat three days later in Minnesota. Not since Billy Martin had a Ranger manager been as visibly upset after losses as was Kennedy, who often would still be openly fuming more than an hour after a defeat. But none of Kennedy's postgame tirades compared with a fifteen-minute tantrum at the Metrodome on June

The End of an Era

1, during which the former minor league catcher hurled a baked potato into his clubhouse mirror, shattering it to smithereens.

The club continued to fall in the standings, landing in fifth place, 6½ games out, when Kennedy called an off-day workout on June 24 following another dreadful road trip. Although Kennedy called frequent team meetings, the off-day session in ninety-one-degree heat was unique.

The Rangers had just lost six straight games and appeared on the verge of descending into the sort of free fall that had brought a premature end to many of their championship hopes in years gone by. But this time, spurred on perhaps by their manager's refusal to accept losing, the Rangers recovered admirably and won 13 of their next 16 games. That surge left Texas just one game behind the White Sox at the All-Star break.

Gonzalez and Rodriguez each left their mark at the midseason classic in Baltimore. Juan's power awed the crowd at Camden Yards on workout day as he won the home run contest, while Rodriguez helped the American League to victory with a line-drive double that became embedded in the left field wall.

After the break, the Rangers stayed in contention, and management beefed up the bullpen by acquiring Cris Carpenter from Florida. But the Rangers had to part with two young pitchers, including Robb Nen, the fireballer who was out of minor league options and still plagued by frequent bouts of wildness. Carpenter would become the primary setup man for Henke, a job that had been handled capably by Whiteside until he tired from overuse.

In a wild five-game series in Kansas City in late July, the Rangers and their

Kevin Kennedy, disagreeing here with John Hirschbeck, was ejected only once in his two years as Ranger manager, but often vented his anger in the clubhouse after losses. (Fort Worth Star-Telegram)

Carlos Martinez's drive bounces off Jose Canseco's head and over the wall for a home run in Cleveland, May 26, 1993. (Ron Kuntz, Reuters)

Jose Canseco meets President Bill Clinton on Opening Day in Baltimore, April 5, 1993, as manager Kevin Kennedy (left) looks on. (Official White House Photograph)

Jose Canseco on the mound at Fenway Park, May 29, 1993, left his best stuff in the bullpen and blew out his elbow. (Barry Chin, *The Boston Globe*)

Tom Henke, lost to Toronto in the free agent compensation draft in '85, returned to Texas in '93 and set a club record with 40 saves. (Texas Rangers Archives)

At age forty-six, Ryan was more than capable of handling an unscheduled visit to the mound by twenty-seven-year-old Robin Ventura, pummeling Ventura with a series of short rights to the head on August 4, 1993. "Self-preservation is all that goes through your mind when something like that happens," said Ryan. (Linda Kaye)

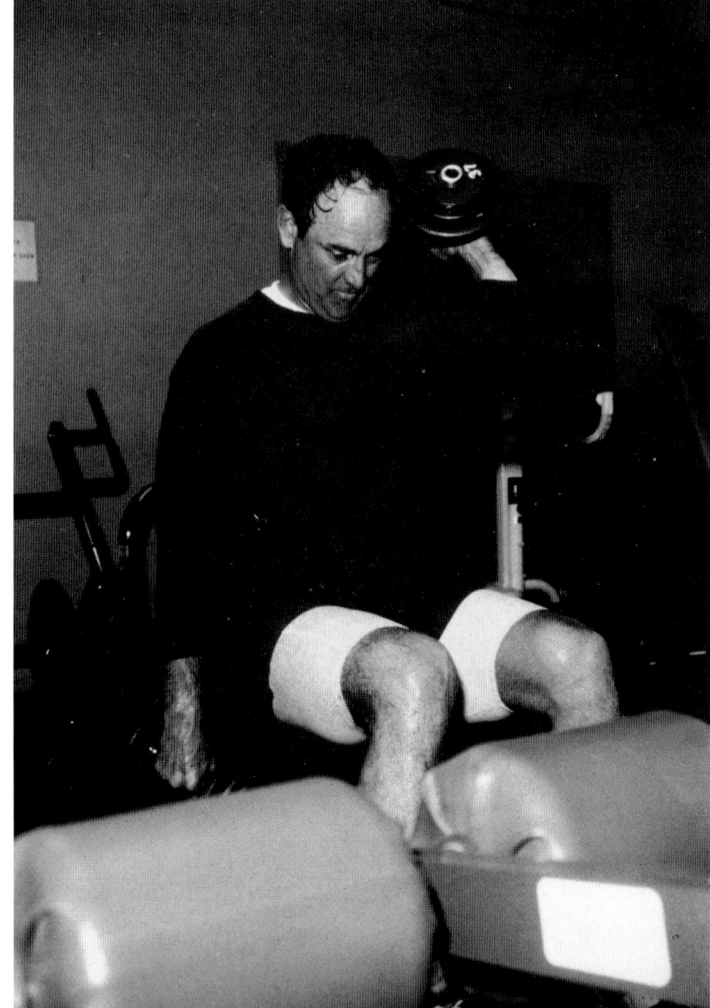

The only man to play in 27 major-league seasons, Ryan adhered to a strict workout regimen which included weight work and countless miles on the exercise bike. (Texas Rangers Archives)

Never has a player been more attentive to his fans than Ryan, shown here on Nolan Ryan Day, September 12, 1993, before taking a farewell ride with his wife, Ruth. (Texas Rangers Archives/*Fort Worth Star-Telegram*)

Ryan leaves the mound for the final time after injuring his elbow in Seattle, September 22, 1993. Ryan pitched five years for the Rangers, earning 51 of his 324 career victories. (Corky Trewin)

The End of an Era

Rafael Palmeiro, pictured on Turn Back the Clock Day in 1993, set a club record for runs (124) and was one of three Rangers with 30 homers as the Rangers led the majors in home runs. (Texas Rangers Archives)

manager again demonstrated a new feistiness. After losing a doubleheader to start the series, the Rangers beat Royals' ace Kevin Appier the next day when Palmeiro's seventh-inning home run was the only Texas hit in a 1–0 combined shutout by Rogers and Henke.

The Rangers then bombed the Royals, 10–3. Palmeiro clubbed two more homers, then was hit in the knee by a ninth-inning pitch from Rick Reed. An irate Kennedy gestured angrily toward the mound and told the press after the game, "We'll take care of it. We'll take care of ourselves."

In the series finale the next day, a 9–4 Kansas City win, Patterson plunked Brian McRae, the son of Royals' manager Hal McRae, in the back with an eighth-inning pitch. Instead of directing his attention toward Patterson, McRae turned and charged the Ranger dugout, with Kennedy as his target. McRae was intercepted and restrained near the top step by Texas hitting coach Willie Upshaw and a few Ranger players. McRae never succeeded in reaching the Texas skipper.

On the ensuing Texas home stand, another hit-by-pitch had alarming consequences.

The White Sox came to town, leading the Rangers by 5½ games at the start of a four-game series. The teams split the first two games before Ryan took the mound on August 4.

In the third inning, with the Sox leading 2–0, a Ryan fastball drilled Chicago cleanup hitter Robin Ventura in the right arm. After a moment's hesitation, the twenty-seven-year-old Ventura charged the mound, then seemed to hesitate just as he arrived. The forty-six-year-old Ryan quickly hog-tied the intruder with a left-arm headlock and proceeded to land a half-dozen short right-handed punches to Ventura's head before a swarm of players from both sides buried the combatants.

Ventura was the only player ejected from the game. Ryan remained on the mound and emerged as the winning pitcher when the Rangers scored five runs in the sixth to win, 5–2.

Texas won again the next night, reducing the deficit to 4½ games as the Sox left town. But Chicago rebounded, extending its lead to seven games over the second-place Rangers in early September.

Again the Rangers refused to fold, winning seven out of eight. When Gonzalez blasted his 44th home run to help beat the Indians on September 13, the Rangers trailed by just 2½ games, their smallest deficit ever that late in a season.

Unfortunately, that long ball was one of the home run champion's final contributions. Plagued by a recurring back injury, Gonzalez missed most of the remaining games.

One last road trip would take the Rangers to California, Seattle, and Chicago. To help replace the bat of Gonzalez, the Rangers acquired veteran outfielder Chris James from Houston, a move that paid immediate dividends when James belted two homers in a winning debut in Anaheim. But the Rangers lost four out of six against the Angels and Mariners.

The series finale in Seattle on September 22 provided a painful farewell to Ryan's incomparable career. The Texas legend tore a right elbow ligament while pitching in the first inning and had to leave the game without retiring a batter.

Having allowed a grand slam to Dan Howitt, Ryan took the loss, dropping his record to 5–5 in a year in which injuries allowed him to start just 13 games. "The whole year has been a frustration and disappointment, and it's disappointing to end up this way… everything that has happened is a body telling me it's time to get out of the game," admitted the future Hall of Famer.

The Rangers limped into Chicago trailing the Sox by six games with 10 to play, needing a sweep of the three-game weekend series to stay in contention. James came up big in the series opener, tying the game with a two-out, two-strike, two-run homer in the ninth off Chicago stopper Roberto Hernandez. But James's hit was wasted when Warren Newson's pinch-hit single won the game for the Sox in the bottom of the ninth.

The Saturday game was rained out, made up as part of a Sunday doubleheader in which Chicago took the opener, 5–3. Champagne was chilling in the White Sox clubhouse, because a win in the nightcap would clinch the division title. The Rangers, however, avoided having to witness the Sox' celebration. Franco's eighth-inning double won the second game, 3–2 and postponed Chicago's clinching until after the Rangers headed home for their final week ever at Arlington Stadium.

On Sunday, October 3, the curtain came down on the former Turnpike Stadium when a sellout crowd saw the Royals beat the Rangers, 4–1, in George Brett's final game. The Royals' star singled off Henke in the last at-bat of his career. Appier got the win, and Texas rookie Steve Dreyer took the loss.

A frequent sight in '93, Juan Gonzalez acknowledges the cheering crowd after belting one of his league-high 46 home runs. (Texas Rangers Archives)

The Rangers finished as runners-up to Chicago with an 86–76 record, their most wins since 1986, despite a string of injuries unprecedented in club history.

Led by Gonzalez, whose 46 homers gave him a club record and a second straight A.L. home run title, the Rangers led the majors in homers (181) for the first time ever and set a club record for runs scored. Palmeiro (37) and Palmer (33) helped fill the home run void left by the injury to Canseco, who hit just 10 HRs in 60 games.

An improved pitching staff ranked sixth in the league in ERA, led by starters Rogers (16–10), Brown (15–12), and Pavlik (12–6) and the thirty-five-year-old Henke, who finished third in the league with a club-record and career-high 40 saves.

Although far from airtight, the Ranger defense took a step forward, improving from 14th to 11th in the league in fielding percentage—despite having to use eight second basemen and eight shortstops.

Arlington Stadium provided a huge home field advantage. The Rangers were 50–31 in their final season there but stumbled to a 36–45 record away from home. That dismal road record cost the Rangers their first title but failed to temper their optimism as they prepared to move into their new home, The Ballpark in Arlington, in 1994.

Groundbreaking for The Ballpark In Arlington, October 30, 1991. From left: Bill Snider, Rusty Rose, Arlington Mayor Richard Greene, George W. Bush, Tom Schieffer, Texas House Speaker Gib Lewis. (Linda Kaye)

August, 1992 (Texas Rangers Archives)

October, 1992 (Texas Rangers Archives)

January, 1993 (Texas Rangers Archives)

November, 1993 (Texas Rangers Archives)

Ivan Rodriguez (batting), Dean Palmer (#16), and Juan Gonzalez (#19) swung for the fences in the summer of '93, as Ballpark workers scrambled for souvenirs. (Texas Rangers Archives)

Ranger brass announces the signing of first baseman Will Clark to a five-year contract on November 22, 1993. From left: Tom Grieve, Rusty Rose, Tom Schieffer, Clark, George W. Bush. "I didn't come here to lose," said Clark, who would provide the Rangers with a take-charge leader in the clubhouse. (Texas Rangers Archives)

TEXAS RANGERS

Club President Tom Schieffer, who oversaw the planning and construction of The Ballpark, speaks at the ribbon-cutting ceremony on Opening Day, April 11, 1994. "Ballparks are the places where sons remember their fathers and where mothers fulfill their children's dreams," said Schieffer. Seated behind the podium, from left: Dr. Luther Felder, Bill Snider, Arlington Mayor Richard Greene, Rusty Rose, George W. Bush. (Texas Rangers Archives)

NO EXCUSES IN '94

All signs seemed to point toward a first-ever division title for the Rangers in '94, and the men in charge were not bashful about expressing their confidence.

"We have no excuses for not winning this year," said Grieve in late February. "We feel like we have a good enough team." Later in the spring, he went even further, telling T.R. Sullivan of the *Fort Worth Star-Telegram,* "We should win it, it's important for us to win it, and we will win it."

Kennedy echoed those sentiments, certain that his team would allow even fewer runs than it had the previous year. "I think our pitching is much better than last year," was the manager's assessment. "We have a lot more pitching depth."

Kennedy's faith in his mound staff arose from a series of free agent signings in which the Rangers had added veterans Bruce Hurst and Jack Armstrong to the rotation and Jay Howell and former Ranger Rick Honeycutt to the bullpen.

Off the mound, the big change was at first base, where former San Francisco star Will Clark had signed a five-year contract to replace the departed Palmeiro. Franco also left via free agency, leaving room for Canseco to return with a reconstructed elbow as the everyday designated hitter.

For the first time ever, major league baseball had expanded to a three-division format, a realignment that seemed to favor Texas. The Rangers would now play in a four-team West Division that

The honor of being the first to enter The Ballpark went to longtime Ranger fans, Sister Maggie Hession (left) and Sister Frances Evans (right). (Linda Kaye)

The End of an Era

did not include defending West champ Chicago.

Sporting new uniforms that featured red as the primary color, the Rangers would also have the advantage of playing before huge crowds in their brand new ballpark, which was unveiled during a pair of exhibition games on the first two days of April.

The Rangers played their first five regular season games on the road, losing three out of five before returning for the official opening of The Ballpark in Arlington on Monday afternoon, April 11.

A capacity crowd of 46,056 waited out a short rain delay before the game began, then saw the Milwaukee Brewers beat the Rangers, 4–3, on a day in which most of the talk was about the ballpark rather than the ball game.

"May you enjoy this ballpark half as much as we enjoyed building it," said Rangers President Tom Schieffer in the opening ceremonies, adding that the ballpark "is destined to become a museum of memories."

Jose Canseco was the A.L. Comeback Player of the Year in '94, blasting 31 HRs and 90 RBI in the strike-shortened season. (Texas Rangers Archives)

Arlington Mayor Richard Greene, who had spearheaded the drive to build the ballpark, stated, "In the history of our city, there has never been a time when more people have more reason to celebrate the life of their community than today."

The new park received rave reviews from players, fans, media, and architectural critics and proved to be more friendly to the home team in game 2 than it had been in the opener. The Rangers pulled out a 10th-inning victory on a single by reserve shortstop Esteban Beltre, dramatically capturing their first home win.

But the wins did not come easily. Arm injuries to newcomers Hurst and Armstrong and to returning starter Roger Pavlik tore apart the Texas rotation early in the season. Bullpen stopper Henke was derailed by back problems, further contributing to the team's 19–25 start. The rest of the West, however, was scuffling, too, allowing the Rangers to slip into first on May 30 despite a 22–26 mark.

Amazingly, Texas never relinquished the top spot despite never climbing more than one game above .500. On June 13, Canseco smacked three home runs, including an Arlington-record, 480-foot bomb to the back of the visitors bullpen, as the Rangers beat Seattle to open a six-game lead with a 31–30 mark. But it was downhill from that point on.

The All-Star break arrived with the Rangers holding a three-game lead and a 42–45 record. Two weeks later, the California Angels came to The Ballpark on July 28, a day marked by concern over a prolonged stalemate between club owners and the players' union over a proposed salary cap.

When Kenny Rogers went to the mound at 7:35 that evening, the big news of the day was the announcement of August 12 as the players' proposed strike date. The twenty-nine-year-old southpaw then stole the headlines by pitching the first perfect game ever thrown by an American League lefty.

Kenny Rogers salutes the crowd at The Ballpark after his perfect game as the scoreboard tells the story, July 28, 1994. "I don't consider myself a great pitcher, but tonight I was," said Rogers. (Texas Rangers Archives)

The End of an Era

Backed by two Canseco homers and one by Rodriguez in a 4–0 win, Rogers struck out eight and went to a three-ball count on only six of the 27 California hitters. The only near-hit came in the tension-packed ninth inning, when Rex Hudler led off with a soft sinking liner to right-center field. Rookie outfielder Rusty Greer, making a rare start in center, raced in and to his left, then dove to snare the ball, saving Rogers's place in history.

"When Rusty did that, I thought, 'Somebody wants me to do this,'" said Rogers after the game. "I never thought he could catch that ball."

Unfortunately, Rogers's heroics failed to ignite a Texas surge. As the strike approached, the Rangers lost nine of their last 11 games, including the final six. Their record stood at 52–62 when play was halted on August 12, although incredibly, the standings showed the Rangers in first place by one game over Oakland.

While waiting for a resolution of the labor dispute and a resumption of play, the Ranger offense had much to be proud of. Canseco was on his way to the A.L. Comeback Player of the Year Award, with 31 homers and 90 RBI. Clark was seventh in the league in hitting at .329, while youngsters Greer and Frye were also hitting above .300. Rodriguez was having another Gold Glove season and started the All-Star Game.

The pitching, however, had sunk below the levels of all previous Texas teams. The staff's 5.45 ERA ranked 13th in the league and was almost a run higher than the previous team high established by the 1973 Rangers, who lost a club-record 105 games. Rogers (11–8) was the only staff member to win more than seven games, and rookie lefty Darren Oliver (4–0, 3.42 ERA) provided the only bright light in the bullpen.

Defensively, the team took a giant step backward, falling all the way to last in the league in fielding percentage and allowing the most unearned runs.

Although their team's performance was undeniably lackluster, Ranger fans filled their new ballpark in record numbers. Total attendance of 2,503,198 in just sixty-two dates broke the club record, an average of forty thousand per game. The strike came with the Rangers seemingly on their way to drawing over three million fans.

On September 14, acting Baseball Commissioner Bud Selig officially canceled the remainder of the regular season, the playoffs, and the World Series.

Although Selig's action was considered inevitable, an announcement by the Rangers that same day was generally unforeseen.

15

Changing Philosophy

In retrospect, it is not surprising that on the day that the 1994 season officially came to an end, so, too, did the decade-long tenure of Tom Grieve as general manager of the Rangers.

Schieffer was brief and blunt in explaining the decision to reassign Grieve to a new post as assistant to the president. "We haven't won, and it's not much more complicated than that," said Schieffer. "At some point in time, we have to say, 'Let's let somebody else take a look at it and see if they can put it together in a different way.'"

Upright and honorable as always, Grieve did not disagree with the change, saying, "I think ownership showed a lot of patience. I think we accomplished a lot of things, but the bottom line is we didn't win. We had a disappointing year."

In less than a month, Schieffer found the man he wanted to rebuild the team. On October 10, Baltimore Assistant General Manager Doug Melvin was introduced as the Rangers' new G.M. A forty-two-year-old native of Chatham, Ontario, Melvin was a former minor league pitcher who vowed to win with pitching and defense.

Desiring a manager who possessed similar priorities, Melvin dismissed Kennedy and hired the only candidate he interviewed. The manager with whom Melvin was most familiar, the man who had recently been fired by the Orioles after three straight winning seasons, forty-eight-year-old Johnny Oates would be the Rangers' 14th full-time manager.

"What this ball club needs is a manager who has experience and who has a winning percentage in the big leagues. This man, Johnny Oates, brings both qualities to the ball club," said the new general manager.

Known as a "players' manager," Oates would be called upon to handle what many considered to be a clubhouse full of difficult personalities, some of whom had clashed with that of Kennedy. A former big league catcher who was born in a small

The all-Texas battery of Kenny Rogers and Pudge Rodriguez teamed up on this strikeout of Reggie Sanders in the All-Star Game. (Fort Worth Star-Telegram)

"WE WANT PLAYERS WHO AREN'T ONE-DIMENSIONAL... WHO CAN DO A NUMBER OF THINGS FOR THE CLUB THAT CANNOT BE MEASURED BY HOMERS AND RBI."

General Manager Doug Melvin, announcing the trade of Jose Canseco on December 10, 1994

Johnny Oates, who was hired with the reputation as a "players' manager," hit .250 while playing 593 games in 10 major league seasons. (Texas Rangers Archives)

town in the mountains of North Carolina, Oates personified the low-key approach best suited for unifying the Rangers in a team effort.

Citing the caring way with which he was treated by manager Dick Howser when Oates was a bench player with the Yankees, the new skipper explained, "I believe in family. I handle ballplayers like I do my own children. They want to be communicated with."

Players whom Oates had managed in Baltimore and in the minors were quick to sing his praises. Some of them would soon have the opportunity to play for Oates again.

Kennedy, in the meantime, had been hired to manage the Red Sox. And he would soon be joined by his favorite outfielder/pitcher. Flying in the face of public opinion, Melvin's first trade shipped the enormously popular Canseco to Boston for swift center fielder Otis Nixon and third baseman Luis Ortiz.

"It's really a change of philosophy," Melvin explained. "We want to go from a club that puts up offensive numbers to a club that has speed and defense and does other things to win. We need to have those kind of players."

Although Melvin was criticized for not receiving pitching help in the deal, the money saved in unloading Canseco's huge salary was used to help sign free agent right-hander Kevin Gross. Melvin then took further steps to aid the defense by signing versatile Mark McLemore—an Oates favorite in Baltimore—and reserve catcher David Valle.

The rest of Melvin's restructuring was put on hold while baseball continued its long-failed attempts to settle the labor stalemate. After an unforgettable spring training in which replacement players competed in a full exhibition schedule, the players' strike finally came to an end on April 2.

Third baseman Dean Palmer went down for the season on June 8 with a biceps injury. (*Fort Worth Star-Telegram*)

Changing Philosophy

A shortened spring training was highlighted by a flurry of player transactions. In one astounding week, Melvin signed starting pitcher Bob Tewksbury, relievers Roger McDowell and former Ranger Jeff Russell, and designated hitter Mickey Tettleton—whose ability to play first base and the outfield supplied the versatility valued by Oates and Melvin.

The club suffered a major blow in spring training when Gonzalez was diagnosed as having a herniated disk in his lower back. When the shortened 144-game season began on April 26, the Rangers were without their cleanup hitter—and their manager, who had been granted a leave of absence to be with his wife Gloria, who was hospitalized.

Oates returned May 1 after the club went 2–3 under interim manager Jerry Narron. But Gonzalez would not rejoin the lineup until June and was restricted almost entirely to DH duties.

By the time the Rangers welcomed back Gonzalez, they were embroiled in a three-team division race with the Mariners and the front-running Angels. But after June 3, Texas would have to play the rest of the year without Palmer. The slugging third baseman was off to his best start ever when he ruptured a biceps tendon while swinging and missing at a Kevin Tapani pitch.

In Palmer's absence, veterans Mike Pagliarulo and Craig Worthington provided solid glove work alongside rookie shortstop Benji Gil, forming a reliable left-side defense. But Palmer's bat was sorely missed.

In early June, the Rangers moved into first place on the strength of a six-game winning streak, highlighted by the franchise's most remarkable comeback ever on June 8 at The Ballpark. Trailing the Royals, 8–1, in the eighth inning, Texas rallied to tie the game at 9–9 on a two-run homer by Gil in the ninth. Then a 10th-inning homer by Greer was the game-winner in the contest now referred to as "the Hallelujah Game."

The Rangers and Angels swapped places in the top spot for most of June, winding up tied for first place as the baseball world turned its attention to Arlington on July 11 for the first All-Star Game hosted by the Rangers.

The National League edged the American, 3–2, before 50,920, the largest crowd ever at The Ballpark. Rodriguez was the A.L.'s starting catcher for the third straight year, becoming the first Ranger to make four consecutive All-Star appearances. Rogers, who had set a club record by hurling 39 consecutive shutout innings in May, pitched the seventh inning and allowed a game-tying homer to Mike Piazza.

After the break, the Rangers won three of their first four in Boston, a series in which Gonzalez stroked his 154th career home run to surpass Sierra's club record. Returning home on July 17 to face the Orioles, the Rangers dropped a 13-inning heartbreaker, 3–2.

With their offense suddenly dormant, the Rangers did not win again until July 27, suffering through a demoralizing 10-game losing streak that sank them eight games behind the Angels.

Otis Nixon had played for Oates as a minor leaguer in the Yankee system. Acquired from Boston in a trade for Canseco, Nixon stole 50 bases in his one season with Texas. (Texas Rangers Archives)

All eyes were on The Ballpark on July 11, 1995, for the 66th All-Star Game, the first ever played in Arlington, which drew the largest crowd ever at The Ballpark—50,920. (Glenn Patterson, Sky Cam)

Changing Philosophy

As it turned out, California's sizable lead was not insurmountable. But it was the Mariners, not the Rangers, who mounted a miraculous September charge to take the division title in a one-game playoff.

The Rangers closed to within four games of the Angels on September 17 but then were swept in a three-game series in Seattle, ending their chances in the first-ever wild-card race as well as all hopes for a division title.

When the Mariners won, 6–2, in the opener of a four-game series at The Ballpark on the final Thursday of the season, Texas was mathematically eliminated from playoff contention. Relegated to the spoiler role, the Rangers beat the M's in the last two games to force the Seattle-California playoff game.

Finishing at 74–70, 4½ games out, the Rangers had come a long way from their 52–62 mark in 1994. The new emphasis on pitching and defense achieved the desired results, with the team ERA improving from 13th to 8th while the fielding percentage climbed all the way from 14th to 4th.

Despite Jeff Russell spending two stints on the disabled list with back trouble, the bullpen was better, thanks in part to the acquisitions of lefties Dennis Cook and Ed Vosberg. Rogers (17–7) and Pavlik (10–10) led the rotation, but a disappointing first half by Gross (9–15) and a back injury to Tewksbury (8–7) limited their contributions.

Oliver appeared to have blossomed as a starter until a shoulder injury ended his season in August. But the reacquisition of Bobby Witt in a trade with Florida helped fill the void.

In a departure from recent seasons, the Rangers were hurt most by an unproductive offense. Nixon (.295, 50 SBs) and Tettleton (32 HRs) had fine years, but the holes created by the injuries to Palmer and Gonzalez (27 HRs in 90 games) were too much for the club to overcome.

Expecting to have the two injured sluggers ready to go in '96, Melvin concentrated his off-season efforts on adding a bullpen stopper and either re-signing or replacing free agents Rogers, Nixon, Witt, McDowell, and Tettleton.

Clearly, Oates was happy with the makeup of his team. "I think the guys hung in pretty good," he said. "They created a lot of chances to win when they didn't have a right to win."

The tenacity that Oates was referring to would be a major factor the next year when Ranger fans finally celebrated a championship.

Will Clark hit .302 and led the team with 92 RBI, but the Rangers could not overcome injuries to Palmer and Gonzalez. (Texas Rangers Archives)

T I M E

Owner: Bob Short, President (1972–74)

Manager: Ted Williams (1972) (Linda Kaye)

General Manager: Dan O'Brien (1973–78)

General Manager: Joe Burke (1972–73) (Kansas City Royals)

Interim Manager: Del Wilber (9/8/73)

Manager: Whitey Herzog (11/2/72–9/7/73)

Manager: Billy Martin (9/8/73–7/21/75)

Owner: Brad Corbett, Chairman of the Board (1974–80)

Manager: Frank Lucchesi (7/21/75–6/22/77)

1972   1973   1974   1975   1976

(All photos are from Texas Rangers Archives except as otherwise noted.)

L I N E

Interim Manager: Eddie Stanky (6/22/77)
(*St. Paul Pioneer Press*)

Interim Manager: Connie Ryan (6/23/77–6/27/77)

General Manager: Eddie Robinson (1978–82)

Owner: Eddie Chiles, Chairman of the Board (1980–89)

Manager: Billy Hunter (6/28/77–9/30/78)

Manager: Pat Corrales (10/1/78–10/5/80)

Manager: Don Zimmer (11/12/80–7/28/82)

1977　　1978　　1979　　1980　　1981 →

T I M E

General Manager: Joe Klein (1982–84)
(Detroit Tigers)

Manager: Darrell Johnson
(7/28/82–10/3/82)

Owner: George W. Bush, General Partner (1989–94)

Manager: Doug Rader
(11/1/82–5/16/85)

General Manager: Tom Grieve (1984–94)

Manager: Bobby Valentine
(5/16/85–7/9/92)

Owner: Edward W. Rose, General Partner (1989–)

1982　1983　1984　1985　1986　1987　1988　1989　1990

L I N E

Manager: Toby Harrah
(7/9/92–10/4/92)

General Manager: Doug Melvin (1994–)

Owner: Tom Schieffer, President (1991–) General Partner (1994–)

Manager: Kevin Kennedy (10/26/92–10/12/94)

Manager: Johnny Oates (10/19/94–)

Interim Manager: Jerry Narron (4/21/95–4/30/95)

1991　1992　1993　1994　1995　1996　1997

Despite a great effort, the ball eluded Oddibe McDowell on this play. (*Fort Worth Star-Telegram*)

Alex Johnson (Linda Kaye)

Bump Wills is hit by a pitch.
(Linda Kaye)

ALL-TIME ROSTER

MANAGERS
CORRALES, Pat ('78–'80)
HARRAH, Toby ('92)
HERZOG, Whitey ('73)
HUNTER, Billy ('77–'78)
JOHNSON, Darrell ('82)
KENNEDY, Kevin ('93–'94)
LUCCHESI, Frank ('75–'77)
MARTIN, Billy ('73–'75)
NARRON, Jerry ('95)
OATES, Johnny ('95–'96)
RADER, Doug ('83–'85)
RYAN, Connie ('77)
STANKY, Eddie ('77)
VALENTINE, Bobby ('85–'92)
WILBER, Del ('73)
WILLIAMS, Ted ('72)
ZIMMER, Don ('81–'82)

COACHES
BOSMAN, Dick ('95–'96)
BROWN, Jackie ('79–'82)
BURRIS, Ray ('92)
CAMACHO, Joe ('72)
COMBS, Merrill ('74–'75)
CORRALES, Pat ('76–'78)
DENT, Bucky ('95–'96)
DONNELLY, Rich ('80, '83–'85)
EGAN, Dick ('88–'89)
ESTRADA, Chuck ('73)
EZELL, Glenn ('83–'85)
FERGUSON, Joe ('86–'87)
FOLI, Tim ('86–'87)
FOWLER, Art ('74–'75)
FOX, Nellie ('72)
GERNERT, Dick ('76)
GOMEZ, Orlando ('91–'92)
HARDY, Larry ('95–'96)
HARRAH, Toby ('89–'92)
HATCHER, Mickey ('93–'94)
HELMS, Tommy ('81–'82)
HILL, Perry ('92–'94, '95)
HILLER, Chuck ('73)
HOUSE, Tom ('85–'92)
HOWE, Art ('85–'88)
HUDSON, Sid ('72, '75–'78)
JARAMILLO, Rudy ('95–'96)
JOHNSON, Darrell ('81–'82)
KOENIG, Fred ('77–'82)
LOPES, Davey ('88–'91)
LUCCHESI, Frank ('74–'75, '79–'80)
MOORE, Jackie ('73–'76, '80, '93–'94)
NAPOLEON, Ed ('95–'96)
NARRON, Jerry ('95–'96)
OLIVER, Dave ('87–'94)
OSTEEN, Claude ('93–'94)
PIERSALL, Jim ('75)
RETTENMUND, Merv ('83–'85)
ROBSON, Tom ('86–'92)
RYAN, Connie ('77–'79)
SCHAFFER, Jim ('78)
SILVERA, Charlie ('74–'75)
SUCH, Dick ('83–'85)
SUSCE, George ('72)
TERWILLIGER, Wayne ('72, '81–'85)
UPSHAW, Willie ('93–'94)

PLAYERS (CAREER STATISTICS WITH TEXAS ONLY)

Batting

PLAYER	AVG	AB	R	H	2B	3B	HR	RBI	BB	SO	SB
ALOMAR, Sandy ('77–'78)	.250	112	24	28	4	0	1	12	9	20	4
ANDERSON, Jim ('83–'84)	.181	149	10	27	1	1	0	7	9	15	1
ASHFORD, Tucker ('80)	.125	32	0	4	0	0	0	0	0	0	0
AULT, Doug ('76)	.300	20	0	6	1	0	0	0	1	3	0
BAINES, Harold ('89–'90)	.288	493	59	142	19	1	16	60	60	90	0
BALBONI, Steve ('93)	.600	5	3	0	0	0	0	0	0	2	0
BANNISTER, Alan ('84–'85)	.278	234	37	65	6	2	3	15	35	34	11
BASS, Randy ('82)	.206	48	5	10	2	0	1	6	1	7	0
BEASLEY, Lew ('77)	.219	32	5	7	1	0	0	3	2	2	1
BELCHER, Kevin ('90)	.133	15	4	2	1	0	0	0	2	6	0
BELL, Buddy ('79–'85, '89)	.293	3623	470	1060	197	21	87	499	335	297	24
BELTRE, Esteban ('94–'95)	.256	223	19	57	13	0	0	19	20	40	2
BENIQUEZ, Juan ('76–'78)	.261	1375	166	359	50	13	21	133	102	158	53
BEVACQUA, Kurt ('77–'78)	.253	344	34	87	19	2	11	58	24	44	1
BIITTNER, Larry ('72–'73, '83)	.259	756	58	196	31	4	4	61	58	74	2
BILLINGS, Rich ('72–'74)	.226	780	60	176	27	1	8	90	53	126	4
BLANKS, Larvell ('79)	.200	120	13	24	5	0	1	15	11	9	0
BOGENER, Terry ('82)	.217	60	6	13	2	1	1	4	4	8	0
BONDS, Bobby ('78)	.265	475	85	126	15	4	29	82	69	111	37
BOSLEY, Thad ('89–'90)	.264	201	21	53	9	0	4	19	17	34	1

Records and Statistics

PLAYER	AVG	AB	R	H	2B	3B	HR	RBI	BB	SO	SB
BRINKMAN, Ed ('75)	.000	2	0	0	0	0	0	0	0	1	0
BROWER, Bob ('86–'88)	.244	513	95	125	18	3	15	57	63	107	26
BROWN, Kevin ('96)	.000	4	1	0	0	0	0	1	2	2	0
BROWN, Larry ('74)	.197	76	10	15	2	0	0	5	9	13	0
BROWNE, Jerry ('86–'88)	.263	692	95	182	27	8	2	58	87	86	34
BRUMMER, Glenn ('85)	.278	108	7	30	4	0	0	5	11	22	1
BUCKLEY, Kevin ('84)	.286	7	1	2	1	0	0	0	2	4	0
BUECHELE, Steve ('85–'91, '95)	.240	2723	337	654	115	13	94	338	248	523	14
BUFORD, Damon ('96)	.283	145	30	41	9	0	6	20	15	34	8
BURROUGHS, Jeff ('72–'76)	.257	2334	311	601	93	5	103	386	311	462	6
CAMPANERIS, Bert ('77–'79)	.230	830	109	191	24	10	6	63	68	125	50
CANGELOSI, John ('92)	.188	85	12	16	2	0	1	6	18	16	6
CANSECO, Jose ('92–'94)	.269	733	126	197	37	3	45	151	100	200	22
CAPRA, Nick ('82–'83, '85, '91)	.200	25	6	5	0	0	1	1	4	4	2
CARDENAS, Leo ('74–'75)	.253	194	20	49	5	0	1	12	16	26	1
CARTY, Rico ('73)	.232	306	24	71	12	0	3	33	36	39	2
CASTLE, Don ('73)	.308	13	0	4	1	0	0	2	1	3	0
CHALK, Ken ('79)	.250	8	0	2	0	0	0	0	0	0	0
CLARK, Will ('94–'96)	.304	1279	227	389	76	6	42	244	203	178	7
CLINES, Gene ('76)	.276	446	52	123	12	3	0	38	16	52	11
COOLBAUGH, Scott ('89–'90)	.216	231	28	50	7	0	4	20	19	59	1
COX, Larry ('81)	.231	13	0	3	1	0	0	0	0	4	0
CUBBAGE, Mike ('74–'76)	.250	190	14	39	6	0	4	21	25	25	0
DASCENZO, Doug ('93)	.199	146	20	29	5	1	2	10	8	22	2
DAUGHERTY, Jack ('89–'92)	.261	687	72	179	36	6	8	77	65	114	5
DAVIS, Butch ('93–'94)	.244	176	26	43	13	4	3	20	5	31	4
DAVIS, Doug ('92)	1.000	1	0	1	0	0	0	0	0	0	0
DAVIS, Odie ('80)	.125	8	0	1	0	0	0	0	0	2	0
DAVIS, Willie ('75)	.249	169	16	42	8	2	5	17	4	25	13
DENT, Bucky ('82–'83)	.233	563	52	131	24	2	3	48	36	41	3
DIAZ, Mario ('91–'93)	.266	418	50	111	18	1	3	47	24	33	1
DOWNING, Brian ('91–'92)	.278	727	129	202	35	2	27	88	120	128	2
DRISCOLL, Jim ('72)	.000	18	0	0	0	0	0	0	2	3	0
DUCEY, Rob ('93–'94)	.254	114	16	29	7	3	2	10	12	18	2
DUNBAR, Tommy ('83–'85)	.231	225	19	52	6	0	3	18	23	32	4
DURAN, Dan ('81)	.250	16	1	4	0	0	0	0	1	1	0
ELLIS, John ('76–'81)	.256	800	65	205	37	1	22	131	48	138	5
ELSTER, Kevin ('96)	.252	515	79	130	32	2	24	99	52	138	4
EPSTEIN, Mike ('73)	.188	85	9	16	3	0	1	6	14	19	0
ESPY, Cecil ('87–'90)	.241	901	122	217	29	13	5	71	69	205	91
FANEYTE, Rikkert ('96)	.200	5	0	1	0	0	0	1	0	0	0
FAHEY, Bill ('72, '74–'77)	.219	320	27	70	9	1	2	27	25	48	5
FARISS, Monty ('91–'92)	.223	197	19	44	8	1	4	27	24	62	0
FLETCHER, Scott ('86–'89)	.280	1947	270	545	95	14	8	182	208	200	34
FLYNN, Doug ('82)	.211	270	13	57	6	2	0	19	4	14	6
FOLEY, Marv ('84)	.217	115	13	25	2	0	6	19	15	24	0
FORD, Ted ('72)	.235	429	43	101	19	1	14	50	37	80	4
FOX, Eric ('95)	.000	15	2	0	0	0	0	0	3	4	0
FRANCO, Julio ('89–'93)	.307	2358	388	725	123	12	55	331	290	342	98
FRAZIER, Lou ('95–'96)	.228	149	24	34	4	1	0	13	15	30	13

PLAYER	AVG	AB	R	H	2B	3B	HR	RBI	BB	SO	SB
FREGOSI, Jim ('73–'77)	.254	582	77	148	18	0	22	84	68	117	2
FRIAS, Pepe ('80)	.242	227	27	55	5	1	0	10	4	23	5
FRYE, Jeff ('92, '94–'95)	.286	717	99	205	44	6	5	59	69	95	10
GAMBLE, Oscar ('79)	.335	161	27	54	6	0	8	32	37	15	2
GARBEY, Barbaro ('88)	.194	62	4	12	2	0	0	5	4	11	0
GIL, Benji ('93, '95–'96)	.210	477	39	100	20	3	9	49	32	170	3
GONZALES, Rene ('96)	.217	92	19	20	4	0	2	5	10	11	0
GONZALEZ, Juan ('89–'96)	.283	3130	480	887	172	13	214	659	214	609	16
GRAY, Gary ('77–'79)	.234	94	8	22	1	0	2	7	3	21	2
GREEN, Gary ('90–'91)	.204	108	10	22	4	0	0	9	7	24	1
GREER, Rusty ('94–'96)	.307	1236	190	380	78	9	41	207	163	198	12
GRIEVE, Tom ('72–'77)	.255	1675	191	427	67	9	60	236	108	362	7
GRUBB, John ('78–'82)	.279	1103	151	300	51	5	26	127	149	146	5
HAMILTON, Darryl ('96)	.293	627	94	184	29	4	6	51	54	66	15
HARE, Shawn ('95)	.250	24	2	6	1	0	0	2	4	6	0
HARGROVE, Mike ('74–'78)	.290	2494	380	724	122	14	47	295	435	278	10
HARRAH, Toby ('72–'78, '85–'86)	.259	4188	582	1086	176	19	122	546	668	527	143
HARRELSON, Bud ('80)	.272	180	26	49	6	0	1	9	29	23	4
HARRIS, Donald ('91–'93)	.205	117	17	24	3	0	2	11	6	36	2
HARRIS, Vic ('72–'73)	.221	741	79	164	19	8	8	54	67	120	20
HART, Mike ('80)	.250	4	1	1	0	0	0	0	1	1	0
HASELMAN, Bill ('90)	.154	13	0	2	0	0	0	3	1	5	0
HATCHER, Billy ('95)	.083	12	2	1	1	0	0	0	1	1	0
HENDERSON, Ken ('77)	.258	244	23	63	14	0	5	23	18	37	2
HERNANDEZ, Jose ('91)	.184	98	8	18	2	1	0	4	3	31	0
HOLLE, Gary ('79)	.167	6	0	1	1	0	0	0	1	0	0
HORN, Sam ('95)	.111	9	0	1	0	0	0	0	1	6	0
HORTON, Willie ('77)	.289	519	55	150	23	3	15	75	42	8	1
HOSTETLER, Dave ('82–'84)	.226	804	91	182	23	6	36	123	97	243	2
HOWARD, Frank ('72)	.244	287	28	70	9	0	9	31	42	8	1
HOWELL, Roy ('74–'77)	.247	935	100	231	44	4	19	107	73	199	3
HULSE, David ('92–'94)	.278	809	143	225	21	14	2	50	50	128	50
HUSON, Jeff ('90–'93)	.273	1027	145	241	35	9	6	80	126	139	38
INCAVIGLIA, Pete ('86–'89)	.248	2449	333	607	120	13	124	388	219	788	26
JACKSON, Chuck ('94)	.000	2	0	0	0	0	0	0	0	0	0
JAMES, Chris ('93–'94)	.274	164	33	45	9	4	10	26	23	44	0
JOHNSON, Alex ('73–'74)	.289	1077	119	311	40	6	12	109	60	141	30
JOHNSON, Bobby ('81–'83)	.197	249	24	49	8	1	9	27	20	79	3
JOHNSON, Cliff ('85)	.257	296	31	76	17	1	12	56	31	44	0
JOHNSON, Lamar ('82)	.259	324	37	84	11	0	7	38	31	40	3
JONES, Bobby ('74–'75, '81, '83–'86)	.226	420	40	95	11	0	13	66	32	82	2
JONES, Dalton ('72)	.159	151	14	24	2	0	4	19	10	31	1
JORGENSEN, Mike ('78–'79)	.213	254	41	54	10	0	7	25	32	39	3
KEMP, Steve ('88)	.222	36	2	8	0	0	0	2	2	9	1
KING, Hal ('72)	.180	122	12	22	5	0	4	12	25	35	0
KIRKPATRICK, Ed ('77)	.188	48	2	9	1	0	0	3	4	11	2
KREUTER, Chad ('88–'91)	.166	235	21	39	6	1	6	16	42	63	0
KUBIAK, Ted ('72)	.224	116	5	26	3	0	0	7	12	12	0

Records and Statistics

PLAYER	AVG	AB	R	H	2B	3B	HR	RBI	BB	SO	SB
KUNKEL, Jeff ('84–'90)	.224	838	88	188	42	9	18	72	37	226	9
LAHOUD, Joe ('76)	.225	89	10	20	3	1	1	5	10	16	1
LEACH, Rick ('89)	.272	239	32	65	14	1	1	23	32	33	2
LEE, Manuel ('93–'94)	.256	540	72	138	21	3	3	50	43	105	5
LISI, Rick ('81)	.313	16	6	5	0	0	0	1	4	0	0
LOVITTO, Joe ('72–'76)	.216	763	70	165	22	4	4	53	80	113	22
LOWENSTEIN, John ('78)	.222	176	28	39	8	3	5	21	37	29	16
MACKANIN, Pete ('73–'74)	.104	96	3	10	2	1	0	2	4	28	0
MADDOX, Elliott ('72–'73)	.247	466	64	115	8	2	1	27	78	81	25
MADLOCK, Bill ('73)	.351	77	16	27	5	3	1	5	7	9	3
MAHLBERG, Greg ('78–'79)	.111	18	2	2	0	0	1	1	2	4	0
MALDONADO, Candy ('95)	.233	30	6	7	3	0	2	5	7	5	0
MANRIQUE, Fred ('89)	.288	191	23	55	12	0	2	22	9	33	4
MARTINEZ, Marty ('72)	.146	41	3	6	1	1	0	3	2	8	0
MARZANO, John ('95)	.333	6	1	2	0	0	0	0	0	0	0
MASON, Jim ('72–'73, '77–'78)	.202	545	52	110	17	2	4	39	43	114	0
MAURER, Rob ('91–'92)	.120	25	1	3	1	0	0	3	3	8	0
MAY, Dave ('77)	.241	340	46	82	14	1	7	42	32	43	4
MAZZILLI, Lee ('82)	.241	195	23	47	8	0	4	17	28	26	11
McDOWELL, Oddibe ('85–'88, '94)	.251	2005	322	503	88	22	57	195	221	424	129
McGINNIS, Russ ('92)	.242	33	2	8	4	0	0	4	3	7	0
McLEMORE, Mark ('95–'96)	.261	984	157	272	43	9	10	87	146	140	48
MEIER, Dave ('87)	.286	21	4	6	1	0	0	0	0	4	0
MENDOZA, Mario ('81–'82)	.224	246	19	55	6	1	0	22	7	29	2
MERCADO, Orlando ('86)	.235	102	7	24	1	1	1	7	6	13	0
MILLER, Eddie ('77)	.333	6	7	2	0	0	0	1	1	1	3
MINCHER, Don ('72)	.236	191	23	45	10	0	6	39	46	23	2
MOATES, Dave ('74–'76)	.260	312	42	81	16	1	3	27	24	33	15
MONTANEZ, Willie ('79)	.319	144	19	46	6	0	8	24	8	14	0
NELSON, Dave ('72–'75)	.250	1629	219	407	54	8	14	128	143	241	125
NEWMAN, Al ('92)	.220	246	25	54	5	0	0	12	34	26	9
NEWSON, Warren ('96)	.255	235	34	60	14	1	10	31	37	82	3
NIXON, Otis ('95)	.295	589	87	174	21	2	0	45	58	85	50
NORMAN, Nelson ('78–'81)	.225	422	42	95	12	3	0	25	21	49	4
NORRIS, Jim ('80)	.247	174	23	43	5	0	0	16	23	16	6
O'BRIEN, Pete ('82–'88)	.273	3351	419	914	161	16	114	487	404	373	19
O'MALLEY, Tom ('87)	.274	117	10	32	8	0	1	12	15	9	0
OLIVER, Al ('78–'81)	.319	2094	283	668	135	13	49	337	128	150	20
ORTIZ, Junior ('94)	.276	76	3	21	2	0	0	9	5	11	0
ORTIZ, Luis ('95–'96)	.235	115	11	27	5	3	2	19	6	19	0
PACIOREK, Tom ('86–'87)	.286	273	23	78	10	0	7	34	4	60	1
PAGLIARULO, Mike ('95)	.232	241	27	56	16	0	4	27	15	49	0
PALMEIRO, Rafael ('89–'93)	.296	2993	471	887	174	19	107	431	316	347	35
PALMER, Dean ('89, '91–'96)	.247	2390	378	590	113	8	140	396	253	673	27
PAPE, Ken ('76)	.217	23	7	5	1	0	1	4	3	2	0
PARENT, Mark ('91)	.000	1	0	0	0	0	0	0	0	1	0
PARRISH, Larry ('82–'88)	.264	3223	419	852	147	9	149	522	272	715	13
PELTIER, Dan ('92–'93)	.255	184	24	47	7	1	1	19	20	30	0
PETRALLI, Geno ('85–'93)	.266	1823	181	485	81	9	24	191	211	256	8

PLAYER	AVG	AB	R	H	2B	3B	HR	RBI	BB	SO	SB
PETTIS, Gary ('90–'91)	.230	705	103	162	23	13	3	50	111	209	67
POQUETTE, Tom ('81)	.156	64	2	10	1	0	0	7	5	1	0
PORTER, Darrell ('86–'87)	.253	285	40	72	9	0	19	50	52	94	1
PRUITT, Ron ('75)	.176	17	2	3	0	0	0	0	1	3	0
PRYOR, Greg ('76)	.375	8	2	3	0	0	0	1	0	1	0
PUJOLS, Luis ('85)	1.000	1	0	1	0	0	0	0	0	0	0
PUTNAM, Pat ('77–'82)	.262	1327	153	348	75	6	42	168	89	164	5
RAGLAND, Tom ('72)	.172	58	3	10	2	0	0	2	5	11	0
RANDLE, Lenny ('72–'76)	.257	1938	229	498	66	18	9	179	145	239	76
REDUS, Gary ('93–'94)	.286	255	30	73	13	4	6	33	27	41	4
REIMER, Kevin ('88–'92)	.262	1018	109	267	63	3	39	144	85	225	2
RICHARDT, Mike ('80, '82–'84)	.225	565	45	127	14	1	4	58	27	61	11
RIPKEN, Bill ('93–'94)	.235	213	21	50	9	0	0	17	14	30	2
RIVERS, Mickey ('79–'84)	.303	1966	276	596	93	13	22	168	73	134	48
ROBERTS, Dave ('79–'80)	.245	319	39	78	6	1	13	44	20	55	1
ROBERTS, Leon ('81–'82)	.268	306	33	82	20	2	5	37	29	52	3
ROBSON, Tom ('74–'75)	.208	48	5	10	1	0	0	4	5	6	0
RODRIGUEZ, Ivan ('91–'96)	.285	2667	347	761	158	11	68	340	143	330	17
RUSSELL, John ('90–'93)	.235	187	21	44	5	0	3	14	15	62	1
SAMPLE, Billy ('78–'84)	.270	2177	330	587	111	9	39	201	172	194	92
SCOTT, Donnie ('83–'84)	.218	239	16	52	9	0	3	20	20	44	0
SCRUGGS, Tony ('91)	.000	6	1	0	0	0	0	0	0	1	0
SEE, Larry ('88)	.130	23	0	3	0	0	0	0	1	8	0
SHAVE, Jon ('93)	.319	47	3	15	2	0	0	7	0	8	1
SIERRA, Ruben ('86–'92)	.280	4043	571	1132	226	43	153	657	284	588	86
SIMS, Duke ('74)	.208	106	7	22	0	0	3	6	8	24	0
SLAUGHT, Don ('85–'87)	.260	894	98	232	49	7	29	97	60	124	8
SMALLEY, Roy ('75–'76)	.227	379	37	86	10	0	4	41	59	69	6
SMITH, Keith ('77)	.239	67	13	16	4	0	2	6	4	7	2
SODERHOLM, Eric ('79)	.279	147	15	41	6	0	4	19	12	9	0
SOSA, Sam ('89)	.238	84	8	20	3	0	1	3	0	20	0
SPENCER, Jim ('73–'75)	.270	1107	121	299	41	8	22	134	91	111	1
STANLEY, Mike ('86–'91)	.251	987	114	248	43	4	16	120	147	215	6
STAUB, Rusty ('80)	.300	340	42	102	23	2	9	55	39	18	1
STEELS, James ('88)	.189	53	4	10	1	0	0	5	0	15	2
STEIN, Bill ('81–'85)	.285	653	64	186	33	2	6	86	33	93	3
STELMASZEK, Rick ('73)	.111	9	0	1	0	0	0	0	1	2	0
STEPHENS, Ray ('92)	.154	13	0	2	0	0	0	0	0	5	0
STEVENS, Lee ('96)	.231	78	6	18	2	3	3	12	6	22	0
STILLWELL, Kurt ('96)	.273	77	12	21	4	0	1	4	10	11	0
STONE, Jeff ('89)	.167	36	5	6	1	2	0	5	3	5	2
STRANGE, Doug ('93–'94)	.242	710	84	172	41	1	12	86	58	107	7
SUAREZ, Ken ('72–'73)	.238	311	27	74	12	0	1	31	34	20	1
SUDAKIS, Bill ('73)	.243	494	58	120	19	0	22	82	48	101	0
SUNDBERG, Jim ('74–'83, '88–'89)	.252	4684	482	1180	200	27	60	480	596	744	18
TABOR, Greg ('87)	.111	9	4	1	1	0	0	1	0	4	0
TETTLETON, Mickey ('95–'96)	.242	920	154	223	45	2	56	161	202	247	2
THOMPSON, Bobby ('78)	.225	120	23	27	3	3	2	12	9	26	7
THOMPSON, Danny ('76)	.214	196	12	42	3	0	1	13	13	19	2
THON, Dickie ('92)	.247	275	30	68	15	3	4	37	20	40	12

Records and Statistics

PLAYER	AVG	AB	R	H	2B	3B	HR	RBI	BB	SO	SB
TOLLESON, Wayne ('81–'85)	.251	1225	156	307	32	9	4	50	94	180	71
TOVAR, Cesar ('74–'75)	.277	989	131	274	40	6	7	86	74	58	29
VALENTINE, Ellis ('85)	.211	38	5	8	1	0	2	4	2	8	0
VALLE, David ('95–'96)	.273	161	21	44	9	1	3	22	15	35	1
VOIGT, Jack ('95)	.155	71	9	11	3	0	2	6	7	10	0
WAGNER, Mark ('81–'83)	.246	264	29	65	8	2	1	22	18	42	2
WALKER, Duane ('85)	.174	132	14	23	2	0	5	11	15	29	2
WALLING, Denny ('91)	.091	44	1	4	1	0	0	2	3	8	0
WALTON, Danny ('80)	.200	10	2	2	0	0	0	1	3	5	0
WARD, Gary ('84–'86)	.293	1575	228	461	64	16	41	200	125	264	45
WASHINGTON, Claudell ('77–'78)	.275	563	64	155	31	2	12	70	26	124	21
WASHINGTON, LaRue ('78–'79)	.238	21	5	5	0	0	0	2	4	1	2
WERNER, Don ('81–'82)	.245	469	55	115	15	2	2	44	35	56	12
WILKERSON, Curtis ('83–'88)	.255	1591	185	406	50	18	3	106	89	241	53
WILLS, Bump ('77–'81)	.265	2611	408	693	110	20	30	264	264	365	161
WORTHINGTON, Craig ('95–'96)	.207	87	6	18	4	0	3	10	13	11	0
WRIGHT, George ('82–'86)	.248	2043	219	507	83	16	42	203	115	287	18
YOST, Ned ('84)	.182	242	15	44	4	0	6	25	6	47	1
ZISK, Richie ('78–'80)	.271	1462	185	396	57	3	59	226	154	223	4

Pitchers

NAME	W–L	ERA	G	SV	IP	H	R	ER	BB	SO
AKERFELDS, Darrel ('89)	0–1	3.27	6	0	11.0	11	6	4	5	9
ALBERRO, Jose ('95–'96)	0–1	6.90	17	0	30.0	40	24	23	19	12
ALEXANDER, Doyle ('77–'79)	31–28	3.89	88	0	541.1	533	252	234	222	213
ALEXANDER, Gerald ('90–'92)	6–3	5.79	36	0	98.0	112	67	63	54	59
ALLARD, Brian ('79–'89)	1–4	4.72	12	0	47.2	49	30	25	23	24
ALLEN, Lloyd ('73–'74)	0–7	8.29	37	1	63.0	82	76	58	57	43
ALVAREZ, Wilson ('89)	0–1	—	1	0	0.0	3	3	3	2	0
ANDERSON, Scott ('87)	0–1	9.53	8	0	11.1	17	12	12	8	6
ARNSBERG, Brad ('89–'91)	8–3	4.00	78	6	200.0	194	103	89	103	120
ARMSTRONG, Jack ('94)	0–1	3.60	2	0	10.0	9	4	4	2	7
BABCOCK, Bob ('79–'81)	2–3	3.00	39	0	57.0	48	20	19	31	39
BACSIK, Mike ('75–'77)	4–4	4.54	32	0	83.1	103	53	42	35	35
BANNISTER, Floyd ('92)	1–1	6.32	36	0	37.0	39	27	26	21	30
BARFIELD, John ('89–'91)	8–8	4.72	65	2	139.1	153	86	73	39	53
BARKER, Len ('76–'78)	6–6	3.62	46	5	114.1	106	50	46	59	91
BARR, Steve ('76)	2–6	5.59	20	0	67.2	70	51	42	44	27
BIBBY, Jim ('73–'75, '84)	30–35	4.26	87	1	528.2	468	268	250	251	341
BITKER, Joe ('91)	1–0	6.75	9	0	14.2	17	11	11	8	16
BLYLEVEN, Bert ('76–'77)	23–23	2.74	54	0	437.0	363	148	133	115	326
BOGGS, Tommy ('76–'77, '85)	1–10	4.48	23	0	124.2	140	69	62	48	57
BOHANON, Brian ('90–'94)	11–13	5.61	87	0	271.0	321	187	169	120	149
BOITANO, Dan ('82)	0–0	5.34	19	0	30.1	33	19	18	13	28

NAME	W–L	ERA	G	SV	IP	H	R	ER	BB	SO
BOSMAN, Dick ('72–'73)	10–15	3.75	36	0	213.1	225	111	89	65	119
BOYD, Dennis ('91)	2–7	6.68	12	0	62.0	81	47	46	17	33
BRANDENBURG, Mark ('95–'96)	1–4	4.20	37	0	75.0	84	40	35	32	58
BRILES, Nelson ('76–'77)	17–13	3.53	60	2	318.1	338	145	125	77	155
BROBERG, Pete ('72–'74)	10–25	5.11	73	1	324.0	312	199	184	164	205
BRONKEY, Jeff ('93)	1–1	4.00	21	1	36.0	39	20	16	11	18
BROWN, Jackie ('73–'75)	23–22	3.76	77	2	354.1	371	165	148	133	214
BROWN, Kevin ('86, '88–'94)	78–64	3.81	187	0	1278.2	1322	629	541	428	742
BRUMLEY, Duff ('94)	0–0	16.20	2	0	3.1	6	6	6	5	4
BURKETT, John ('96)	5–2	4.06	10	0	68.2	75	33	31	16	47
BURNS, Todd ('92–'93)	3–9	4.13	6	1	168.0	160	90	77	64	90
BURROWS, Terry ('94–'95)	2–2	6.50	29	1	45.2	61	38	33	20	22
BUTCHER, John ('80–'83)	11–16	3.81	67	6	283.1	282	128	120	96	143
CARPENTER, Cris ('93–'94)	6–6	4.75	74	6	91.0	104	50	48	32	66
CECENA, Jose ('88)	0–0	4.78	22	1	26.1	20	16	14	23	27
CHIAMPARINO, Scott ('90–'92)	2–6	3.27	15	0	85.1	87	36	31	29	40
CLAY, Ken ('80)	2–3	4.60	8	0	43.0	43	24	22	29	17
CLEVELAND, Reggie ('78)	5–7	3.09	53	12	75.2	65	33	26	23	46
CLYDE, David ('73–'75)	7–18	4.60	47	0	217.0	241	130	111	107	128
COMER, Steve ('78–'82)	39–29	3.80	151	13	575.0	605	280	243	210	205
COOK, Dennis ('95–'96)	5–4	4.06	95	2	115.1	100	57	52	51	104
COOK, Glen ('85)	2–3	9.45	9	0	40.0	53	42	42	18	19
CORREA, Edwin ('86–'87)	15–19	5.09	47	0	272.1	250	165	154	178	250
COX, Casey ('72)	3–5	4.41	35	4	65.0	73	41	32	26	27
CREEL, Keith ('87)	0–0	4.66	6	0	9.2	12	5	5	5	5
CRUZ, Victor ('83)	1–3	1.44	17	5	25.0	16	7	4	10	18
CUELLAR, Bobby ('77)	0–0	1.35	4	0	6.2	4	1	1	2	3
DARWIN, Danny ('78–'84, '95)	55–52	3.71	224	15	872.2	833	405	360	298	566
DETTMER, John ('94–'95)	0–6	4.47	12	0	54.1	65	43	27	20	27
DEVINE, Adrian ('77, '80)	12–7	3.84	69	15	133.2	151	65	57	40	75
DREYER, Steve ('93–'94)	4–4	5.71	15	0	58.1	67	41	37	28	34
DUKES, Jan ('72)	0–0	4.50	3	0	2.0	1	2	1	5	0
DUNNING, Steve ('73–'74)	2–6	5.70	24	0	96.1	104	68	61	55	39
DURHAM, Don ('73)	0–4	7.59	15	1	40.1	49	35	34	23	23
ELLIS, Doc ('77–'79)	20–18	3.83	54	0	354.2	353	175	151	104	145
FAJARDO, Hector ('91, '93–'95)	5–9	6.79	28	0	118.0	139	93	89	35	70
FARMER, Ed ('79)	2–0	4.36	11	0	33.0	30	21	16	19	25
FARR, Jim ('82)	0–0	2.50	5	0	18.0	20	8	5	7	6
FIGUEROA, Ed ('80)	0–7	5.90	8	0	39.2	62	29	26	12	9
FOSSAS, Tony ('88)	0–0	4.76	5	0	5.2	11	3	3	2	0
FOUCAULT, Steve ('73–'76)	26–25	3.22	206	35	382.2	341	165	137	151	231
GLEATON, Jerry Don ('79–'80)	0–1	4.86	10	0	16.2	20	9	9	6	4
GIDEON, Jim ('75)	0–0	7.94	1	0	5.2	7	6	5	5	2
GOGOLEWSKI, Bill ('72–'73)	7–17	4.23	85	8	274.2	275	141	129	106	172
GOSSAGE, Rich ('91)	4–2	3.57	44	1	40.1	33	16	16	16	28
GROSS, Kevin ('95–'96)	20–23	5.41	59	0	313.0	351	202	188	139	184
GUANTE, Cecilio ('88–'89)	6–6	3.79	57	3	73.2	74	36	31	40	73
GUZMAN, Jose ('85–'88, '91–'92)	66–62	3.90	159	0	1013.2	983	498	439	395	715

Records and Statistics

NAME	W–L	ERA	G	SV	IP	H	R	ER	BB	SO
HALL, Drew ('89)	2–1	3.70	38	0	58.1	42	24	24	33	45
HAND, Rich ('72–'73)	12–17	3.72	38	0	212.2	188	95	88	122	123
HANDS, Bill ('74–'75)	8–7	3.79	20	0	123.2	129	61	52	31	71
HARGAN, Steve ('74–'77)	30–27	3.93	111	1	512.2	554	275	224	153	264
HARRIS, Greg ('85–'87)	20–22	3.50	173	31	365.0	334	167	142	141	312
HAYWARD, Ray ('88)	4–6	5.46	12	0	62.2	63	44	38	35	37
HELLING, Rick ('94–'96)	4–6	6.38	18	0	84.2	104	62	60	35	46
HENKE, Tom ('82–'84, '93–'94)	11–12	3.54	144	58	172.2	154	70	68	71	169
HENNEMAN, Mike ('96)	0–7	5.79	49	31	42.0	41	28	27	17	34
HENNINGER, Rick ('73)	1–0	2.74	6	0	23.0	23	8	7	11	6
HENRY, Dwayne ('84–'88)	3–4	5.54	54	4	65.0	62	42	40	54	56
HEREDIA, Gil ('96)	2–5	5.89	44	1	73.1	91	50	48	14	43
HEREDIA, Wilson ('95)	0–1	3.75	6	0	12.0	9	5	5	15	6
HILL, Ken ('96)	16–10	3.63	35	0	250.2	25	110	101	95	170
HINTON, Rich ('72)	0–1	2.45	5	0	11.0	7	10	3	10	4
HOERNER, Joe ('76)	0–4	5.14	41	8	35.0	41	22	20	19	15
HOFFMAN, Guy ('88)	0–0	5.24	11	0	22.1	22	14	13	8	9
HONEYCUTT, Rick ('81–'83, '94)	31–33	3.84	117	1	491.2	526	232	210	117	178
HOOTON, Burt ('85)	5–8	5.23	29	0	124.0	149	78	72	40	62
HOOVER, John ('90)	0–0	11.57	2	0	4.2	8	6	6	3	0
HOUGH, Charlie ('80–'90)	139–123	3.68	344	1	2307.2	1995	1086	943	965	1452
HOWARD, Chris ('95)	0–0	0.00	4	0	4.0	3	0	0	1	2
HOWE, Steve ('87)	3–3	4.31	24	1	31.1	33	15	15	8	19
HOWELL, Jay ('94)	4–1	5.44	40	2	43.0	44	29	26	16	22
HUDSON, Charley ('73)	4–2	4.62	25	1	62.1	59	35	32	31	34
HURST, Bruce ('94)	2–1	7.11	8	0	38.0	53	30	30	16	24
HURST, James ('94)	0–0	10.13	8	0	10.2	17	12	12	8	5
JANESKI, Jerry ('72)	0–1	2.77	4	0	13.0	11	5	4	7	7
JEFFCOAT, Mike ('87–'92)	19–19	4.71	149	6	357.2	423	208	187	100	177
JENKINS, Fergie ('74–'75, '78–'81)	93–72	3.56	197	0	1410.0	1339	611	558	315	895
JOHNSON, John Henry ('79–'81)	7–9	3.86	72	6	144.2	125	69	62	57	98
JONES, Odell ('83–'84)	5–10	3.35	75	12	126.1	118	56	47	45	78
KAINER, Don ('80)	0–0	1.83	4	0	19.2	22	7	4	9	10
KEKICH, Mike ('75)	0–0	3.73	23	2	31.1	33	16	13	21	19
KERN, Jim ('79–'81)	17–18	2.59	132	37	236.0	185	83	68	129	196
KILGUS, Paul ('87–'88)	14–22	4.15	57	0	292.2	285	150	135	102	130
KNOWLES, Darold ('77)	5–2	3.22	42	4	50.1	50	22	18	23	14
KREMMEL, Jim ('73)	0–2	9.00	4	0	9.0	15	10	9	6	6
LACEY, Bob ('81)	0–0	9.00	1	0	1.0	1	1	1	0	0
LACHOWITZ, Al ('83)	0–1	2.25	2	0	8.0	9	2	2	2	8
LAWSON, Steve ('72)	0–0	2.81	13	1	16.0	13	6	5	10	13
LEARY, Tim ('94)	1–1	8.14	6	0	21.0	26	19	19	11	9
LEFFERTS, Craig ('93)	3–9	6.05	52	0	83.1	102	57	56	28	58
LEIBRANDT, Charlie ('93)	9–10	4.55	26	0	150.1	169	84	76	45	89
LEWALLYN, Dennis ('80)	0–0	7.94	4	0	5.2	7	5	5	4	1
LINDBLAD, Paul ('72, '77–'78)	10–14	3.43	126	15	238.2	239	97	91	73	122
LOYND, Mike ('86–'87)	3–7	5.82	35	2	111.3	131	83	72	57	81
LYLE, Sparky ('79–'80)	8–10	3.84	116	21	175.2	175	84	75	56	91
MAHLER, Mickey ('86)	0–2	4.14	29	3	63.0	71	31	29	29	28

NAME	W–L	ERA	G	SV	IP	H	R	ER	BB	SO
MALLOY, Bob ('87)	0–0	6.55	2	0	11.0	13	11	8	3	8
MANON, Ramon ('90)	0–0	13.50	1	0	2.0	3	3	3	3	0
MANUEL, Barry ('91–'92)	2–0	2.08	11	0	21.2	13	5	5	7	14
MARSHALL, Mike ('77)	2–2	4.04	12	1	35.2	42	19	16	13	18
MASON, Mike ('82–'87)	25–37	4.38	118	0	561.0	574	302	273	217	328
MATHEWS, Terry ('91–'92)	6–4	4.61	74	1	99.2	102	53	51	49	77
MATLACK, John ('78–'83)	43–45	3.42	158	3	915.1	964	413	348	219	493
MAY, Scott ('88)	0–0	8.59	3	0	7.1	8	7	7	4	4
McCALL, Larry ('79)	1–0	2.16	2	0	8.1	7	2	2	3	3
McDOWELL, Roger ('95)	7–4	4.02	64	4	85.0	86	39	38	34	49
McLAUGHLIN, Joey ('84)	2–1	4.41	15	0	32.2	33	17	16	13	21
McMURTRY, Craig ('88–'90)	3–6	3.90	74	3	124.2	109	62	54	67	63
MEDICH, Doc ('78–'82)	50–43	3.94	132	2	789.2	834	384	346	251	322
MERCER, Mark ('81)	0–1	4.70	7	2	7.2	7	4	4	7	8
MERIDITH, Ron ('86–'87)	2–0	5.71	16	0	23.2	27	19	15	13	19
MERRITT, Jim ('73–'75)	5–13	3.98	66	1	196.2	240	97	87	40	83
MIELKE, Gary ('87, '89–'90)	1–3	3.56	79	1	93.2	97	37	37	41	42
MIRABELLA, Paul ('78–'82)	4–3	5.15	50	4	78.2	76	46	45	39	52
MOHORCIC, Dale ('86–'88)	11–16	3.24	175	28	230.1	236	94	83	54	102
MOORE, Tommy ('75)	0–2	8.14	12	0	21.0	31	21	19	12	15
MORET, Roger ('77–'78)	3–4	3.93	25	5	87.0	82	49	38	40	44
MOYER, Jamie ('89–'90)	6–15	4.31	48	0	196.1	199	110	94	79	102
MURRAY, Dale ('85)	0–0	18.00	1	0	1.0	3	2	2	0	0
NELSON, Gene ('93)	0–0	3.38	6	1	8.0	10	3	3	1	4
NEN, Robb ('93)	1–1	6.35	9	0	22.2	28	17	16	26	12
NICHTING, Chris ('95)	0–0	7.03	13	0	24.1	36	19	19	13	6
NOLES, Dickie ('84–'85)	6–11	5.09	46	1	168.0	189	105	95	63	98
NOLTE, Eric ('91)	0–0	3.38	3	0	2.2	3	1	1	3	1
OLIVER, Darren ('93–'96)	22–8	4.34	92	2	276.0	279	147	133	144	203
PANTHER, Jim ('72)	5–9	4.12	58	0	94.0	101	55	43	46	44
PATTERSON, Bob ('93)	2–4	4.78	52	1	52.2	59	28	28	11	46
PATTERSON, Danny ('96)	0–0	0.00	7	0	8.2	10	4	0	3	5
PAUL, Mike ('72–'73)	13–13	3.14	85	3	249.1	253	105	87	88	157
PAVLIK, Roger ('92–'96)	43–33	4.65	115	0	671.1	668	360	347	315	483
PERRY, Gaylord ('75–'77, '80)	48–43	3.26	112	0	827.0	787	345	300	190	575
PERZANOWSKI, Stan ('75–'76)	3–3	4.06	17	0	77.2	79	40	35	29	32
PETERSON, Fritz ('76)	1–0	3.60	4	0	15.0	21	7	6	7	4
PETKOVSEK, Mark ('91)	0–1	14.46	4	0	9.1	21	16	15	4	6
PINA, Horacio ('72)	2–7	3.20	60	15	76	61	33	27	43	60
POLONI, John ('77)	1–0	6.43	2	0	7	8	5	5	1	5
POOLE, Jim ('91)	0–0	4.50	5	1	6.0	10	4	3	3	4
RAJSICH, Dave ('79–'80)	3–4	4.68	51	2	102.0	112	59	53	40	67
REED, Rick ('93–'94)	2–1	5.22	6	0	20.2	23	14	12	8	14
ROGERS, Kenny ('89–'95)	70–51	3.88	376	28	943.1	925	468	407	370	680
ROLAND, Jim ('72)	0–0	8.10	5	0	3.0	7	3	3	2	4
ROSENTHAL, Wayne ('91)	1–4	5.40	42	1	75.0	79	47	45	38	62
ROZEMA, Dave ('85–'86)	3–7	4.38	40	7	98.2	119	54	48	25	45
RUSSELL, Jeff ('85–'92, '95–'96)	41–40	3.76	408	114	720.0	699	337	301	293	433
RYAN, Nolan ('89–'93)	51–39	3.30	129	0	840.0	593	362	320	353	939

NAME	W–L	ERA	G	SV	IP	H	R	ER	BB	SO
SCHIRALDI, Calvin ('91)	0–1	11.57	3	0	4.2	5	6	6	5	1
SCHMIDT, Dave ('81–'85)	20–22	3.14	172	26	344.0	341	142	120	92	203
SCHOOLER, Mike ('93)	3–0	5.55	17	0	24.1	30	17	15	10	16
SEBRA, Bob ('85)	0–2	7.52	7	0	20.1	26	17	17	14	13
SHELLENBACK, Jim ('72–'74)	2–4	4.17	33	1	82.0	76	42	38	28	44
SIEBERT, Sonny ('73)	7–11	3.99	25	2	119.2	120	68	53	37	76
SINGER, Bill ('76)	4–1	3.48	10	0	64.2	56	31	25	27	34
SKOK, Craig ('76)	0–1	12.60	9	0	5.0	13	7	7	3	5
SMITH, Dan ('92, '94)	1–5	4.66	17	0	29.0	36	19	15	20	14
SMITHSON, Mike ('82–'83)	13–18	4.10	41	0	270.0	284	128	123	84	159
STANHOUSE, Dan ('72–'74)	4–17	4.28	63	1	206.0	181	109	98	134	146
STANTON, Mike ('96)	0–1	3.22	22	0	22.1	20	8	8	4	14
STEWART, Dave ('83–'85)	12–22	4.44	82	4	332.2	329	174	164	141	207
SURHOFF, Rich ('85)	0–1	7.56	7	2	8.1	12	7	7	3	8
TANANA, Frank ('82–'85)	31–49	3.60	107	0	677.2	678	329	271	210	367
TAYLOR, Scott ('95)	1–2	9.39	3	0	15.1	25	16	16	5	10
TERPKO, Jeff ('74–'76)	3–3	2.26	35	0	59.2	48	16	15	33	27
TEWKSBURY, Bob ('95)	8–7	4.58	21	0	129.2	169	75	66	20	53
THOMAS, Stan ('74–'75)	4–4	3.59	58	3	95.1	94	46	38	40	54
TOBIK, Dave ('83–'84)	3–7	3.65	51	14	86.1	80	38	35	30	60
UMBARGER, Jim ('75–'78)	24–28	3.90	121	3	439.0	472	215	190	153	220
VANDE BERG, Ed ('88)	2–2	4.14	26	2	37.0	44	19	17	11	18
VAUGHN, DeWayne ('88)	0–0	7.63	8	0	15.1	24	15	13	4	8
VOSBERG, Ed ('95–'96)	6–6	3.00	96	12	80.0	83	32	28	97	163
WAITS, Rick ('73)	0–0	9.00	1	1	1.0	1	1	1	1	0
WALLACE, Mike ('77)	0–0	7.56	5	0	8.1	10	7	7	10	2
WELSH, Chris ('85)	2–5	4.13	25	0	76.1	101	40	35	25	31
WHITEHOUSE, Len ('81)	0–1	16.20	2	0	3.1	8	7	6	2	2
WHITESIDE, Matt ('92–'96)	10–9	4.48	181	9	247.1	263	133	123	92	150
WILLIAMS, Matt ('85)	2–1	2.42	6	0	26.0	20	7	7	10	22
WILLIAMS, Mitch ('86–'88)	18–19	3.70	232	32	274.2	180	124	113	220	280
WILMET, Paul ('89)	0–0	15.43	3	0	2.1	5	4	4	2	1
WILSON, Steve ('88)	0–0	5.87	3	0	7.2	7	5	5	4	1
WITT, Bobby ('86–'92, '95–'96)	87–88	4.60	228	0	1402.1	1309	807	735	894	1254
WRIGHT, Clyde ('75)	4–6	4.44	25	0	93.1	105	56	46	47	32
WRIGHT, Ricky ('83–'86)	1–2	5.09	35	0	63.2	69	36	36	38	38

RANGERS YEAR-BY-YEAR

YEAR	WON	LOST	PCT.	POS.	GA/GB	MANAGER	HOME ATT.
1972	54	100	.351	6	–38.5	Ted Williams	662,974
1973	57	105	.352	6	–37	Whitey Herzog (47–91)	686,085
						Del Wilber (1–0)	
						Billy Martin (9–14)	
1974	*84	76	.525	2	–5	Billy Martin	1,193,902
1975	79	83	.483	3	–19	Billy Martin (44–51)	1,127,924
						Frank Lucchesi (35–32)	

YEAR	WON	LOST	PCT.	POS.	GA/GB	MANAGER	HOME ATT.
1976	76	86	.469	T4	−14	Frank Lucchesi	1,164,982
1977	94	68	.580	2	−8	Frank Lucchesi (31–31)	1,250,721
						Eddie Stanky (1–0)	
						Connie Ryan (2–4)	
						Bill Hunter (60–33)	
1978	87	75	.537	T2	−5	Bill Hunter (86–75)	1,447,963
						Pat Corrales (1–0)	
1979	83	79	.512	3	−5	Pat Corrales	1,519,654
1980	**76	85	.472	4	−20.5	Pat Corrales	1,198,175
1981	57	48	.543	2	−5	Don Zimmer	850,076
1982	64	98	.395	6	−29	Don Zimmer (38–58)	1,154,432
						Darrell Johnson (26–40)	
1983	*77	85	.475	3	−22	Doug Rader	1,363,469
1984	69	92	.429	7	−14.5	Doug Rader	1,102,471
1985	62	99	.385	7	−28.5	Doug Rader (9–23)	1,112,497
						Bobby Valentine (53–76)	
1986	87	75	.537	2	−5	Bobby Valentine	1,692,021
1987	75	87	.463	T6	−10	Bobby Valentine	1,763,053
1988	70	91	.435	6	−33.5	Bobby Valentine	1,581,901
1989	83	79	.512	4	−16	Bobby Valentine	2,043,993
1990	83	79	.512	3	−20	Bobby Valentine	2,057,887
1991	85	77	.525	3	−10	Bobby Valentine	2,297,720
1992	77	85	.475	4	−19	Bobby Valentine (45–41)	2,198,231
						Toby Harrah (32–44)	
1993	86	76	.531	2	−8.0	Kevin Kennedy	2,244,616
1994	52	62	.456	@1	+1.0	Kevin Kennedy	2,503,198
1995	74	70	.514	3	−4.5	Johnny Oates	1,985,910
1996	*90	72	.556	1	+4.5	Johnny Oates	2,889,020
TOTALS	1881	2032	.481	—	—		39,092,875

* One Tie Game   **Two Tie Games

@Recognized as A.L. West leader through games of Aug. 11. No division titles were awarded.

RANGERS ALL-TIME MANAGERS' WON-LOST RECORDS

MANAGER	YEARS	GAMES	WON	LOST	PCT.
Pat Corrales	1978–80	++326	160	164	.494
Toby Harrah	1992	76	32	44	.421
Whitey Herzog	1973	138	47	91	.341
Billy Hunter	1977–78	254	146	108	.575
Darrell Johnson	1982	66	26	40	.394
Kevin Kennedy	1993–94	276	138	138	.500
Frank Lucchesi	1975–77	291	142	149	.488
Billy Martin	1973–75	+279	137	141	.493
Johnny Oates	1995–96	+307	164	142	.536
Doug Rader	1983–85	+356	155	200	.437
Connie Ryan*	1977	6	2	4	.333
Eddie Stanky	1977	1	1	0	1.000
Bobby Valentine	1985–92	1186	581	605	.490
Del Wilbur*	1973	1	1	0	1.000
Ted Williams	1972	154	54	100	.351
Don Zimmer	1981–82	201	95	106	.473

*Interim   +One Tie   ++Two Ties

Veteran slugger Don Mincher hit his last six home runs with Texas in 1972, finishing his career with exactly 200. (Courtesy *Fort Worth Star-Telegram*, Special Collections Division, University of Texas at Arlington Libraries.)

Rich Billings' tag is late on Baltimore's Don Buford (father of current Ranger Damon Buford) as umpire Larry Napp makes the call. (Courtesy *Fort Worth Star-Telegram*, Special Collections Division, University of Texas at Arlington Libraries.)

RANGERS ALL-TIME MISCELLANEOUS WON-LOST RECORDS

						VS. EAST DIVISION		
YEAR	ONE-RUN GAMES	TWO-RUN GAMES	HOME	ROAD	TOTAL	HOME	ROAD	
1972	19–28	8–20	31–36	23–54	26–46	14–22	12–24
1973	14–23	14–22	35–46	22–59	25–47	13–23	12–24
1974	22–13	18–14	42–38	42–38	39–33	20–16	19–17
1975	33–21	13–21	39–41	40–42	37–35	18–17	19–18
1976	33–29	11–19	39–42	37–44	30–42	14–22	16–20
1977	30–29	15–10	44–37	50–31	42–30	18–18	24–12
1978	33–29	13–14	52–30	35–45	35–37	19–17	16–20
1979	23–30	16–11	44–37	39–42	39–45	24–18	15–27
1980	20–30	11–16	39–41	37–44	46–38	24–18	22–20
1981	13–15	9–7	32–24	25–24	27–27	17–12	10–15
1982	20–26	13–20	38–43	26–55	28–56	16–26	12–30
1983	23–28	15–24	44–37	33–48	34–50	19–23	15–27
1984	25–29	11–20	34–46	35–46	33–50	17–24	16–26
1985	11–27	18–18	37–43	25–56	29–54	16–25	13–29
1986	28–26	14–13	51–30	36–45	40–44	23–19	17–25
1987	18–21	19–19	43–38	32–49	37–47	23–19	14–28
1988	21–31	14–12	38–43	32–48	36–47	21–21	15–26
1989	20–18	18–15	45–36	38–43	41–43	23–19	18–24
1990	37–22	13–19	47–35	36–44	45–39	25–17	20–22
1991	21–23	18–13	46–35	39–42	42–42	25–17	17–25
1992	25–22	18–16	36–45	41–40	38–36	16–26	22–20
1993	22–23	16–14	50–31	36–45	49–35	26–16	23–19
1994	16–18	9–14	31–32	21–30	21–20	14–7	7–13
1995	21–18	11–13	41–31	33–39	25–20	13–8	12–12
1996	20–21	16–13	50–31	40–41	42–20	25–5	17–15
TOTALS	568–600	351–397	1028–938	853–1094	886–983	483–455	403–538

			EXTRA	DOUBLE-		VS. WEST DIVISION		
YEAR	DAY	NIGHT	INNINGS	HEADERS	TOTAL	HOME	ROAD	
1972	20–30	34–70	5–11	3–4–3	28–54	17–24	11–30
1973	10–30	47–75	10–6	2–7–5	32–58	22–23	10–35
1974	21–19	63–57	16–9	1–3–7	45–43	22–22	23–21
1975	18–15	61–68	16–10	2–4–7	42–48	21–24	21–24
1976	17–20	59–66	13–13	1–5–6	46–44	25–20	21–24
1977	23–18	71–50	14–6	7–4–4	52–38	26–19	26–19
1978	15–20	72–55	9–7	6–2–6	52–38	33–13	19–25
1979	15–12	68–67	5–4	1–3–4	44–34	20–19	24–15
1980	19–19	57–66	9–9	1–2–4	30–47	15–23	15–24
1981	13–18	44–30	4–4	0–1–1	30–21	15–12	15–9
1982	14–20	50–78	6–6	2–1–5	36–42	22–17	14–25
1983	12–21	65–64	8–11	1–3–2	43–35	25–14	18–21
1984	13–22	56–70	7–10	0–0–2	36–42	17–22	19–20
1985	12–25	50–74	1–8	0–1–1	33–45	21–18	12–27
1986	17–17	70–58	10–8	3–0–0	47–31	28–11	19–20
1987	12–21	63–66	8–9	1–0–3	38–40	20–19	18–21
1988	15–20	55–71	7–5	0–1–1	34–44	17–22	17–22
1989	17–13	66–66	8–4	1–2–0	42–36	22–17	20–19
1990	13–16	70–63	8–5	0–2–1	38–40	22–18	16–22
1991	18–13	67–64	14–10	0–1–3	43–35	21–18	22–17
1992	17–14	60–71	9–7	1–0–1	39–39	20–19	19–20

Records and Statistics

YEAR	DAY	NIGHT	EXTRA INNINGS	DOUBLE-HEADERS	VS. WEST DIVISION TOTAL	HOME	ROAD
1993	21–16	65–60	6–5	1–1–3	37–41	24–15	13–26
1994	10–18	42–44	5–8	1–0–0	8–22	4–13	4–9
1995	14–17	60–53	6–6	0–0–1	18–21	10–9	8–12
1996	28–16	62–56	5–7	1–0–0	18–21	10–10	8–11
TOTALS	404–470	1477–1562	209–188	36–47–70	911–959	499–441	412–518

YEAR	VS. CENTRAL DIVISION TOTAL	HOME	ROAD
1994	23–20	13–12	10–8
1995	31–29	18–14	13–15
1996	30–31	15–16	15–15
TOTALS	84–80	46–42	38–38

RANGERS STANDING AT ALL-STAR BREAK

YEAR	RECORD	POS.	GB/GA	YEAR	RECORD	POS.	GB/GA
1972	37–53	6th	18.5	1985	32–56	7th	20.5
1973	34–62	6th	20.5	1986	47–41	2nd	1.5
1974	48–50	4th	8.0	1987	41–45	6th	6.5
1975	41–49	4th	15.5	1988	40–46	6th	13.0
1976	44–38	2nd	7.0	1989	47–39	4th	5.5
1977	46–44	4th	8.0	1990	40–44	6th	12.0
1978	42–41	3rd	2.5	1991	44–33	T1st	——
1979	52–39	2nd	2.0	1992	48–42	3rd	6.5
1980	37–42	3rd	9.5	1993	44–42	T2nd	1.0
1981	33–22	2nd	1.5	1994	42–45	1st	3.0
1982	35–46	5th	11.5	1995	39–30	T1st	——
1983	44–34	1st	2.0	1996	51–36	1st	4.0
1984	38–49	7th	7.5				

TIE GAMES AND FORFEITS

DATE	OPPONENT	SCORE	SITUATION
September 12, 1974	at Chicago	2–2	Game called after 6 innings–rain
June 2, 1980	at Chicago	1–1	Game called in bottom of 6th inning–rain
July 262, 1980	at Chicago	1–1	Game called in bottom of 6th inning–rain
May 24, 1983	at Kansas City	2–2	Game called after 5 innings–rain
June 17, 1996	at Baltimore	1–1	Game called in bottom of 6th inning–rain

In addition, the Rangers have won one game by forfeit, June 4, 1974 at Cleveland. Trailing, 5–3, entering the bottom of the ninth inning, the Indians scored twice to tie the game. With runners on first and third and two out in the bottom of the ninth, a large number of fans attending the Ten-Cent Beer Night at Municipal Stadium swarmed onto the field. After about 15 minutes of unruly action, umpire Nestor Chylak declared the Rangers a winner by a 9–0 forfeit.

SUSPENDED GAMES

DATE	OPPONENT	SITUATION
May 14, 1975	Vs. Milwaukee	Game started 1:13 late due to rain and was suspended after 14 innings due to curfew. Resumed on May 15 and won by Milwaukee in 15 innings, 3–2.

May 26, 1976	Vs. Kansas City	Second game of doubleheader suspended after 9 innings. Resumed on May 27 and won by Texas in 10 innings, 5–4.
April 28, 1989	Vs. Boston	Game suspended after 10 innings due to curfew at 1:21 AM following rain delay of 2:02. Resumed on April 29 and won by Texas in 12 innings, 7–6.
May 11, 1990	Vs. Cleveland	Game suspended at 10:31 PM due to rain in the top of the 6th inning with score tied, 4–4. Resumed on May 12 and won by Cleveland in 9 innings, 5–4.
May 10, 1994	Vs. California	Game suspended after 8 innings due to curfew at 1:10 AM following rain delay of 2:48 with score tied at 5–5. Resumed on May 11 and won by Angels, 8–6 in 10 innings.

RANGERS LONGEST STREAKS

WINNING STREAKS

YEAR	NO.	DATES
1972	5	May 17–21
1973	6	July 20–27
1974	5	April 14 (2nd gm.)–20
1975	6	April 24–May 2
1976	8	April 29–May 9
1977	7	Sept. 21–28
1978	7	April 25–May 3; June 20–27; Sept. 21–25
1979	8	June 23–30
1980	5	April 14–19
1981	5	May 22–26; Sept. 28–Oct. 3
1982	4	April 14–18
1983	6	June 21–26; Sept. 17–23
1984	6	June 8–13
1985	5	Sept. 20–24
1986	7	June 2–8
1987	6	April 23–29
1988	8	May 6–14
1989	8	April 8–16
1990	7	July 5–14
1991	14	May 12–27
1992	7	May 22–29
1993	6	July 8–16; Sept. 6–11
1994	4	June 7–10
1995	6	June 6–12
1996	7	April 1–9; Aug. 9–16

LOSING STREAKS

YEAR	NO.	DATES
1972	15	Sept. 13–30
1973	8	August 7 (2nd gm.)–15
1974	6	May 5 (2nd gm.)–10
1975	6	May 23–29
1976	10	July 7–17
1977	4	April 13–18; Sept. 3–6
1978	8	April 11–23; July 18–25
1979	6	August 12–17
1980	8	Sept. 19–26
1981	4	Sept. 5–8
1982	12	April 20–May 6
1983	8	July 25–August 3
1984	7	April 23–May 1
1985	7	May 11–17
1986	7	July 17–23
1987	9	April 9–19
1988	6	Aug. 31–Sept. 5
1989	4	May 4–7; May 12–17; May 29–June 1; Aug. 5–8
1990	5	May 13–18; May 25–29
1991	8	June 1–10
1992	5	May 10–16; Aug. 14–19
1993	6	June 18–23
1994	6	June 14–19; Aug. 5–10
1995	10	July 17–26
1996	5	September 16–20

RANGERS TOP 10 — ALL-TIME BATTING

GAMES		AT–BATS		RUNS		HITS		DOUBLES		TRIPLES	
Sundberg	1,512	Sundberg	4,684	Harrah	582	Sundberg	1,180	Sierra	226	Sierra	43
Harrah	1,220	Harrah	4,188	Sierra	568	Sierra	1,132	Sundberg	200	Sundberg	27
Sierra	1,033	Sierra	4,032	Sundberg	482	Harrah	1,086	Bell	197	McDowell	22
Bell	958	Bell	3,623	Gonzalez	480	Bell	1,060	Harrah	176	Bell	21
O'Brien	946	O'Brien	3,351	Bell	471	O'Brien	914	Palmeiro	174	Wills	20
Buechele	889	Parrish	3,223	Palmeiro	471	Gonzalez	887	Gonzalez	172	Harrah	19
Parrish	872	Gonzalez	3,130	O'Brien	419	Palmeiro	887	O'Brien	161	Palmeiro	19
Gonzalez	817	Palmeiro	2,993	Parrish	419	Parrish	852	Rodriguez	158	Randle	18
Palmeiro	788	Buechele	2,723	Wills	408	Rodriguez	761	Parrish	147	Wilkerson	18
Petralli	784	Rodriguez	2,667	Franco	388	Hargrove	730	Oliver	135	Ward, O'Brien, Wright	16, 16

Records and Statistics

HOME RUNS		RBI		BATTING PCT. (300 or more games)		STOLEN BASES		EXTRA BASE HITS		TOTAL BASES	
Gonzalez	214	Gonzalez	659	Oliver	.319	Wills	161	Sierra	422	Sierra	1,903
Sierra	153	Sierra	656	Franco	.30746	Harrah	143	Gonzalez	399	Gonzalez	1,727
Parrish	149	Harrah	546	Greer	.30744	McDowell	129	Harrah	317	Harrah	1,666
Palmer	140	Parrish	522	Clark	.304	Nelson	125	Parrish	306	Sundberg	1,614
Incaviglia	124	Bell	499	Rivers	.303	Franco	98	Bell	305	Bell	1,562
Harrah	122	O'Brien	487	Palmeiro	.296	Sample	92	Palmeiro	300	O'Brien	1,489
O'Brien	114	Sundberg	480	Hargrove	.2927	Espy	91	O'Brien	291	Parrish	1,465
Palmeiro	107	Palmeiro	431	Ward	.2926	Sierra	86	Sundberg	287	Palmeiro	1,420
Burroughs	103	Palmer	396	Bell	.2925	Tolleson	79	Palmer	261	Rodriguez	1,145
Buechele	94	Incaviglia	388	Rodriguez	.285	Randle	76	Incaviglia	257	Palmer	1,139

WALKS

Harrah, 668; Sundberg, 542; Hargrove, 435; O'Brien, 404; Bell, 335; Palmeiro, 316; Burroughs, 311; Sierra, 298; Franco, 290; Parrish, 272.

RANGERS TOP 10—SINGLE SEASON BATTING

AVERAGE			AT–BATS			HITS			RUNS		
Franco	.341	1991	Bell	670	1979	Rivers	210	1980	Palmeiro	124	1993
Rivers	.333	1980	Sierra	661	1991	Oliver	209	1980	Rodriguez	116	1996
Greer	.332	1996	Oliver	656	1980	Palmeiro	203	1991	Palmeiro	115	1991
Clark	.32905	1994	Sierra	643	1987	Sierra	203	1991	Sierra	110	1991
Bell	.32857	1980	Rodriguez	639	1996	Franco	201	1991	Franco	108	1991
Oliver	.324	1978	Wright	634	1983	Bell	200	1979	McDowell	105	1986
Oliver	.323	1979	Sierra	634	1989	Sierra	194	1989	Wills	102	1980
Palmeiro	.322	1991	Palmeiro	631	1991	Rodriguez	192	1996	Sierra	101	1989
Palmeiro	.3194	1990	Rivers	630	1980	Palmeiro	191	1990	Hargrove	98	1977
Oliver	.3186	1980	Hamilton	627	1996	Hamilton	184	1996	Palmer	98	1996

DOUBLES			TRIPLES			HOME RUNS			RBI		
Palmeiro	49	1991	Sierra	14	1989	Gonzalez	47	1996	Gonzalez	144	1996
Rodriguez	47	1996	Sierra	10	1986	Gonzalez	46	1993	Sierra	119	1989
Sierra	44	1991	Hulse	10	1993	Gonzalez	43	1992	Gonzalez	118	1993
Oliver	43	1980	Pettis	8	1984	Palmer	38	1996	Burroughs	118	1974
Bell	42	1979	Ward	7	1984	Palmeiro	37	1993	Oliver	117	1980
Parrish	42	1984	Harris	7	1973	Palmer	33	1993	Sierra	116	1991
Greer	41	1996	Ward	7	1985	Tettleton	32	1995	Sierra	109	1987
Palmeiro	40	1993	Randle	7	1975	Parrish	32	1987	Gonzalez	109	1992
Sierra	37	1990	Campaneris	7	1977	Canseco	31	1994	Palmer	107	1996
Bell	36	1984	McDowell	7	1986	Burroughs	30	1973	Palmeiro	105	1993
			Espy	7	1989	Incaviglia	30	1986	Gonzalez	102	1991
									Sierra	30	1987

WALKS			STRIKEOUTS			STOLEN BASES			GAMES		
Harrah	113	1985	Incaviglia	185	1986	Wills	52	1978	Oliver	163	1980
Harrah	109	1977	Incaviglia	168	1987	Nelson	51	1972	Bell	162	1979
Tettleton	107	1995	Burroughs	155	1975	Nixon	50	1995	Wright	162	1983
Hargrove	107	1978	Parrish	154	1987	Espy	45	1989	Sierra	162	1989
Hargrove	103	1977	Palmer	154	1993	Sample	44	1983	Harrah	161	1974
Harrah	98	1975	Palmer	154	1992	Nelson	43	1973	Sierra	161	1991
Hargrove	97	1976	Incaviglia	153	1988	Pettis	38	1990	Palmeiro	160	1993
Tettleton	95	1996	Gil	147	1995	Bonds	37	1978	Harrah	159	1977
Burroughs	91	1974	Incaviglia	146	1990	Franco	36	1991	O'Brien	159	1987
Harrah	91	1976	Palmer	145	1996	Wills	35	1979	Sierra	159	1990
									Palmeiro	159	1991
									Palmeiro	159	1992

RANGERS YEAR-BY-YEAR BATTING LEADERS

(*Led League)

YEAR	AVERAGE		HOME RUNS		RBI		STOLEN BASES	
1972	Harrah	.25934	Ford	14	Billings	58	Nelson	51
	Biittner	.25916						
1973	A. Johnson	.287	Burroughs	30	Burroughs	85	Nelson	43
1974	Burroughs	.301	Burroughs	25	Burroughs	*118	Randle	26
1975	Hargrove	.303	Burroughs	29	Burroughs	94	Harrah	23
1976	Hargrove	.287	Grieve	20	Burroughs	86	Randle	30
1977	Hargrove	.305	Harrah	27	Harrah	87	Wills	28
1978	Oliver	.324	Bonds	29	Oliver	89	Wills	52
1979	Oliver	.323	Bell	18	Bell	101	Wills	35
			Putnam	18				
			Zisk	18				
1980	Rivers	.333	Oliver	19	Oliver	117	Wills	34
			Zisk	19				
1981	Oliver	.309	Bell	10	Bell	64	Wills	12
1982	Bell	.296	Hostetler	22	Bell	67	Mazzilli	11
					Hostetler	67		
1983	Bell	.277	Parrish	26	Parrish	88	Sample	44
1984	Bell	.315	Parrish	22	Parrish	101	Tolleson	22
1985	Ward	.287	O'Brien	22	O'Brien	92	Ward	26
1986	Fletcher	.300	Incaviglia	30	Parrish	94	McDowell	33
1987	Fletcher	.287	Parrish	32	Sierra	109	Browne	27
1988	Fletcher	.276	Sierra	23	Sierra	91	Espy	33
							McDowell	33
1989	Franco	.316	Sierra	29	Sierra	*119	Espy	45
1990	Palmeiro	.319	Incaviglia	24	Sierra	96	Pettis	38
1991	Franco	*.341	Gonzalez	27	Sierra	116	Franco	36
1992	Sierra	.278	Gonzalez	*43	Gonzalez	109	Huson	18
1993	Gonzalez	.310	Gonzalez	*46	Gonzalez	118	Hulse	29
1994	Clark	.329	Canseco	31	Canseco	90	Hulse	18
1995	Rodriguez	.303	Tettleton	32	Clark	92	Nixon	50
1996	Greer	.332	Gonzalez	47	Gonzalez	144	McLemore	27

YEAR	HITS		DOUBLES		TRIPLES		WALKS	
1972	Billings	119	Ford	19	Nelson	3	Nelson	67
1973	A. Johnson	179	A. Johnson	26	Harris	7	Burroughs	67
1974	Burroughs	167	Burroughs	33	Hargrove	6	Burroughs	91
					Tovar	6		
1975	Randle	166	Harrah	24	Randle	7	Harrah	98
			Randle	24				
1976	Hargrove	155	Hargrove	30	Randle	6	Hargrove	*97
1977	Hargrove	160	Washington	31	Campaneris	7	Harrah	*109
1978	Oliver	170	Oliver	35	Sundberg	6	Hargrove	*107
1979	Bell	200	Bell	42	Oliver	4	Zisk	57
					Sundberg	4		
1980	Rivers	210	Oliver	43	Rivers	6	Sundberg	64
1981	Oliver	130	Oliver	29	Five with	2	Sundberg	50
1982	Bell	159	Bell	27	Sundberg	5	Bell	70
					Wright	5		
1983	Wright	175	Bell	35	Wright	6	O'Brien	58
1984	Parrish	175	Parrish	42	Ward	7	Bell	63

YEAR	HITS		DOUBLES		TRIPLES		WALKS	
1985	Ward	170	O'Brien	34	Ward	7	Harrah	113
1986	O'Brien	160	Fletcher	34	Sierra	10	O'Brien	87
1987	Fletcher	169	Sierra	35	Browne	6	Browne	61
	Sierra	169					Fletcher	61
1988	Sierra	156	Sierra	32	Espy	6	O'Brien	72
1989	Sierra	194	Sierra	35	Sierra	*14	Franco	66
1990	Palmeiro	*191	Sierra	37	Pettis	8	Franco	82
1991	Palmeiro	203	Palmeiro	*49	Pettis	5	Palmeiro	68
	Sierra	203			Sierra	5		
1992	Palmeiro	163	Reimer	32	Sierra	6	Palmeiro	72
1993	Palmeiro	176	Palmeiro	40	Hulse	10	Palmeiro	73
1994	Clark	128	Clark	24	Gonzalez	4	Clark	71
					Hulse	4		
1995	Nixon	174	Rodriguez	32	McLemore	5	Tettleton	107
1996	Rodriguez	192	Rodriguez	47	Greer	6	Tettleton	95

RANGERS TEAM BATTING, 1972–1996

YR	AVG	G	AB	R	H	TB	2B	3B	HR	RBI	SH	SF	HP	BB	SO	SB	CS	GIDP
1972	.217	154	5029	461	1092	1460	166	17	56	424	84	34	30	503	926	126	73	100
1973	.255	162	5488	619	1397	1980	195	29	110	574	45	50	27	503	791	91	53	132
1974	.272	161	5449	690	1482	2055	198	39	99	643	81	47	38	508	710	113	80	155
1975	.256	162	5599	714	1431	2075	208	17	134	675	64	41	25	613	863	102	62	125
1976	.250	162	5555	616	1390	1895	213	26	80	574	72	45	29	568	809	87	45	141
1977	.270	162	5541	767	1497	2245	265	39	135	704	116	50	39	596	904	154	85	118
1978	.253	162	5347	692	1353	2037	216	36	132	650	83	55	32	624	779	196	91	115
1979	.278	162	5562	750	1549	2273	252	26	140	718	78	59	33	461	607	79	51	135
1980	.284	163	5690	756	1616	2305	263	27	124	720	70	56	23	480	589	91	49	156
1981	.270	105	3581	452	968	1323	178	15	49	418	36	39	21	295	396	46	41	84
1982	.249	162	5445	590	1354	1955	204	26	115	558	64	32	32	447	750	63	45	134
1983	.255	163	5610	639	1429	2055	242	33	106	587	38	42	29	442	767	119	60	123
1984	.261	161	5569	656	1452	2097	227	29	120	618	47	43	20	420	807	81	50	130
1985	.253	161	5361	617	1359	2041	213	41	129	578	34	45	33	530	819	130	85	133
1986	.267	162	5529	771	1479	2365	248	43	184	725	31	42	35	511	1088	103	85	133
1987	.266	162	5564	823	1478	2394	264	35	194	772	42	51	24	567	1081	120	71	116
1988	.252	161	5479	637	1378	2020	228	39	112	589	48	53	35	542	1023	130	57	111
1989	.263	162	5438	695	1433	2151	260	46	122	654	63	40	34	503	989	101	49	151
1990	.259	162	5469	676	1416	2057	257	27	110	641	54	44	34	575	1054	115	48	142
1991	.270	162	5703	829	1539	2420	288	31	177	774	59	41	42	596	1039	102	50	128
1992	.250	162	5537	682	1387	2176	266	23	159	646	56	45	50	550	1036	81	44	115
1993	.267	162	5510	835	1472	2377	284	39	181	780	69	56	48	483	984	113	67	111
1994	.280	114	3983	613	1114	1738	198	27	124	582	41	34	36	437	730	82	35	95
1995	.265	144	4913	691	1304	2013	247	24	138	651	49	45	33	526	877	90	47	112
1996	.284	163	5702	928	1622	2672	323	32	221	890	32	69	31	660	1041	83	26	128

Opening Day, 1990, Rangers vs. Toronto Blue Jays. (*Fort Worth Star-Telegram*)

Nolan Ryan
(Texas Rangers Archives)

RANGERS CAREER PITCHING LEADERS

ERA (400 IP)		STRIKEOUTS		GAMES		LOSSES		SAVES ('75 rule applied)		WON–LOST PCT. (50 or more decisions)		
Blyleven	2.74	Hough	1,452	Russell	445	Hough	123	Russell	134	Rogers	.579	(70–51)
Perry	3.26	Witt	1,254	Rogers	376	Witt	88	Henke	58	Comer	.574	(39–29)
Matlack	3.41	Ryan	939	Hough	344	Jenkins	72	Kern	37	Ryan	.567	(51–39)
Ryan	3.43	Jenkins	895	Williams	232	Brown	64	Foucault	35	Pavlik	.566	(43–33)
Jenkins	3.56	Brown	742	Witt	228	Guzman	62	Williams	32	Jenkins	.564	(93–72)
Hough	3.68	Guzman	715	Darwin	224	Darwin	52	Henneman	31	Brown	.540	(78–64)
Darwin	3.71	Rogers	680	Foucault	206	Rogers	51	Harris	31	Medich	.538	(50–43)
Russell	3.73	Perry	575	Jenkins	197	Tanana	49	Mohorcic	28	Hough	.531	(139–123)
Comer	3.80	Darwin	566	Brown	187	Matlack	45	Rogers	28	Perry	.527	(48–43)
Brown	3.81	Matlack	493	Whiteside	181	Medich	43	Schmidt	26	Hargan	.526	(30–27)
						Perry	43					

WINS		INNINGS		BASES ON BALLS		COMPLETE GAMES		SHUTOUTS	
Hough	139	Hough	2,307.2	Hough	965	Hough	98	Jenkins	17
Jenkins	93	Jenkins	1,410.0	Witt	894	Jenkins	90	Perry	12
Witt	87	Witt	1,402.1	Brown	428	Perry	55	Blyleven	11
Brown	78	Brown	1,278.2	Guzman	395	Brown	40	Hough	11
Rogers	70	Guzman	1,013.2	Rogers	370	Matlack	32	Bibby	8
Guzman	66	Rogers	943.1	Ryan	353	Witt	30	Medich	7
Darwin	55	Matlack	915.0	Pavlik	315	Blyleven	29	Ryan	6
Ryan	51	Ryan	840.0	Jenkins	315	Bibby	26	Brown	6
Medich	50	Darwin	872.2	Darwin	298	Guzman	24	Darwin	5
Perry	48	Perry	827.0	Russell	296	Medich	22	Honeycutt	5
								Umbarger	5
								Witt	5

RANGERS TOP 10—SINGLE SEASON

ERA (100 innings)			VICTORIES			LOSSES			GAMES		
Kern	1.57	1979	Jenkins	25	1974	Bibby	19	1974	Williams	85	1987
Paul	2.17	1972	Brown	21	1992	Jenkins	18	1975	Rogers	81	1992
Foucault	2.24	1974	Bibby	19	1974	Tanana	18	1982	Williams	80	1986
Matlack	2.30	1978	Jenkins	18	1978	Honeycutt	17	1982	Mohorcic	74	1987
Comer	2.30	1978	Hough	18	1987	Hough	16	1985	Harris	73	1986
Honeycutt	2.42	1983	Alexander	17	1977	Hough	16	1988	Rogers	73	1989
Harris	2.47	1985	Jenkins	17	1975	Tanana	15	1984	Kern	71	1979
Lindblad	2.61	1972	Comer	17	1979	Mason	15	1985	Russell	71	1989
Darwin	2.63	1980	Hough	17	1986	Guzman	15	1986	Jeffcoat	70	1991
Blyleven	2.72	1977	Witt	17	1990	Gross	15	1995	Foucault	69	1974
			Rogers	17	1995				Rogers	69	1990

STARTS			COMPLETE GAMES			SHUTOUTS			SAVES		
Jenkins	41	1974	Jenkins	29	1974	Jenkins	6	1974	Henke	40	1993
Bibby	41	1974	Jenkins	22	1975	Blyleven	6	1976	Russell	38	1989
Hough	40	1987	Perry	21	1976	Bibby	5	1974	Henneman	31	1996
Jenkins	37	1979	Matlack	18	1978	Blyleven	5	1977	Russell	30	1991
Jenkins	37	1976	Hough	17	1984	Medich	4	1981	Kern	29	1979
Comer	36	1979	Jenkins	16	1978	Jenkins	4	1978	Russell	28	1992
Hough	36	1984	Perry	15	1975	Jenkins	4	1975	Harris	20	1986
Tanana	35	1984	Blyleven	15	1977	Perry	4	1975	Russell	20	1995
Brown	35	1992	Blyleven	14	1976	Perry	4	1977	Williams	18	1988
Hill	35	1996	Hough	14	1985	Six tied	3		Mohorcic	16	1987

INNINGS			WALKS			STRIKEOUTS			HR ALLOWED		
Jenkins	328.0	1974	Witt	143	1986	Ryan	301	1989	Jenkins	40	1979
Hough	285.1	1987	Witt	140	1987	Ryan	232	1990	Jenkins	37	1975
Matlack	270.0	1978	Correa	126	1986	Jenkins	225	1974	Hough	36	1987
Jenkins	270.0	1975	Hough	126	1988	Hough	223	1987	Hough	32	1986
Hough	266.0	1984	Hough	124	1987	Witt	221	1990	Tanana	30	1984
Brown	265.2	1992	Hough	119	1990	Ryan	203	1991	Guzman	30	1987
Bibby	264.0	1974	Witt	114	1989	Correa	189	1986	Hough	28	1989
Jenkins	259.0	1979	Bibby	113	1974	Blyleven	182	1977	Pavlik	28	1996
Hough	252.0	1983	Witt	110	1990	Guzman	179	1992	Witt	28	1996
Hough	252.0	1988	Bibby	106	1973	Perry	177	1977	Jenkins	27	1974
									Gross	27	1995

RANGERS YEAR-BY-YEAR PITCHING LEADERS

(*Led League; **Tied for League Lead)

YEAR	WON		LOST		INNINGS		ERA (162 IP)	
1972	Hand	10	Hand	14	Broberg	176.0	Paul	2.17
1973	Bibby	9	Merritt	13	Bibby	180.1	Bibby	3.24
1974	Jenkins	**25	Bibby	19	Jenkins	328.0	Jenkins	2.83
1975	Jenkins	17	Jenkins	18	Jenkins	270.0	Perry	3.03
1976	Perry	15	Perry	14	Perry	250.1	Blyleven	2.76
1977	Alexander	17	Blyleven	12	Perry	238.0	Blyleven	2.72
			Perry	12				
1978	Jenkins	18	Matlack	13	Matlack	270.0	Matlack	2.30
1979	Comer	17	Jenkins	14	Jenkins	259.0	Comer	3.68
1980	Medich	14	Jenkins	12	Matlack	234.2	Matlack	3.68
1981	Honeycutt	11	Darwin	9	Darwin	146.0	Medich	3.08
1982	Hough	16	Tanana	18	Hough	228.0	Hough	3.95
1983	Hough	15	Smithson	14	Hough	252.0	Honeycutt	*2.42
1984	Hough	16	Tanana	15	Hough	266.0	Tanana	3.25
1985	Hough	14	Hough	16	Hough	250.1	Hough	3.31
1986	Hough	17	Guzman	15	Hough	230.1	Hough	3.79
1987	Hough	18	Guzman	14	Hough	*285.1	Hough	3.79
1988	Hough	15	Hough	16	Hough	252.0	Hough	3.32
1989	Ryan	16	Hough	13	Ryan	239.1	Ryan	3.20
			Witt	13				
1990	Witt	17	Hough	12	Witt	222.0	Witt	3.36
1991	Guzman	13	Brown	12	Brown	210.2	Ryan	2.91
1992	Brown	**21	Witt	13	Brown	*265.2	Brown	3.32
1993	Rogers	16	Brown	12	Brown	233.0	Pavlik	3.41
1994	Rogers	11	Brown	9	Brown	170.0	Rogers	4.46
1995	Rogers	17	Gross	**15	Rogers	208.0	Rogers	3.38
1996	Hill	16	Witt	12	Hill	250.2	Hill	3.63
	Witt	16						

YEAR	SAVES		STRIKEOUTS		APPEARANCES		COMPLETE GAMES	
1972	Pina	15	Broberg	133	Lindblad	*66	Broberg	3
1973	Foucault	8	Bibby	155	Gogolewski	49	Bibby	11
1974	Foucault	12	Jenkins	225	Foucault	69	Jenkins	*29
1975	Foucault	10	Jenkins	157	Foucault	59	Jenkins	22
1976	Hoerner	8	Blyleven	144	Foucault	46	Perry	21
1977	Devine	15	Blyleven	182	Devine	56	Blyleven	15
1978	Cleveland	12	Jenkins	157	Cleveland	53	Matlack	18
			Matlack	157				

Records and Statistics

YEAR	SAVES		STRIKEOUTS		APPEARANCES		COMPLETE GAMES	
1979	Kern	*29	Jenkins	164	Kern	71	Jenkins	10
1980	Lyle	8	Matlack	142	Darwin	53	Jenkins	12
	Darwin	8						
1981	Comer	6	Darwin	98	Comer	36	Honeycutt	8
	Kern	6						
1982	Darwin	7	Hough	128	Darwin	56	Hough	12
1983	Jones	10	Hough	152	O. Jones	42	Hough	11
1984	Schmidt	12	Hough	164	Schmidt	43	Hough	*17
1985	Harris	11	Hough	141	Harris	58	Hough	14
1986	Harris	20	Correa	189	Williams	*80	Hough	7
1987	Mohorcic	16	Hough	223	Williams	85	Hough	13
1988	Williams	18	Hough	174	Williams	67	Witt	13
1989	Russell	*38	Ryan	*301	Rogers	73	Brown	7
1990	Rogers	15	Ryan	*232	Rogers	69	Witt	7
1991	Russell	30	Ryan	203	Jeffcoat	70	Guzman	5
1992	Russell	28	Guzman	179	Rogers	*81	Brown	11
1993	Henke	40	Brown	142	Henke	66	Brown	12
1994	Henke	15	Brown	123	Carpenter	47	Rogers	6
					Whiteside	47		
1995	Russell	20	Pavlik	149	McDowell	64	Gross	4
							Tewksbury	4
1996	Henneman	31	Hill	170	Cook	60	Pavlik	7
							Hill	7

RANGERS TEAM PITCHING, 1972–1996

YEAR	W–L	ERA	G	REL	CG	SHO	SV	IP	H	R	ER	HR	BB	SO	HB	WP	BK
1972	54–100	3.53	154	324	11	8	34	1374.2	1258	628	539	92	613	868	48	44	4
1973	57–105	4.64	162	298	35	10	35	1430.0	1430	844	737	130	680	831	44	62	3
1974	84–76	3.82	161	224	62	16	12	1433.2	1423	698	609	126	449	871	40	51	4
1975	79–83	3.86	162	224	60	16	17	1465.2	1456	733	629	123	518	792	43	49	7
1976	76–86	3.45	162	196	63	15	15	1472.0	1464	652	565	106	461	773	31	46	9
1977	94–68	3.56	162	200	49	17	31	1472.1	1412	657	583	134	471	864	31	44	2
1978	87–75	3.36	162	170	54	12	25	1456.1	1431	632	543	108	421	776	24	35	3
1979	83–79	3.86	163	256	26	10	42	1437.0	1371	698	617	135	532	773	28	37	2
1980	76–85	4.02	162	217	35	6	25	1451.2	1561	752	649	119	519	890	37	58	5
1981	57–48	3.40	105	142	23	13	18	940.1	851	389	355	67	322	488	17	18	2
1982	64–98	4.28	162	214	32	5	24	1431.0	1554	749	681	128	483	690	41	34	4
1983	77–85	3.31	163	190	43	11	32	1466.2	1392	609	540	97	471	826	38	36	6
1984	69–92	3.91	161	190	38	6	21	1438.2	1443	714	625	148	518	863	34	62	11
1985	62–99	4.56	161	264	18	5	33	1411.2	1479	785	715	173	501	863	36	43	7
1986	87–75	4.11	162	328	15	8	41	1450.1	1356	743	662	145	736	1059	41	94	13
1987	75–87	4.63	162	329	20	3	27	1444.1	1388	849	743	199	760	1103	55	61	26
1988	70–91	4.05	161	251	41	11	31	1438.2	1310	735	647	129	654	912	56	72	57
1989	83–79	3.91	162	321	26	7	44	1434.1	1279	714	623	119	654	1112	48	65	16
1990	83–79	3.83	162	302	25	9	36	1444.2	1343	696	615	113	623	997	44	61	6
1991	85–77	4.47	162	386	9	10	41	1479.0	1486	814	734	151	662	1022	45	77	12
1992	77–85	4.09	162	359	19	3	42	1460.1	1471	753	663	113	598	1034	48	72	6
1993	86–76	4.28	162	314	20	6	45	1438.1	1476	751	684	144	562	957	44	52	14
1994	52–62	5.45	114	301	10	4	26	1023.0	1176	697	620	157	394	683	32	50	5
1995	74–70	4.66	144	360	14	4	34	1285.0	1385	720	665	152	514	838	36	60	6
1996	90–72	4.65	165	347	19	6	43	1449.1	1569	799	749	168	582	976	43	38	9

RANGERS A.L. PLAYER/PITCHER OF THE MONTH AWARDS

Year	Player	Month
1979	Jim Kern, p	May
1983	Rick Honeycutt, p	April
	Charlie Hough, p	June
1984	Charlie Hough, p	June
	Gary Ward, of	August
1986	Scott Fletcher, ss	July
1987	Larry Parrish, dh	May
1989	Ruben Sierra, of	July
1990	Bobby Witt, p*	July
1991	Ruben Sierra, of	May
1993	Rafael Palmeiro, 1b	July
1995	Kenny Rogers, p	May
1996	Juan Gonzalez, of	July

NOTE: In 1979, the American League started a Pitcher of the Month Award in addition to the Player of the Month.
*Shared Award with California's Chuck Finley

RANGERS MAJOR AWARD WINNERS

Most Valuable Player, A.L. (BBWAA): Jeff Burroughs (1974), Juan Gonzalez (1996)

Player of the Year, A.L. (*The Sporting News*): Jeff Burroughs (1974), Ruben Sierra (1989)

Manager of the Year, A.L. (BBWAA): Johnny Oates (1996*)

Manager of the Year, A.L. (AP): Billy Martin (1974)

Manager of the Year, A.L. (UPI): Billy Martin (1974), Bobby Valentine (1986)

Manager of the Year, A.L. (*The Sporting News*): Johnny Oates (1996)

Executive of the Year, Major League (*The Sporting News*): Doug Melvin (1996)

Rookie of the Year, A.L. (BBWAA): Mike Hargrove (1974)

Rookie of the Year, A.L. (*The Sporting News*): Mike Hargrove (1974), Pat Putnam (1979)

Comeback Player of the Year, A.L. (*The Sporting News*): Ferguson Jenkins (1974), Jose Guzman (1991), Jose Canseco (1994), Kevin Elster (1996)

Comeback Player of the Year, A.L. (United Press International): Ferguson Jenkins (1974)

Fireman of the Year, A.L. (*The Sporting News*, Rolaids): Jim Kern (1979), Jeff Russell (1989)

*Shared award with Joe Torre (N.Y.)

RANGERS SELECTED TO TOPPS ROOKIE ALL-STAR TEAMS

1974	Mike Hargrove, 1b	1986	Pete Incaviglia, of
1977	Bump Wills, 2b	1988	Cecil Espy, of
1979	Pat Putnam, 1b	1990	Jeff Huson, ss
	Billy Sample, of	1991	Ivan Rodriguez, c
1985	Oddibe McDowell, of		

RANGERS SELECTED TO THE SPORTING NEWS SILVER SLUGGER TEAM

1980	Al Oliver, of	1991	Julio Franco, 2b
1981	Al Oliver, dh	1992	Juan Gonzalez, of
1984	Buddy Bell, 3b	1993	Juan Gonzalez, of
1989	Harold Baines, dh	1994	Ivan Rodriguez, c
1989	Julio Franco, 2b	1995	Ivan Rodriguez, c
1989	Ruben Sierra, of	1996	Ivan Rodriguez, c
1990	Julio Franco, 2b	1996	Juan Gonzalez, of

DALLAS-FORT WORTH BBWAA CHAPTER AWARD WINNERS

YEAR	PLAYER OF THE YEAR	PITCHER OF THE YEAR	ROOKIE OF THE YEAR	HAROLD McKINNEY GOOD GUY
1973	Jeff Burroughs	Jim Bibby	—	—
1974	Jeff Burroughs	Ferguson Jenkins	Mike Hargrove	—
1975	Toby Harrah	Gaylord Perry	Roy Howell	Tom Grieve
1976	Tom Grieve	Nelson Briles	Tommy Boggs	Danny Thompson*
1977	Jim Sundberg	Doyle Alexander	Bump Wills	Dave May
1978	Al Oliver	Ferguson Jenkins	Steve Comer	Jim Sundberg
1979	Buddy Bell	Jim Kern	Pat Putnam	Burt Hawkins
1980	Mickey Rivers	Danny Darwin	John Butcher	Buddy Bell
1981	Buddy Bell	Steve Comer	Dave Schmidt	Bill Stein
		Rick Honeycutt		
1982	Buddy Bell	Charlie Hough	Dave Hostetler	Larry Parrish
1983	George Wright	Charlie Hough	Mike Smithson	Bill Zeigler
1984	Larry Parrish	Frank Tanana	Curtis Wilkerson	Dave Stewart
1985	Pete O'Brien	Charlie Hough	Oddibe McDowell	Charlie Hough
1986	Larry Parrish	Charlie Hough	Pete Incaviglia	Pete O'Brien
1987	Ruben Sierra	Charlie Hough	Jerry Browne	Steve Buechele
1988	Ruben Sierra	Charlie Hough	Cecil Espy	Art Howe
1989	Ruben Sierra	Nolan Ryan	Kevin Brown	Mike Stanley
1990	Rafael Palmeiro	Bobby Witt	Jeff Huson	Charlie Hough
1991	Ruben Sierra	Jose Guzman	Ivan Rodriguez	Jack Daugherty
1992	Juan Gonzalez	Kevin Brown	Jeff Frye	Jose Guzman
1993	Juan Gonzalez	Tom Henke	David Hulse	Geno Petralli
1994	Jose Canseco	Kenny Rogers	Rusty Greer	Tom Grieve
1995	Ivan Rodriguez	Kenny Rogers	Benji Gil	Bob Tewksbury
1996	Juan Gonzalez	Ken Hill	Mark Brandenburg	David Valle

*Awarded posthumously

(Fort Worth Star-Telegram)